4D Living with FASD:

Shared Voices, Clearer Understanding

Patricia Kasper, MA

4D Living with FASD:

Shared Voices, Clearer Understanding

Patricia Kasper, MA

Better Endings New Beginnings

Minneapolis, USA

Patricia Kasper, MA

Also by author
Sip by Sip: Candid Conversations with Adults Living with FASD

Paperback — ISBN# 9781971663067

Library of Congress # 2026919286

Dedication

To all those affected by Prenatal Alcohol Exposure who have felt misunderstood and bewildered.

To all those who have raised children with challenging and complex behaviors who have not found the help they desperately searched for.

To all those who have been called to this field, wanting desperately to help but who have been frustrated by what seemed like failure.

Thank you for never giving up, for continuing to hope, and for giving of your time to read this book.

Advance Praise & Endorsements

Angela (AJ) Locashio

Chapter 12 alone is reason for owning this book. Kasper names something the neurodiversity movement doesn't acknowledge: that FASD has been sidelined within neurodivergent spaces, not just outside them. This is a form of gatekeeping our community claims to reject everywhere except at its own door; however unintentional, it is what happens. That matters to me because at Umbrella ND, we don't define neurodivergence by diagnosis; we define it by whether a nervous system has had to adapt to survive an unsafe or unsustainable environment. By that measure, FASD was never on the margins; it was always clearly embedded. And the 4D Framework doesn't stop at FASD—Kasper builds it explicitly to hold the whole neurodivergent experience (unique to context), which means this book belongs on the shelf of anyone doing this work, whatever experience brought them to it. 4D Living with FASD is rigorous, whole-body, and long overdue—a framework I'll be citing for years.

— AJ Locashio, Founder & Executive Director, Umbrella ND

Dr. Jennifer Fraser

"Patricia Kasper's 4D model should be required reading for all who work with children because not only does it provide well-researched insight into what it is like for those with Fetal Alcohol Spectrum Disorder, but it reveals the harmful approach we apply to individuals who are suffering and need support, not moralizing labels. Our 2D model is outdated, as Kasper reveals from multiple angles. It does not account for harm done in utero to the brain, energy levels, and physical systems that impact how a child develops and behaves. We are quick with moral judgments, when the invisible damage done to brain and body can be far better identified and supported with medically informed insights. Kasper's book presents multiple voices and angles ranging from diverse

experts to those who live with FASD. The reading experience is an excellent balance of studies, data, and lived experience that brings research alive. Kasper's approach is one of profound empathy that transfers beautifully to other areas such as ADHD, ASD, and chronic illness. I look forward to a 4D way of assessing, thinking, and supporting in the future."

—Dr. Jennifer Fraser, Best-selling Author and Educator

Dr. William Curran

"4D Living with FASD: Shared Voices, Clearer Understanding offers an important and timely contribution to the evolving conversation about Fetal Alcohol Spectrum Disorder and, most importantly, about the people who live with the effects of prenatal alcohol exposure. Patti Kasper brings together professional knowledge, personal experience, and the voices of individuals and families who have often been spoken about rather than listened to. Her work through the Living with FASD podcast has created an important space for these experiences to be heard, challenging stigma and encouraging a more nuanced understanding of the diversity of FASD experiences.

What makes this book particularly valuable is its willingness to look beyond the familiar narratives that have shaped FASD for decades. The 4D Framework provides a way of bringing together dimensions that are often considered separately, while the inclusion of lived experience reminds us that FASD cannot be adequately understood through diagnosis, impairment, or professional observation alone. The voices of those living with PAE add an essential dimension to the evidence base, helping readers to consider not only what FASD is, but what it actually means to live with it across different environments, relationships, and stages of life.

This is an important book because it asks us to pause and reconsider assumptions that have become embedded in FASD practice, research, and policy. It encourages the reader to move from asking 'What is wrong?' toward asking

'What are we not yet understanding?' That shift has significant implications for families, educators, health and social care professionals, researchers, and policymakers. In bringing together recognized knowledge with voices of lived experience, Patti Kasper offers an opportunity to see familiar information differently, and that is precisely where meaningful change can begin.

I would recommend 4D Living with FASD: Shared Voices, Clearer Understanding to anyone seeking to deepen their understanding of FASD beyond diagnostic labels and conventional professional narratives. It is a valuable reminder that clearer understanding does not come simply from accumulating more information; it comes from listening differently, connecting what we already know, and taking seriously the experiences of those living with PAE every day."

—Dr. William Curran, M.Sc., LCSW, Adjunct Professor of Social Work

Professor Jerrod Brown, Ph.D.

"Patricia Kasper's book, 4D Living with FASD: Shared Voices, Clearer Understanding, brings together multidisciplinary, caregiver, and lived-experience perspectives to increase awareness and enhance understanding of FASD among professionals, caregivers, and anyone seeking to learn more about the condition. It is a practical, go-to resource for understanding the complexities of FASD through the perspectives of professionals, caregivers, and individuals living with FASD. Thoughtful and impressive, this book is a valuable resource for anyone seeking to deepen their understanding of FASD and more effectively support individuals living with FASD."

—Professor Jerrod Brown, Ph.D.

Dr. Inyang Takon, MD

"As a neurodevelopmental paediatrician involved in FASD assessments for almost two decades, the diagnostic framework has historically been based on

quantifying the presence of static deficits. The 4D approach is a vital paradigm shift that moves from focusing on quantifying deficits to understanding the dynamic interplay of somatic foundations, energy, and environment. A truly practical, compassionate roadmap for families and a highly recommended resource for clinicians."

—Dr. Inyang Takon, MD, Consultant Neurodevelopmental Paediatrician, United Kingdom

Sandra Flach

"As an adoptive mom of two adult sons, both diagnosed with Fetal Alcohol Syndrome, and as an FASD trainer and parent support group moderator, I believe 4D Living with FASD is groundbreaking work. Patti brings over thirty years of professional experience—as well as lived experience as an individual diagnosed with an FASD. 4D Living with FASD brings this hidden yet prevalent disability into clear focus. Patti's book is a vital resource for professionals, adults living with FASD, and parents and caregivers raising children prenatally exposed to alcohol."

—Sandra Flach, Adoptive Parent, Author, FASD Trainer, Host of The Adoption & Foster Care Journey Podcast, and Founder of Hope for the FASD Journey

Ana Morales, MS, PPSC

"4D Living with FASD: Shared Voices, Clearer Understanding offers an intellectual yet deeply personal exploration of FASD, written with compassion and a strong emphasis on restructuring how we understand, support, and care for individuals living with FASD. Comprehensive and thorough, Patti examines FASD from diagnosis through different stages of the lifespan and across a variety of settings.

As a school psychologist, I found the research especially valuable in understanding how FASD can affect learning, behavior, executive functioning, and social-emotional development. The information offers meaningful insight that can directly inform assessment and support for students. The 'Pivot Points' at the end of each chapter provide a valuable opportunity for reflection for caregivers, professionals, and individuals living with FASD, highlighting how the research can be meaningfully applied to each person and setting."

—Ana Morales, MS, PPSC, School Psychologist

"A valuable resource for anyone seeking to understand and advocate for neurodivergence. Drawing on contemporary research, clinical expertise, and lived experience, it offers an integrated framework that highlights the realities of neurodivergent lives and informs more effective advocacy."

—Evangelia Markopoulou, PhD, Greece

Living-Experience & Community Endorsements

"Patricia's 4D model as a framework to understanding FASD is the first concept that finally covers all aspects of the complexity of the disorder. It resonated deeply with me as both a caregiver and as an individual living with FASD. The use of the 4D framework would have significantly reduced the gaslighting of my co-morbid medical issues and possibly eliminated the mental health issues I endured throughout most of my life. For those of us living with FASD who are now in the later stages of life—while our brains are suddenly functioning at a heightened level beyond anything in our past, our bodies have prematurely outpaced it. Just when we are able to create our life's work, our bodies are physically failing us. This book guides us to the pathway of improved lifelong outcomes when the 4D framework is applied as part of early intervention and woven throughout the lifespan. I relate strongly to Patricia's analogy of being a wildflower that has risen from the ashes of a forest fire." —Mary Byrnes

"This is an exhausting read—but in a GREAT way! I keep having to pause to recall this and that about my own family because so much applies directly. Patti would be the first to tell you that if you've met and learned about one person with FASD, you know a little about that one person—for that day, in that hour in particular. There are so many dynamics! The 4D Framework will help you stop chasing squirrels and formulate actionable descriptives that those affected, carers, and practitioners can use to make meaningful accommodations for today and achievable growth pathways to improve human lives tomorrow. Imagine the benefits of not devaluing or dehumanizing 1/20 or even 1/12 of the population of our planet! This book matters. Read on!"

—David Hambleton

Foreword

It is one thing to know and understand a condition such as Fetal Alcohol Spectrum Disorder (FASD). It is another thing entirely to encounter a framework that changes the angle from which you see nearly everything you thought you already understood.

Before reading Patricia Kasper's 4D Framework, I wasn't in the dark about FASD—years of living experience, family experience, advocacy, professional work, and study had already shaped how I understood many of the challenges individuals with FASD face, and the families and professionals who support them.

I use the term *living experience* intentionally. I have FASD. My youngest child also has FASD. We share a diagnosis, but our viewpoints, challenges, strengths, and experiences within that shared diagnosis are not the same. FASD is not a single story, and no one person's experience should be treated as representative of everyone else's.

Reading the 4D Framework, however, was like someone replacing the lightbulb with something much brighter.

Nothing about the people had changed. Neither had the challenges or the systems surrounding them. What changed was my ability to see relationships and patterns that had previously been much harder to distinguish.

My viewing angle changed as well. Rather than replacing what I already knew, the framework reorganized it. My perspective shifted perhaps ninety degrees or more, causing me to revisit long-held assumptions about behavior, capacity, support, accountability, health, education, and the environments in which people with FASD are expected to function.

That kind of shift is rare.

Patricia's 4D Framework gave me a way to view FASD from an angle I hadn't considered before. I will leave it to her to explain the framework in the pages that follow. What I can speak to is what happened to my own thinking after I encountered it.

For me, the implications were immediate.

Education was the first place my mind went.

Much of my work has involved helping families and professionals think about what happens when a child with FASD enters a system that expects relatively consistent performance. Schools understandably depend upon routines, expectations, deadlines, rules, and demonstrations of learning. Yet a student may perform a task successfully under one set of conditions and struggle significantly with the same task under another.

Such differences are easy to interpret as unwillingness.

- A student did it yesterday, so why not today?
- A student explained the rule, so why did the student fail to follow it?
- A student performed the skill in one classroom, so why was it not used somewhere else?

Through the 4D Framework, I began asking those questions differently.

- What was happening for the student at that moment?
- What conditions were present?
- What had happened earlier in the day, earlier in the week, or over a longer period of time?
- What might we be missing if we judge only the behavior or performance in front of us?

Those questions do not remove expectations. They help us understand whether those expectations are accessible under the conditions in which the person is being asked to meet them.

That distinction matters tremendously in education.

It also changed how I thought about Individualized Education Programs and other forms of educational planning. Rather than looking only at isolated behaviors, academic performance, or individual deficits, I found myself thinking more deliberately about the interaction between the student and the conditions surrounding the student.

Families came next.

I began developing questions designed to help parents describe what they actually observe across daily life: when their child functions well, when capacity appears to diminish, which environments improve functioning, which environments create greater difficulty, what recovery looks like, and how performance changes over time.

My goal was not to label behavior. It was to understand the person more fully.

From there, my thinking moved into juvenile justice.

That may be where the framework challenged me most.

Young people involved in juvenile justice are often evaluated primarily through what can be observed: what happened, which rule was violated, whether a condition was followed, whether an appointment was missed, whether an account changed, or whether behavior escalated.

All of those things matter.

- Accountability matters.
- Safety matters.
- Other people's rights and safety matter.

Yet the framework raised another set of questions for me.

- What did the young person actually understand?
- What was the young person able to access in that moment?

- What conditions were present?
- Could the young person state the rule while still being unable to carry it out reliably in daily life?
- Had a consequence actually produced learning, or had the system simply repeated the same response to the same failure?

None of those questions require us to excuse unlawful or unsafe behavior. They may instead help us construct accountability in a way that has a greater chance of producing safety, repair, learning, and future success.

That distinction has become increasingly important to me.

A behavior can be an accountable act while still requiring us to examine whether neurodevelopmental impairment contributed to what occurred. Those two ideas do not have to be mutually exclusive.

Professional training has also begun to look different to me.

For years, much FASD training has understandably focused on helping people recognize characteristics associated with the condition. That remains important. But I now want to move beyond simply asking professionals to know more about FASD.

I want them to look differently.

For a social worker, teacher, therapist, probation officer, physician, caregiver, or other professional, the question cannot always stop with, "What behavior am I seeing?"

We also need to ask, "What are the conditions where I am seeing it?"

That shift changes the conversation.

It changes how we interpret inconsistency, how we think about support, how we respond when a person appears capable in one moment and significantly less capable in another, and how we understand the difference between possessing an ability and accessing that ability when it is needed.

At some point, I realized the framework had affected me deeply because I had stopped simply reading it and started applying it.

Cross-system questions and functional-profile tools followed. I began thinking about how psychological testing, school information, caregiver observations, and justice-system records might be brought together to create a more complete functional picture of a young person.

Its influence also reached work I was already doing in the education and FASD space. The distinction between capability and moment-specific capacity became richer when viewed through Patricia's 4D lens.

I mention that not to draw attention to my own work, but because it demonstrates the depth of Patricia's influence on my thinking. Her framework did not remain something I read and appreciated. It changed how I approached problems I had been working on for years.

Eventually, the impact became even more personal.

I began looking at my own life differently. Living with FASD and navigating my own health journey has forced me to confront the complicated relationship between what I may be capable of doing and what my brain and body can actually sustain under particular conditions.

Patricia's framework gave me another way to examine those experiences.

It also caused me to look again at my son's journey through the criminal justice system.

Questions emerged that I wish I had known to ask years earlier.

- What was his capacity at particular moments?
- What was happening around him?
- What demands were being placed upon him?
- What did he genuinely understand?
- Which abilities were available to him at one point but inaccessible at another?
- What might have been different if the systems around him had understood those questions differently?

No framework can rewrite the past. But a framework can change how we understand it, and it can influence what we choose to do differently in the future.

That may be the greatest value I have found in Patricia Kasper's work.

I came to this framework with years of experience and an established understanding of FASD.

I leave it asking different questions.

- Different questions of educators.
- Different questions of social workers.
- Different questions of the juvenile justice system.
- Different questions of families.
- And different questions of myself.

The people have not changed. The realities were there all along.

For me, though, the light is brighter, and I am looking from a different angle.

That kind of change in perspective deserves our attention.

It is also why I believe the pages that follow are worth reading carefully.

Carl Young,

Author, FASD advocate, trainer with living experience

Table of Contents

Part III: Reclaiming the Language of Lived Experience

Part IV: FASD Within Neurodiversity

Part V: Rethinking the Framework

Preface

One of the greatest privileges of my life is hosting my podcast, *Living with FASD: Candid Conversations with Patti Kasper.* I am so blessed that week by week I have conversations with some of the coolest people on earth, all of whom are connected to FASD, either by profession or because either they or a family member lives with the effects of prenatal alcohol exposure (PAE) or other significant neurodiversity or developmental conditions.

From the beginning of the podcast, I sensed it would be important to save the transcripts, possibly for a book, though I had no idea at the time what that might look like. Over time, I knew that it would be an expansion of my first book, *Sip by Sip: Candid Conversations with Adults Living with FASD.* That book was designed to be a mirror for the reader, so that they might consider if PAE could be a key part of the explanation for their life's struggles.

This book, along with its sequel, launching in 2027, is designed to close the gap between living experience with FASD and how society thinks about it and deals with us who live with it. These books, along with their companion workbooks, are written with AI assistance: I had AI sift through the 130+ transcripts for quotes to seed into each identified chapter of my outline.

The voices of my podcast contemporaries are not the only voices that I share within the pages of this series. I also share the voices of professionals and visionaries from decades past, whose work was not adopted into the dominant dialogue and approach by noteworthy members of the scientific community, yet which formed a parallel body of data which informs direction of future policy and practice. I acknowledge these other sources of insight and information in honor of my father, who as a visionary engineer with several patents to his name, was not widely recognized because his ideas were decades ahead of public perceptions. Remembering him, I feel fortunate to have found certain visionaries in our field of FASD, whose ideas I have gathered and woven into the tapestry of this book, along with the many guests from my podcast.

The basis of my writing is these collective voices. As I introduce each quote or summary of a guest's position on an idea, I include the episode number, so that you, dear reader, can easily go back and watch or listen to the full conversation. To all my podcast guests, thank you! You have turned this work from the opinions of one person to a qualitative analysis of our experiences, as those who live and work with the effects of PAE.

My hope is that the timing of our collective living wisdom applied though the lens of the 4D framework rounds out the perspectives towards FASD, offering a truly inclusive picture informed by all who contributed to understanding, intervention and prevention.

Introduction

Fetal Alcohol Spectrum Disorder (FASD) remains one of the most pervasive yet profoundly invisible disabilities of our time. It affects millions of individuals across the globe, yet it goes largely unrecognized by the very systems designed to support them. Recent findings reveal that one in every seven pregnancies is exposed to alcohol, meaning that a staggering 14.28% of pregnancies involve exposure to this widely accepted substance. While conservative North American prevalence rates are estimated at 5% to 8% (representing 1 in 20 to 1 in 12 people, as reported by the CDC and CanFASD, respectively), our formal diagnostic rate hovers at an abysmal 0.01%. This means approximately 99.99% of people with FASD walk through life completely undiagnosed, navigating a world that constantly misinterprets their neurological challenges as intentional behavioral choices or character flaws.

These stats, these facts, have been the underpinning of everything I have done in recent years. FASD is like that. Once you learn about it, it profoundly changes you; there is no un-ringing that bell.

This profound invisibility is not accidental. It stems from a perfect storm of cultural normalization, systemic medical inertia, and a heavy cloak of misdirected stigma. Society treats alcohol simply as a beverage, willfully ignoring its reality as a potent neurotoxin and solvent capable of permanently altering brains and bodies while developing in utero. When unrecognized, the fallout lands heavily at the front doors of child welfare, our educational systems, and the judicial machine. You will see that these systems are structurally blind, relying upon rigid, compliance-based behavior modification. They attempt to apply standard psychological "software updates" to what is actually a physical, biological "hardware gap" created before birth.

In *4D Living with FASD: Shared Voices, Clearer Understanding*, we delve deeply into the factors that contributed to our current way of viewing FASD, and supporting, or not, those who live with the effects of Prenatal Alcohol Exposure (PAE). The threads that I have gathered to weave this tapestry are not new. You, the reader, will resonate with much in this book. But I have gathered things previously recognized but not pondered long enough, along with the voices of living experience, from my Living with FASD podcast, and woven them into my 4D Framework. This evolution in my thinking has been fueled by a spirit of curiosity, a passion to share understanding, and a firm belief that the wisdom of lived experience is just as vital as empirical testing. In the second edition of *Sip by Sip: Candid Conversations with Adults Living with FASD*, I introduced a 3D Model of spectrums.

In the year since that edition was published, I have deepened and clarified this understanding. To truly tailor support for those impacted by PAE, we must map their whole-body functioning along 4 dimensions. *4D Living with FASD: Shared Voices, Clearer Understanding* thoroughly explains my framework. Also available to help you apply this framework to your life, is the companion study guide, *Discover Your 4D Life: the FASD Living Experience*. So many people do not like workbooks with a single expected answer to each question. This study companion is different. Just as no two people are impacted by PAE in the same manner or to the same degree, so too will no two people gain the same insights about themselves from this book or its companion study guide.

These tools are for you.

This book is also for those who love and support those living with FASD, as well as professionals of every discipline. We must examine the whole-body medical reality of this condition, respect the immense metabolic energy tax paid by differently wired brains, and transition from clinical correction to environmental connection.

Within these pages, you will hear a chorus of authentic, lived-experience voices. Together, we will dismantle the shadows of this hidden epidemic, replacing the shadows with guiding clarity, validation, and practical hope.

— Part 1 —

WHY FASD IS STILL IN THE SHADOWS?

— CHAPTER 1 —

The Diagnostic Desert

"You simply cannot motivate a tree to grow by painting its leaves gold."

- Jodee Kulp

The Mirage and the Wildflower:

The Diagnostic Desert is a landscape defined not only by the absence of specialized care, but by shimmers of false hope. For individuals and family members navigating this space, finding a knowledgeable, neuro-informed provider is like chasing a desert mirage. From a distance, a local clinic, a general therapist, or a standard community program appears as a life-saving oasis. Yet, because true specialty clinics are locked behind massive, multi-year waitlists, families are forced to rely on local systems that routinely get it wrong. In these local settings, the system defaults to standard, top-down behavioral modifications, suggests a "close enough" label like ADHD or Autism for administrative convenience, or dismisses the physical, whole-body complexity of the condition entirely. Even when families attempt to travel hundreds of miles across state lines to reach an actual specialty oasis, the wait is so long that simply surviving until they reach that point in time is an agonizing struggle. It is a cruel, systemic illusion that leaves the seeker parched, exhausted, and questioning their own reality. But we must look past the mirage to understand the true nature of this desert terrain. A desert is not a wasteland devoid of life; it is a place where life simply goes underground to survive. Beneath the parched, highly alkaline soil of Death Valley lies a hidden marvel: millions of dormant wildflower seeds waiting for the precise conditions to explode into a vibrant "Superbloom of Desert Gold." These desert wildflowers (ephemerals) don't try to survive the harsh summer heat by growing year-round; they spend most of their lives completely invisible, buried in the dust. To protect themselves from premature sprouting, these seeds are wrapped in a thick, protective chemical coating. A passing, superficial drizzle is not enough to wake them; in fact, a small amount of moisture is a direct threat, as it might cause them to sprout only to wither immediately under the blistering sun. The seeds must wait for a deep, soaking rain to thoroughly wash away their protective chemical coating, followed by gentle warmth. When this specific sequence of environmental scaffolding occurs, the barren valley floor transforms almost overnight into a breathtaking sea of gold, purple, and white. The individuals stranded in our diagnostic desert are not broken; they are wildflowers waiting for their true conditions. They do not need to be genetically modified or forced into a neurotypical mold to be worthy of space. They simply require the deep, metabolic hydration of sensory safety, predictable routines, and relational connection. By shifting the burden of support to the environment, we wash away the friction and provide the protective conditions that allow their innate, hard-wired **wildflower nature** to finally rise, take root, and bloom beautifully on its own terms.

Defining the Landscape:

Fetal Alcohol Spectrum Disorder (FASD) is a lifelong, whole-body neurodevelopmental disability caused by prenatal alcohol exposure (PAE). It can affect physical health, cognition, sensory processing, regulation, social communication, learning, and daily functioning. It affects people across the lifespan, yet many systems meant to support human wellbeing overlook it. Wildflowers do grow in deserts, and do not become less valuable because they do not resemble the plants arranged in a formal garden. Their intelligence lies in their capacity to respond to their conditions, find a place in altered soil, and contribute to a living ecosystem in ways a manicured landscape may not recognize. This is what I call **Wildflower Intelligence**: the distinctive, adaptive intelligence of people whose neurotypes do not fit narrow, neurotypical expectations.

The Diagnostic Desert:

FASD is widely under-recognized. The result is a diagnostic desert: a landscape in which many people live with brain-based and body-based differences without an explanation, appropriate support, or language that accurately describes their experience. Public-health estimates make the scale of prenatal alcohol exposure difficult to ignore. The Centers for Disease Control and Prevention reports that approximately 14% of pregnancies involve alcohol exposure, and that 1 in 20 pregnant women reported binge drinking in the month before the survey. A common misunderstanding is that only daily or heavy drinking affects fetal development. Dr. Susan Rich cautions, "Even a single high-concentration alcoholic beverage consumed during the earliest weeks of gestation, before a pregnancy is often even confirmed, can result in permanent neurodevelopmental injury." Estimates for FASD prevalence in North America vary. The CDC has cited a conservative estimate of 5 percent, and CanFASD has pointed to estimates closer to 8 percent. In research for my first book, *Sip by Sip: Candid Conversations with Adults Living with FASD*, I found a 2020 article by Svetlana Popova, Danijela Dozet, and Larry Burd that stated that "99.99% of people with FASD are undiagnosed." Put another way, the diagnostic rate was described as 0.01 percent.

Numbers matter, but they cannot fully describe the human cost of being unseen. The gap between prevalence and recognition is not simply clinical oversight. It reflects decades of limited professional knowledge, narrow diagnostic assumptions, and systems that often fail to recognize neurological differences when they are not visible on a face, scan, or basic laboratory test—as I learned when I discovered FASD in My Life. If you listen to my podcast, *Living with FASD: Candid Conversations with Patti Kasper*, or have read my first book, *Sip by Sip: Candid Conversations with Adults Living with FASD*, you know that FASD entered my own life through my work. As a foster and adoption social worker, I watched families struggle, and children experience repeated placements. Families were often asked to meet needs they weren't prepared to understand. I became certified in Trust-Based Relational Intervention (TBRI) and trained parents in my community using this trauma-informed approach.

Still, I sensed that something more was needed. A friend told me that her three adopted children were affected by FASD, and I invited her to speak to my post-adoption support group. That conversation changed the way I understood behavior. I completed hours of FASD training through FASCETS and later enrolled in its year-long neurobehavioral certification program. Then my husband said, with characteristic sarcasm, "Oh, is *that* what's wrong with you?" I turned to my mother and asked whether she had used alcohol while pregnant with me. "Oh yeah," she answered, apparently surprised by the question, as if to say, "Doesn't everybody?" She gave birth to me in the 1960s, before people understood the effects of prenatal alcohol exposure. Drinking and smoking were woven into ordinary life (in cocktail culture, doctors' offices, public buildings, and workplaces). Over the following months, pieces of my own story began to fit together. I understood more about my physical struggles, my need for workarounds, and the profile of both challenges and abilities that shaped my life. Understanding replaced some judgment with compassion.

What Systems Fail to See

FASD has often been missed because medicine has placed too much weight on what can be easily seen or measured. When a person does not show selected facial features, an obvious intellectual disability, or a simple biological marker, differences in regulation, sensory processing, executive functioning, learning, and health can be misread as misconduct, lack of effort, or attention-seeking. This is why the first question needs to change. Instead of asking, "What is wrong with you?" we can ask, "What happens for you, and what helps?"

The Cost of Inaction

The consequences of under-recognition reach far beyond diagnosis. People with FASD may encounter avoidable difficulty in healthcare, education, employment, housing, relationships, and justice systems when their neurotype is mistaken for noncompliance or poor character. Prenatal alcohol exposure is associated with many co-occurring health conditions, though we must be careful not to assume that exposure is the definitive cause of every diagnosis. While future clinical research will likely find causative links for some of these conditions, we are not there yet; for now, this high rate of co-occurrence clearly shows a complex bodily relationship we need to study more closely. As research continues to clarify these whole-body connections, the need for prevention, early recognition, accommodation, and lifelong support becomes more urgent. The cost of ongoing systemic negligence is not merely harmful to individuals who are born with FASD; it has an astronomical impact on our entire society. Beyond the immediate, well-documented secondary effects, which can include struggles with the revolving door of substance use, family instability, and difficulty maintaining long-term employment, we must confront the reality of the 428 potential co-morbid health conditions that frequently co-occur with FASD (a massive clinical overlap that is rarely investigated as a unified physical profile). When we view PAE through the lens of this costly medical and societal fallout, the economic and public health imperative for prevention and intervention becomes undeniable. Public and government systems often find themselves holding the bag, absorbing the massive costs of managing chronic, lifelong disabilities and the associated loss of economic productivity. Yet these same systems frequently underfund or ignore primary prevention, prenatal education, and robust public health awareness campaigns. This is not a matter of charity; it is a matter of fiscal and public health honesty, accountability, and intelligence, especially when the system itself begins to fracture under the strain. The cost is not merely financial, although systems do bear substantial costs when needs are ignored until crisis. The greater cost is human: people spend years being blamed for difficulties that could have been understood and supported. A society that invests in accurate information and practical accommodation does more than save money; it treats people with honesty and dignity.

From the Fire, Wildflowers:

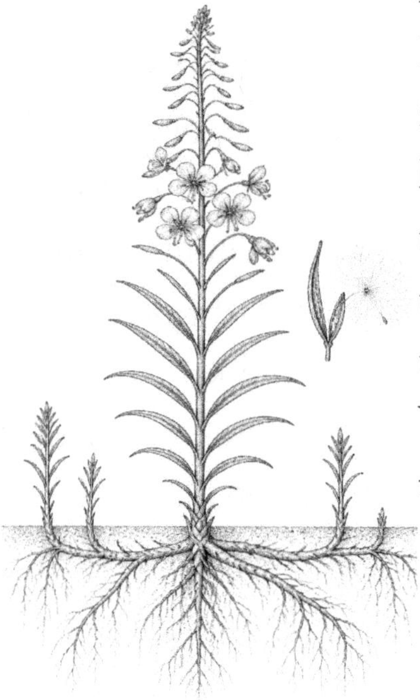

Alcohol has sometimes been called "firewater." Prenatal alcohol exposure can alter development in lasting ways. The effects are real, and the losses can be profound. Fire imagery tells the truth about injury without ending the story there. After a wildfire, the land does not return unchanged. The burn remains part of its history. Yet wildflowers are often among the first living things to emerge in fire-altered soil.

We do not see a scorched wasteland;
we see altered soil
built to sprout something beautiful.

The iconic **Alaskan Fireweed (*Chamerion angustifolium*)** is designed for this very reclamation, its seeds sleeping deep in the soil for years, waiting for the intense heat of a forest fire to clear the canopy and crack open their possibility. They do not erase what happened. They reveal life's capacity to respond, adapt, and become visible in a changed landscape. That is the heart of our Wildflower Nature. People with FASD are not failed versions of neurotypical people. They are people with distinct neurotypes (people who may need different supports, pacing, sensory conditions, communication tools, and ways of participating). Their lives do not need to resemble a formal garden to hold beauty, contribution, purpose, and worth. Society often recognizes only familiar forms of intelligence: those that are easily measured, predictable, and rewarded by schools, workplaces, and institutions. But a meadow is more than the blooms we recognize first. Its health relies on a range of plants with different needs, rhythms, strengths, and contributions. Human communities work the same way. A narrow definition of intelligence overlooks the focused interests, persistence, honesty, fairness, creativity, sensory awareness, and unconventional problem-solving that many people with FASD bring to the world. For example, what is often labeled "perseveration" can also be experienced as profound tenacity, commitment, and the ability to stay with a concern others abandon too quickly. The neurological pattern may be the same; the meaning changes when we move from deficit-only thinking to a fuller view of the person.

When Systems Prune Instead of Support:

The macro-system (our bureaucratic corporate landscaping conglomerate) is designed to shear, spray, and pull us up because we refuse to conform to a manicured lawn schedule. Frontline caretakers in this system, including many passionate social workers, find themselves trapped under a rigid corporate contract that prioritizes uniform compliance over organic, individualized care. As social work professor William "Liam" Curran summarizes this systemic friction: "I know there are good social workers out there that are pushing the needle, but they're doing it at a cost because the system is not pushing the needle with them. Yes, I nudge, I nudge,

I nudge, but it has to be systemic in terms of the response." I remember times when I advised parents to withhold rewarding activities as a bribe for "good" behavior. That was before I understood that behavior is not moral, and it is all too often reflexive. It is data: a reflection of how a brain and body are managing the conditions of the moment. When a person is overwhelmed, punished, or shamed for a stress response, the demand becomes heavier. When the environment is adjusted, the person has a better chance to regulate and participate. The goal is not to force a wildflower to imitate a garden plant. The goal is to understand what conditions allow that wildflower to grow.

From Compliance to Accommodation:

Environmental accommodation changes the question from "How do we make this person comply?" to "What support makes participation possible?" This difference matters at every age. Adults with FASD may benefit from the same clear communication, sensory awareness, organizational tools, breaks, predictable expectations, and environments that respect a finite metabolic battery. FASD does not end with childhood, and neither does the need for accommodation. The question remains: "What happens for you, and what helps?"

Pivot Points: Putting Chapter 1 into Practice

- **For the Professional** —Treat challenging moments as opportunities for investigation rather than control. When a person is struggling, ask what underlying need, sensory condition, communication barrier, stress response, or battery drain may be contributing. Let accommodation, not compliance, guide the next step.

- **For Caregivers** — For one week, notice opportunities to replace rigid compliance tools with environmental supports. Try visual steps, transition warnings, shared routines, sensory resets, or fewer demands during low-energy periods. Observe whether regulation changes when the goal shifts from hiding stress signals to finding a workable reset.
- **For Those Living with FASD** —Name one part of your Wildflower Intelligence: a strength, talent, way of noticing, value, or ability that is meaningful to you. When the world pressures you to fit a shape that does not fit, choose one form of self-support. That might mean declining a battery-draining task, asking for clearer steps, taking a sensory reset, using a reminder system, or giving yourself more time.

Up Next

This chapter has named why FASD remains in the shadows: systems often view a complex, lifelong neurophysiological reality through a narrow lens. We have entered the diagnostic desert and begun to see how a different understanding can make room for Wildflower Intelligence. In Chapter 2, we leave linear categories behind and begin mapping the 4D Framework. We will move from asking people to fit a false standard toward understanding neurodiversity as part of the broader range of human capacity.

Sources and Resources

Maternal Exposure and Prevalence Data: Centers for Disease Control and Prevention (CDC) Maternal Self-Report Surveys on Alcohol Use During Pregnancy. These reports confirm that approximately 14.28% (1 in 7) of pregnant individuals report alcohol exposure, with 5% engaging in binge drinking. https://www.cdc.gov/alcohol-pregnancy/data-research/facts-stats/index.html

Clinical Prevalence Studies: May, P. A., et al. (2018). Prevalence of Fetal Alcohol Spectrum Disorders in 4 US Communities. Journal of the American Medical Association (JAMA). This landmark study establishes the conservative active-case prevalence of FASD at 5% of the general population (1 in 20).

North American Prevalence Rates: Canada FASD Research Network (CanFASD) Issue Papers. These policy briefs estimate the broad North American prevalence of the spectrum at up to 8% of the population (1 in 12). https://canfasd.ca/2024/12/18/updated-issue-papers-on-the-prevalence-of-fasd/

The 99.99% Diagnostic Gap: Popova, S., Dozet, D., and Burd, L. (2020). Fetal Alcohol Spectrum Disorder: Can We Change the Future? Alcoholism: Clinical and Experimental Research.

Chapter 1
Podcast Guests

- **Susan Rich, MD**, Episode 23 *(A Candid Conversation with Dr. Susan Rich)*
- **William "Liam" Curran, LCSW,** Episode 101 *(The Invisible Struggle of Addressing FASD in Child Welfare)*
- **Claire Coles, MD,** Episode 132 *(FASD Across the Lifespan: A Longitudinal Perspective with Dr. Claire Coles)*

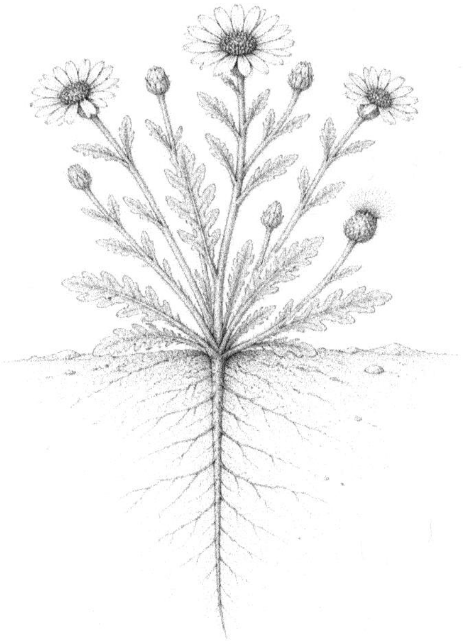

The Desert Gold flower requires a specific sequence of environmental triggers in order to bloom;
likewise, our wildflower intelligence
requires the right environment for us to bloom

— CHAPTER 2 —

The Functional Fingerprint

"Acceptable ranges do not magically make life easy or erase problems that the declaration of normalcy eliminates from care."

The Linear Illusion

When we hear the word "spectrum" in medical or psychological diagnostics, we often picture a straight line, a continuum from "low functioning" on the left to "high functioning" on the right. This linear scale typically uses an arbitrary IQ score over 75 as a gatekeeper to deny support services, oversimplifying human capacity. But your biological reality is not a flat line. As first responder and self-advocate Jake Tjapkes put it plainly, "Flat lines only fit dead people." You are a multifaceted, three-dimensional being whose unique profile is as intricate as a precious, custom-cut gemstone or geometric crystal, resulting in a naturally jagged, scattered pattern across multiple functional domains.

This flat, binary default stuck because of the way medicine evolved from studying cadavers, battlefield wounds, and early public health (rough contrasts of alive vs. dead, healthy vs. sick. In those eras, the impact of a poison was confined to a few overt symptoms, like detecting arsenic on a corpse. While a binary, linear scale works for positive or negative blood tests, it is a dangerous yardstick for measuring the multi-systemic damage of a gestational neurotoxin. How a person functions reflects a complex biological interplay among organs coordinating within our bodies and how those capacities fit our surroundings. As society shifted from an agricultural world of manual labor to an industrial world of machines, and finally to a technological world of sedentary, increasingly abstract cognitive tasks, the fit of our biological systems became entirely dependent on what activities are demanded of us. This is why relying on a flat IQ score as the pivot for determining capacity and contribution is so fundamentally broken.

The Fallacy of Normal

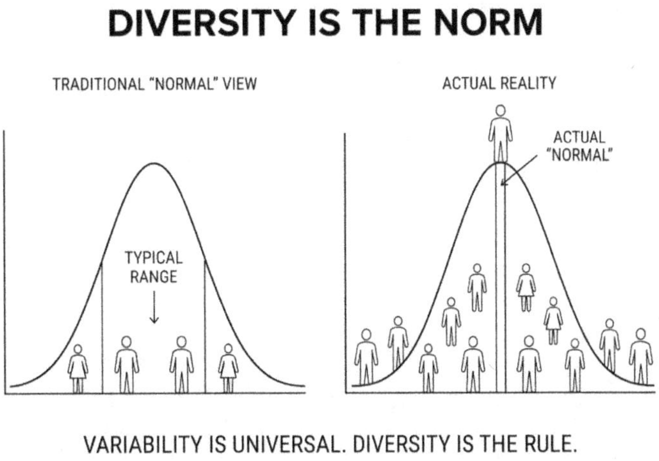

When we rely on a linear diagnostic spectrum, we tend to look to the middle, implicitly treating that broad range as "neurotypical". This is a fallacy.

As AJ Locashio suggested in our discussion, neurotypicality represents only the narrow, central peak of the human variation curve. Most of the world interprets the bell curve as a central "normal" eighty percent, reserving the far tails of the graph as the only true outliers. But classifying those who are truly neurodiverse (as demonstrated by their severe daily struggles and the massive, exhausting metabolic cost of masking as "normal" simply because their standardized scores fall within that broad middle range is needlessly cruel. True neurotypicality (an individual who sits perfectly at the median across every single cognitive, sensory, and somatic domain) is a statistical illusion. In reality, the sought-after "normal" at the center of the bell curve represents only a tiny fraction of humanity, a narrow one percent peak. (Maybe it's me, but I don't even use the "normal" setting on my washing machine!) Multi-dimensional diversity across the lifespan is the true biological norm, not an anomaly. In this light, diversity is the norm, and the rigid one percent ideal is the true outlier.

It is fundamentally misguided to try to "fix" an individual so they match this narrow peak. We are not dealing with a deviation from a standard; we are dealing with human variability as a natural fact. Neurotoxins heighten variability, which is already extant. Within the larger neurodivergent community, we use the term ***neurotype*** to describe various biological configurations of neurodivergence (such as Autism Spectrum Disorder (ASD), Attention Deficit Hyperactivity Disorder (ADHD), the combined profile of AuDHD, or Fetal Alcohol Spectrum Disorder (FASD). I further use the term "**neuroprint**" to refer to the individual's unique combination of strengths, challenges, and learning preferences, as unique to them as their fingerprint. Ultimately, whether society celebrates that neuroprint as a highly specialized asset or pathologizes it as a catastrophic deficit depends entirely on what it demands of us.

When we force an individual to fit the linear model, we flatten their identity and ignore a range of capacities by failing to capture who they are. Instead of asking how we can push an individual toward the center high point of that bell curve, our perspective must shift to understanding the individual's unique profile and providing the environment they need to function and thrive. This requires a transition from a diagnostic "sieve" focused on isolating and curing a problem to a multidimensional system of support that respects the complexity of the whole person. We are more than just extremes on a spectrum, high or low, givers or takers, workers or unemployable in a human economy! What each of us can do also depends on what kind of human economy we participate in. We must evaluate a society's capacity to be a place where all have a stake in shaping and participating in it, rather than simply judging the individual.

The Convergence of Evidence

For years, skeptics in medical and social services have dismissed the voices of the diversity community. They label our findings as anecdotal. They call it "soft" literature instead of "hard" science, arguing that because this data comes from people living with the condition, it lacks scientific rigor.

They are wrong. In the field of FASD, we now have strong scientific validation. By combining our community-led data with massive institutional datasets and independent clinical studies, we now see a clear convergence of evidence. This is no longer a matter of opinion. It is a matter of documented record.

Three distinct methods confirm the systemic health challenges faced by individuals with FASD:

1. **A Community-Driven Record:** The ALC "Lay of the Land" survey captured data on 428 health conditions associated with prenatal alcohol exposure. This perspective captures daily

realities that clinical snapshots often miss. It shows the breadth of what we face across the lifespan.

2. **A Clinical Longitudinal Study:** Dr. Claire Coles, who has researched this field for five decades, has tracked cohorts over many years. This clinical backbone confirms that the individual profile of one's living experience does not occur in isolation. The variable pattern of neurophysiological impact is indeed present and predictable across persons living with FASD.
3. **A Massive Institutional Analysis:** Brandon Nattel from the University of Georgia conducted a landmark study published in *Nature*. He used the H-Cup database. This medical repository contains records for about 35 million people. By reviewing hospital discharge records and standardized diagnostic codes, he mapped the health issues of individuals diagnosed with Fetal Alcohol Syndrome on a national level.

Dr. Coles confirmed that when these three diverse methods are compared, the findings are identical. As she noted, "What he found in that large data set and what we found from the self-report of our people and what they found in the 'Lay of the Land' are all the same."

This convergence and confirmation of evidence form the basis of the 4D Framework, ending the debate over whether these 428 health conditions are merely coincidental. As Dr. Coles emphasizes, we have three valid methods for collecting information, all of which raise the same concerns. We are no longer pleading for recognition. We present irrefutable evidence of the effects of the neurotoxin alcohol on human health throughout the lifespan.

The 4D Perspective

Dimension 1: Neuroprint (D1)

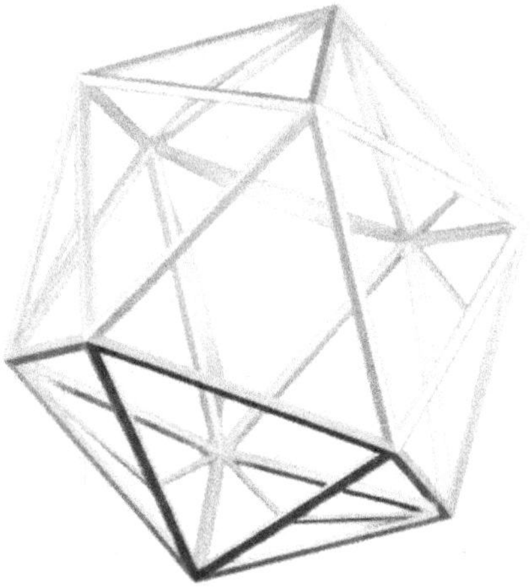

Let us correct the lens that FASD is a "brain-based" disorder. Alcohol acts as a solvent that, during gestation, disrupts the cellular signaling required to build *every* organ system in the body. FASD is a systemic condition with individualized effects across all organs and networks within the body. The brain extends its functions throughout the body, not just to the mind's operations above the neck. Physical co-morbidities are clinical signatures of FASD. When we view the individual through the 4D Framework, the physical body is an equal partner within the neurodevelopmental profile. This reality is part of the condition's neurotype, but each individual's neuroprint is the unique expression of that neurotype.

As a straight line cannot accurately represent the realities of Fetal Alcohol Spectrum Disorder, we will use a multi-dimensional Framework. To help people visualize the nature of the individualized profile of vulnerabilities and capacities left in the wake of prenatal alcohol exposure, imagine a shape with many facets, each representing a different domain of human function. One facet is working memory. Another is processing speed. Others represent abstract reasoning, sensory integration, emotional regulation, impulse control, or expressive language. Still others reflect aspects of physical functioning, such as the HPA Axis, motor coordination, and visual cortex function, to name a few.

This multi-dimensional concept explains the scattered findings that often frustrate families seeking a diagnosis. When a person with prenatal alcohol exposure undergoes comprehensive testing, evaluators often look for a recognized pattern characteristic of a specific diagnosis. However, because alcohol affects the body across many domains and to varying degrees, test results show a scattered pattern of vulnerabilities and capacities that do not fit neatly into accepted diagnostic patterns. School psychologists and clinicians often feel confused. They might say, "We cannot make sense of this. It is behavioral; mental health can address this." Except it does not (not effectively). They fail to realize that scattered findings reflect the unique neurotype, the primary pattern of FASD. Often, the portrait can look a bit like a hybrid between varying aspects typically seen under diagnoses of ADHD, CPTSD (complex post-natal trauma), the Autism Spectrum or other diagnoses, however with three rather problematic features in addition; memory impairments, fatigue, and sensory overwhelm which are more commonly recognized with localized head injuries and cognitive impairments seen in aging, such as stroke and dementia, or Alzheimer's. Alcohol's impact has significantly damaged the regulatory bandwidth of the child exposed in utero, and this hit to the bodily battery life of the person remains a challenge over the course of development.

This brings us to the most significant pitfall in diagnostic assessment: the averaging effect. Standard assessment tools create an average score. This suppresses the inconsistencies and spread of functional differences that define an FASD profile. By seeking an average, clinicians ignore the individual neuroprint revealed by this wide scatter.

My colleagues, Deb Evensen in education, Jodee Kulp in family advocacy, and clinician Antonia Rathbun Lindsey, each bring decades of deep experience to this field. Our rich conversations over the years reflect our shared passions through our respective lenses and hold many of the essential pioneer threads I have woven into the 4D Framework. By moving away from linear spectrum concepts, we can better capture how our strengths and vulnerabilities coexist without forcing us into a neurotypical mold.

This multidimensional Framework is a powerful tool for accurately conceptualizing this health condition and for optimizing recognition of how to build workarounds based on our capacities. By visualizing each area of function and capacity, we acknowledge the whole person: the body culture of the individual's neurotype and way of functioning. We are not points on a flat line. We are complex, multi-dimensional beings living in a variety of settings with different expectations and potential outcomes. Some individuals may have a high level of verbal expression yet struggle with sensory regulation. These contradictions are normal for us. They are the signatures of our individual profile. We must shift our focus. Instead of trying to fix the individual to match some abstract normalcy, support needs to match the specific neuroprint and build on its capacities.

As my friend Carl Young articulated, "People keep trying to categorize me by my cognitive deficits, but my FASD is *far more physical* than it is cognitive. My body has been fighting a war since before I was born." This war for survival and rebuilding is a constant physical demand. When the body suffers from systemic inflammation or immune dysfunction, the whole system is sapped of the surplus fuel required to manage complex cognitive tasks.

Dimension 2: Metabolic Energy (D2)

Think of our metabolism as a battery with a fixed lifespan that fuels mental and physical stamina. For a person without FASD, a full battery often signals 'normalcy'. For a person with FASD's unique changes, the battery is chronically drained by persistent physical demands. Invisible pressures draining the battery can include gastrointestinal distress, skeletal and neuromuscular anomalies that challenge posture and motor activities when moving through the daily routine, autoimmune flare-ups, and chronic pain. These are not separate diseases so much as integral, developmental system characteristics of life following PAE.

We can advocate for diagnostic assessments that include our physical co-morbidities, which chronically drain our battery. By centering on this biological reality and the reality of fluctuating battery life in our 4D Framework, and bearing in mind that the functions that occur within our bodies have a metabolic energy price tag, we stop asking the individual to "try harder". Instead, we provide support that aligns with their physical reality. We recognize that executive function is directly tied to the integrity of the body's internal systems and to those systems' fluctuating capacity relative to load.

Dimension 3: Environment (D3)

For someone living with FASD, the environment is rarely neutral: it is either a source of support or a source of strain. Nature teaches that it is completely unrealistic to expect individuals to force themselves to adapt to one-size-fits-all surroundings. Environmental design draws on principles of nature, adapting surroundings to accommodate variation among individuals. This is the core concept of "goodness of fit". When environmental demand exceeds a person's biological capacity, the organism fails. We see this as behavioral dysregulation. It is not a moral failing. It signals a mismatch between the person and their surroundings. Shifting the responsibility for adaptation from the vulnerable person's brain to the room's physical and sensory architecture is the real work of habilitation.

When we fail to do this, we force the individual into constant, unsustainable effort. This preserves battery capacity for learning, connection, and success. Instead of asking why someone cannot handle a space, we must ask what in that space is causing a system crash. We then change the environment from draining to sustaining the individual.

Dimension 4: Time (D4)

D4 is Time. This reality pushes us beyond static, diagnostic snapshots. Fetal Alcohol Spectrum Disorder is not a fixed state. It is a lifelong journey. The interaction between prenatal alcohol exposure and environmental load creates a perpetually shifting capacity for functioning over the lifespan. As life roles change, such as moving into a new job, starting a

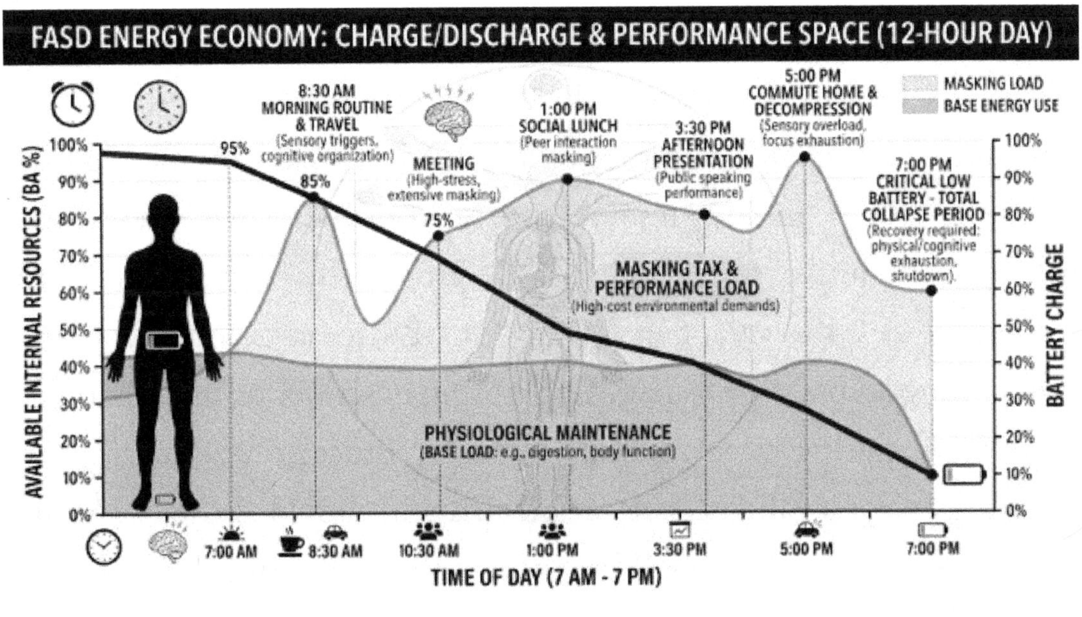

relationship, becoming a parent, or navigating middle-age health shifts, novel environmental demands render old workarounds obsolete.

The cumulative wear of allostatic load means the stamina we had at twenty is not the stamina we have at forty. While all people experience physical changes, those of us with FASD find our physical bodies and nervous systems burning out prematurely. This biological reality is not a personal failure; it is the physical manifestation of living a lifetime in a body programmed by prenatal alcohol exposure. In midlife, many self-advocates experience a profound "cognitive bloom," developing deep wisdom, emotional intelligence, and creative self-advocacy. However, just as their intellectual clarity peaks, their physical bodies hit a wall of somatic burnout from carrying decades of unaccommodated load. As Dr. Tamara Bodnar notes, "Environment matters so much, and there's really a lot of room to modulate and treat and support and prevent." This means that aging with FASD is not a fixed, doomed trajectory, but an ongoing process of creative resilience and supportive adjustments.

For many adults, the path toward this creative resilience begins with a search for answers after decades of unexplained struggle. While a formal diagnostic evaluation can be difficult to access in adulthood, self-advocates can begin their journey of self-discovery using online cognitive screening tools. One such resource is **BrainOnline**, a free, scientifically validated cognitive screening tool developed by researchers at the University of California, San Diego (UCSD) to assess neurocognitive functioning across the lifespan. Carl Young describes using this "online brain scan" during his own adult discovery process, recalling that the resulting analysis validated his suspicions and provided the exact push he needed: "I did it as myself because I suspected, but I didn't know...

the resulting email that I received from the university was, 'You really must speak to a clinician to get the diagnosis, because these factors are telling us that you have this condition or this disorder'." By taking this test at home and sharing the results with a clinician, adults can bypass initial gate keeping and secure a targeted referral. (The direct link to this screening tool is provided in the Sources and Resources section at the end of this chapter).

The 4D Mandate

The 4D Framework is not merely theoretical; it is a diagnostic and systemic mandate. If we acknowledge that FASD reflects a multi-faceted neurodevelopmental profile (**D1**), a unique physical metabolism with distinctive functional energy parameters (**D2**), the need to match environmental load to our functional profile (**D3**), and a lifelong, shifting maturational trajectory (**D4**), then our current systems, built on linear, silo thinking, are fundamentally unfit for purpose.

This book is built on qualitative data from hundreds of hours of interviews with people with lived experience, from which themes emerge that link personal and collective public health concerns. For years, we have parsed out symptoms in isolation, treating the gut, then the mind, then the behavior, without ever acknowledging that we were looking at the same 4D shape from different angles. People are finally beginning to put two and two together. The pieces have always been there; what was missing was the framework to hold them in relation to one another.

We can now leverage this growing understanding to drive systemic policy change towards alcohol use during the reproductive years, and towards those of us living with the health condition of FASD throughout our lives. We can mandate that every intake assessment accounts for the full 4D profile, treating physical health and its neurocognitive parameters, and ensuring support plans are longitudinal rather than time-limited. This points to the need to update public health practices and ultimately revise global health policy to protect human reproduction.

Shifting the Paradigm

The transition from a static diagnostic view to a 4D systems-based Framework requires a complete reorientation of our values and expectations.

Feature	Traditional View (Static/2D)	4D Framework (Dynamic/Systems)
Problem Definition	Behavioral issue	Biological architecture issue
Expectations	Consistent expectations	Energy-aware pacing and parameters
Support Strategy	Accommodations as permanent	Habituation-based growth & flexed accommodations across key environments
Development	Aging as a chronological event	Allostatic load & lifespan management

While finalizing this manuscript, I discovered that my 4D Framework, built on the dimensions of Neuroprint/Physical (D1), Metabolism/Energy (D2), Environment (D3), and Time (D4), is not a solitary invention but part of a wider, emerging shift in neurodevelopmental science. Researchers with neurodivergence, such as Lori Hogenkamp and her colleagues, are independently formulating methodologies that describe this same perspective. They have identified that human regulation operates through a multi-system interplay among the autonomic, neuroendocrine, immune, and metabolic domains. By formalizing these dimensions, mapping the physical baseline, measuring the regulatory bandwidth of energy, accounting for environmental tuning, and tracking longitudinal cumulative burden, we are contributing to the mandate of a new paradigm. It is now clear that traditional behavioral and medical models that rely on linear measures miss manifold effects and fall short because they view functions in isolation. A truly effective framework must account for the interplay among all four dimensions; without them, we miss the mechanisms that dictate functional stability and define the 'breaking point' of the human system. (Lori Hogenkamp has produced a wonderful YouTube video for those who want to learn more without spending hours poring through scientific journals, which is referenced in the Sources and Resources section at the end of this chapter).

Pivot Points: Chapter 2 in Practice

- **For the Professional** —It is time to discard the lens of "behavioral conformity". If you are still using tools designed for a 1% neurotypical standard, you are not treating the patient; you are managing a myth. The new clinical imperative is to shift from asking "Why won't they behave?" to "What is this unique 4D biological system communicating?" When you abandon the expectation of conformity and start mapping the system through symptoms and strengths to manage each unique profile, you create an authentic therapeutic alliance in place of masking; you team up in effective clinical collaboration to build and sustain resilience.

- **For Caregivers** — When you witness a breakdown or inconsistent performance, stop treating it as a behavioral choice. View it an inevitable result of a depleted battery. Start monitoring your loved one's energy levels the way a system engineer monitors a server load. Identify their most frequent energy drains, such as sensory over-stimulation high-stakes social interaction, or complex processing tasks, and create a charging plan. Your role is no longer to correct them; it is to map out where the environment can be modified, and what supports sensory and energetic resets for living with a battery difference. Strengths bloom where stamina is used for growth instead of mere survival.
- **For Those Living with FASD** —You have been told your entire life that your fluctuating abilities would even out if only you applied yourself. It is time to reject that story. Knowing that inconsistent performance is actually a physiological sign of the energy tax on your body's unique system changes everything. Your task is to know your signals and how to reset when needed. When you feel the masking tax start to drain your battery, map and manage the signals in your body, permit yourself to pause, reset, and unmask, even if only for five minutes. You are not failing; you are managing your unique maintenance and refueling for resilience. Trust your strengths as sources of relief, comfort, and creativity that help you sustain. Fun is good for your health.

Up Next

We have established the necessity of a 4D Framework, one that accounts for the whole body, the metabolic engine, the reality of an energy-taxed nervous system, and the need for environmental accommodations to help reset and build resilience over time. However, the path to implementing this new Framework is currently blocked by a broken gatekeeper: the diagnostic process itself.

We cannot successfully treat a 4D system with 2D diagnostic tools. The current landscape of FASD is littered with the fallout of a system that is either blind to the condition, looking for the wrong markers, or pathologizes the symptoms as moral failures or separate medical diseases rather than biological outcomes of a central whole-body condition. Having established what the condition *is*, we must now confront the chaos of how it is currently identified, or more often, misunderstood, and/or entirely ignored. In the next chapter, we will dissect the disastrous cycle within the diagnostic mirage, revealing how our current screening "sieve" lets the most vulnerable fall through the cracks, and discuss what we do about it.

Sources and Resources

- **BrainOnline Cognitive Screening Tool:** Developed by researchers at the University of California, San Diego (UCSD) to assess neurocognitive functioning across the lifespan, providing an accessible, free starting point for adult self-discovery and clinical collaboration. Available at: https://research.sc/participant/login/dynamic/6E1C35D8-9F3C-4234-A2A9-B6187B6B90FF

- **Lori Hogenkamp's Autonomic Mapping Overview:** An overview video exploring how human regulation operates through a dynamic multi-system interplay among autonomic, neuroendocrine, immune, and metabolic domains. Available at: https://youtu.be/YHg9l0G-J6Q?si=RI16xPAQse69QNSS

Chapter 2
Podcast Guests

- **AJ Locashio** - Episode 110 *(Understanding Emotional Regulation in Neurodivergent Individuals)*
- **Carl Young** - Episode 129 *(Aging with FASD: Insights, Challenges, and Hope with Carl Young)*
- **Dr. Tamara Bodnar** - Episode 135 *(Navigating Life with FASD: A Personal Journey with FASD podcaster & educator Jake Tjapkes)*
- **Jake Tjapkes** - Episode 119 *(Navigating Life with FASD: A Personal Journey with FASD podcaster & educator Jake Tjapkes)*

— Chapter 3 —

Diagnosis, Misdiagnosis, and "No Diagnosis"

"The Desert Gold flower does not make
a moral choice to close; its petals fold automatically
to protect its delicate core
from sudden, freezing temperatures."

Moving Without a Map

Moving through the world with a neuroprint that functions differently is challenging, but doing so without an accurate map can feel nearly impossible. Standard medical training is designed to provide a reliable guide, yet for millions of individuals living with Fetal Alcohol Spectrum Disorder (FASD), standard diagnostic tools simply do not fit their reality. The status of "no diagnosis" or misdiagnosis does not reflect a person's truth, but rather a flaw in our systemic maps.

FASD is incredibly common, yet the formal diagnostic rate remains at just 0.01 percent. The millions in the 99.99 percent muddle through life without understanding their struggles or why they cannot do what others expect. This leaves their brains sensitive to judgment, progressively obscuring the true nature of their biological needs. To build a hopeful path forward, we can shift to the 4D Perspective. This lens allows us to see the whole person through four unassailable dimensions: Neuroprint/Physical (D1), Metabolism/Energy (D2), Environment (D3), and Time (D4).

Cacti, Wildflowers, and the Wrong Field Guide

In the medical and therapeutic fields, clinicians are trained with a field guide designed almost exclusively for cacti and tough desert scrub. When faced with developmental challenges, they look for the familiar, deeply rooted surface-survivalists they studied in college: the obvious needles of ADHD, or the rigid, protective structures of Autism. Because their standard field guide lacks a category for delicate, underground ephemerals, professionals routinely mistake a struggling wildflower shoot for a stunted cactus or a defiant weed. They try to apply standard "cactus care" (standardized behavior plans, token economies, and superficial behavioral drizzles) to a sensitive biological seed that actually requires a deep, soaking rain of physical safety and specialized environmental scaffolding to survive. We cannot blame these professionals for reaching for the tools they were given; they are simply trying to manage a wildflower using a manual written for a cactus.

To understand why our standard diagnostic maps are so severely limited, we must recognize that we are recovering from what can only be described as a medical dark age. When many of today's adults were being carried in the womb, the medical establishment was completely blind to the dangers of prenatal exposure. Dr. Ken Jones recalls a striking illustration of this ignorance from 1971, when he and Dr. David Smith first began investigating cases of infant exposure at King County Hospital in Seattle. A pediatric resident named Christy Uland was on call when an obstetric resident asked her to research what alcohol actually did to a developing fetus quickly. She ran across the street to the medical library, pulled the only authoritative pediatric textbook available, and found a passage stating that alcohol was actually good for the baby. She rushed back to the delivery room to share her findings, and as Ken recalls, "they both rolled their eyes back, and they went running in and delivered this baby." This historical context explains why an entire generation of adults grew up feeling "weird" or "different" without ever receiving an explanation: their mothers were actively assured that their social drinking was entirely harmless.

Examining the history of this clinical bottleneck helps explain why standard diagnostics remain so narrow. When the criteria for Fetal Alcohol Syndrome (FAS) were first established in the 1970s, researchers focused exclusively on the most severe, visible, and catastrophic presentations. Those early observations were locked into institutional systems as the gold standard for what prenatal exposure looks like. If a child does not display the specific sentinel facial features (small eye openings, smooth philtrum, and thin upper lip) or score low enough on a standard IQ test, standard diagnostic checklists fail to see them. This historical bottleneck created a persistent myth: the idea that a typical face means a lack of brain-based impact.

To be fair, clinical diagnosticians must work with the formal criteria legally available to them within standard administrative systems. Today, three primary diagnostic frameworks are in use globally: the Diagnostic and Statistical Manual of Mental Disorders (DSM), the International Classification of Diseases (ICD), and the updated Canadian and Australian guidelines. While the DSM and ICD remain heavily anchored to older, more rigid checklists, the Canadian and Australian systems have simplified this beautifully by defining the condition simply as FASD *with* or *without* sentinel facial features. If the rest of the world adopted this practical approach, it would immediately simplify the clinical landscape and bridge the gap for thousands of families. But until that global alignment occurs, standard clinical assessments often miss the **Scattered Profile**. When a vibrant child walks into a clinic with an average IQ and exceptional verbal fluency, but struggles with daily Metabolism/Energy (D2) management, standard checklists show nothing. The old diagnostic models were built on a deficit-only framework designed to find what was "broken" or "missing" based on neurotypical standards, leaving absolutely no room for the unique, resilient, and often highly specialized capabilities of an individual with prenatal alcohol exposure.

Yet, people do not grow in manicured, predictable greenhouse environments. An individual with FASD adapts to their surroundings, creates their own internal architecture, and blooms in unexpected, beautiful ways. This capacity for creative survival and these unexpected assets represent what I call **Wildflower Intelligence**. This intelligence is marked by incredible out-of-the-box thinking, deep empathy, artistic brilliance, or intense focus in areas of interest. But because standard assessments were historically designed to look only for "weeds" (behaviors that disrupt a classroom or home), they completely miss the beauty of this intelligence. They use a child's actual strengths as an excuse to deny them scaffolding, leaving them to navigate a hostile, behavior-heavy environment entirely on their own.

Desert Wildflowers: Understanding the "Protective Shutdown"

In the third dimension of the 4D Perspective (Environment (D3)), we pay close attention to how the body and brain react when the environmental load becomes too heavy. When an individual with prenatal alcohol exposure (PAE) screams, throws things, or flees a room, their internal alarm system has gone off. They are not choosing to behave poorly; they are experiencing an automatic, involuntary survival reflex triggered when their physical stress threshold is exceeded. This indicates a mismatch between their unique biological baseline and the sensory or relational demands of their immediate environment.

By adding the Metabolism/Energy (D2) dimension to our lens, we shift from judging these meltdowns as willful defiance to recognizing them as vital physiological indicators of a biological battery running on empty. This intense state of alarm floods the brain with stress hormones, temporarily wiping the short-term working memory clean. If the individual cannot explain what happened afterward, they are experiencing a physical inability to perceive their own memory gaps (anosognosia). Their subconscious mind often fills those voids with plausible but incorrect details, a neurological symptom called confabulation. They are not intentionally lying. Demanding logical answers, a detailed explanation, or an immediate apology during or after this crisis only increases the trauma and prolongs the panic. Just like the Desert Gold flower tightly folding its petals against the dropping temperatures of the desert night, this protective shutdown is an automatic physical reflex to survive when the environment becomes too hostile to bear.

The Desert Gold flower does not make a moral choice to close; its petals fold automatically to protect its delicate core from sudden, freezing temperatures. (For the full biological profile of this wildflower, see Appendix: The Wildflower Field Guide).

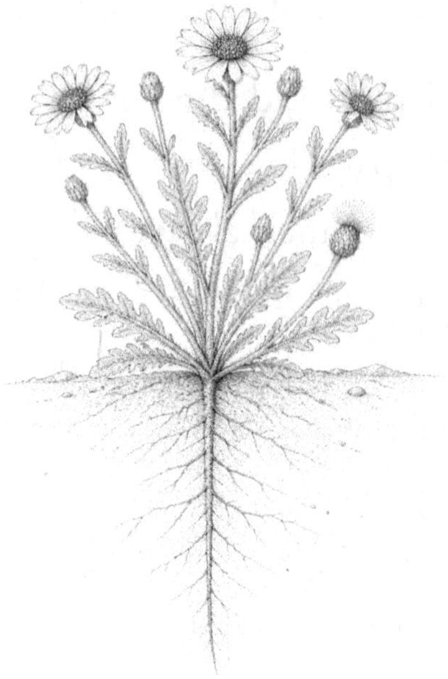

FASD vs. ADHD

In neurodiversity, ADHD is the first familiar profile clinicians recognize. Because ADHD and FASD both involve impulsivity, regulation struggles, and inattention, ADHD is often the default label. While ADHD certainly brings its own deep challenges, standard clinical medicine diagnoses it based entirely on behavioral criteria: how a person thinks and acts. Just like the obvious needles of a desert cactus that draw a clinician's immediate attention, these behavioral symptoms are the first things noticed, leading providers to default to the cactus care section of their standard field guide.

To understand why these physical differences are so deeply etched into the body, we must look at the unique, invasive behavior of alcohol as a teratogen. Unlike many other substances, alcohol crosses both the placenta and the blood-brain barrier with absolute ease, actively saturating the developing cells of the fetal brain. Dr. Ken Jones highlights this devastating reality, drawing a stark contrast between alcohol and other substances: "You can take all of the illicit drugs you can think of, heroin, marijuana, methamphetamine, cocaine, and wrap them up in a single bag, and they don't hold a candle to alcohol and its impact on a developing baby."

FASD, by contrast, is a physical, body-wide condition rooted in an organic brain and body injury. These differences are written directly into the body's biology, which explains why standard ADHD strategies often fail. With FASD, we see physical signs that standard ADHD does not have: physical survival reflexes that remain stuck in an active loop, and structural changes to the brain's physical architecture. Beyond the diagnosis itself, FASD also carries a lifelong predisposition to a wide array of potential physical health struggles over a person's lifetime, spanning 428 potential co-morbidities across all systems of the body. Whichever bodily system was actively developing at the exact time of the alcohol exposure is the one that takes the physical hit, meaning these vulnerabilities can affect anything from the heart to the immune system. Many of these issues may never develop, or may only appear years or decades later.

So, while standard ADHD describes someone who struggles with focus, FASD represents those same executive challenges wrapped inside a complex, full-body physical injury. As Dr. Kathryn Page states:

"Suppose you don't have any cognitive, adaptive, regulatory, or sensory issues or problems with abstract concepts, even if you have prenatal alcohol exposure. In that case, you don't have FASD, just a good solid case of garden-variety ADHD... But if you have ADHD and also have many of the other issues, with alcohol exposure involved, you probably have FASD."

This distinction matters. When a clinician applies standard ADHD protocols to an individual with FASD, they are using tools designed for a different biological engine. Stimulants are the go-to treatment for ADHD, but if the challenges stem from prenatal alcohol exposure, stimulants may not help. For instance, one common effect of prenatal exposure is Cortical Visual Impairment (CVI) or other oculomotor challenges. Pediatric occupational therapist Kokeb McDonald points out that children are sometimes misdiagnosed with ADHD when they are actually experiencing these physical visual skill challenges. If your vision cannot focus, your eyes struggle to team or track smoothly across the midline. Trying to read or navigate a room under these conditions requires immense conscious effort, causing profound physical fatigue that is easily misunderstood as a learning challenge or hyperactivity. Stimulants will not coordinate eye muscles or fix a brain's visual-processing loop.

Furthermore, the research behind these medications is historically flawed. Dr. Kathryn Page notes that almost all clinical trials evaluating ADHD medications were conducted in a "contaminated field" because they never screened for or weeded out individuals who had been prenatally exposed to alcohol:

"Up until very recently, nobody was sorting out who among the ADHD research subjects was exposed to alcohol vs not. So, most of the research done on the effectiveness of ADHD medication was done in a 'contaminated field'. There were no controls for prenatal alcohol exposure. No one knows what proportion.

Even when stimulants do help, perhaps because the prenatal injury resulted in a baseline deficit in their dopamine systems, standard clinical doses are often far too overwhelming. Dr. Paul Connor notes that standard clinical doses are often too much for people with FASD, causing intense side effects with very little cognitive benefit.

This trial-and-error cycle of medication-switching is not new. In his early work, Dr. Daniel Amen spent years distinguishing among different subtypes of ADHD to explain why some individuals responded beautifully to standard stimulants while others struggled, including one specific profile that required holistic, sensory-based support rather than pharmaceuticals. He noted that without expensive, specialized brain scans, doctors are often left to prescribe by rote, switching drugs simply to chase behavioral relief. But when we look back at these subtypes today through our 4D lens, a simple question remains: In those early years, before the biological overlap with FASD was ever questioned, how many of those "treatment-resistant" profiles were actually individuals with unrecognized prenatal exposure? Rather than looking for a completely different biological engine, the clinical community was simply doing its best to distinguish among complex subtypes within the ADHD label.

FASD vs. Autism

Autism is another common clinical profile that can easily be confused with FASD, as both conditions share a strong tendency to hyperfocus, experience sensory sensitivities, and rely on predictable daily routines. However, standard autism typically shows a narrowed, highly specific cognitive profile, whereas FASD exhibits a highly scattered array of executive function and memory gaps. While an autistic individual may find genuine comfort in drilling down into specific routines, an individual with FASD may get stuck in a repetitive perseveration loop that represents a physical, brain-based stress response rather than a comforting preference. When clinical evaluations default to autism, they often overlook the highly individualized, scattered nature of an FASD profile. While some individuals on the spectrum may experience hidden processing delays or language-processing struggles despite high verbal fluency, these challenges are highly unique to the individual and are never a universal template.

Carl Young, a fellow FASD self-advocate and father, noted that most people with FASD have prior diagnoses, such as ADHD, autism, trauma, or OCD, due to providers' unfamiliarity with FASD or their having rationalized the misdiagnosis. As Carl shared, providers often say, "Well, we can get you services if we use this other label instead."Choosing a more familiar label for services may seem practical, but it carries long-term, devastating risks. Speech-language pathologist Elizabeth Kriston warned: "If we keep misdiagnosing, then it just increases the autism numbers... which don't need to be increased." Doctors often assign autism or ADHD to access services, avoiding FASD's stigma. However, while these alternative diagnoses might secure school accommodations, they leave a person completely blind to their true medical history. While they do not contribute to the diagnosis of FASD itself, and many may never develop, there are 428 potential physical co-morbidities linked to prenatal alcohol exposure that can emerge across any system of the body depending on the timing of prenatal exposure. Recognizing FASD on a medical chart ensures these biological predispositions are actively monitored long term, rather than missed or mismanaged as unrelated health crises years or decades later. Behavioral strategies for autism or ODD, like rigid token economies, sticker charts, or ABA (Applied Behavior Analysis), often backfire spectacularly with FASD, resulting in more trauma, anxiety, burnout, and family hardship.

In the Absence of a Diagnosis: From Early Frameworks to 4D Matrix Mapping

In 2010, educator Jody Allen Crowe introduced a pioneering model for FASD identification, rather than clinical diagnosis, to foster a better understanding of students and their unique needs within the educational system. While his framework offered a valuable, non-shaming path, his approach never fully caught on. This was likely because it was so strongly tied to childhood and academic settings, and because the broader field was simply not yet ready to receive a non-diagnostic, needs-based model. For adults, families, or professionals navigating daily life outside a school setting, we need a simpler, more universally applicable, non-diagnostic tool to map support.

This universal compass is the **4D Matrix Mapping System**. The Matrix Map is a simple, non-diagnostic tool that allows us to bypass the clinician's signature and immediately start auditing our needs and engineering supportive environments. Instead of waiting years in the Diagnostic Desert, we can map any challenging situation across the four dimensions:

- **Neuroprint/Physical (D1):** Mapping the individual's unique physical wiring, sensory integration, and brain-body baseline, recognizing that behaviors are reflective data rather than moral choices.
- **Metabolism/Energy (D2):** Auditing the somatic battery, tracking the heavy metabolic energy tax of masking, and identifying active energy reserves to prevent regulatory collapse.
- **Environment (D3):** Analyzing the rooms we move through and shifting the burden of adaptation from the brain to the physical, sensory, and relational architecture of our surroundings.

- **Time (D4):** Factoring in slow processing speeds, chronic fatigue, and developmental pacing, while respecting the need for strategic pauses and transitions.

By using this simple matrix, individuals and families can immediately reclaim their sovereignty, translate their complex lived experiences into plain prose, and identify the exact environmental scaffolding they need to grow and bloom beautifully.

The Trauma of Authority and "Progressive Lenses"

Gaslighting happens when someone in a position of power repeatedly downplays, dismisses, or explains away our reality, symptoms, and experiences, causing us to doubt our own sanity. Dr. Jennifer Fraser offered deep explanations of how our societal systems shape us for this vulnerability, simply stating: "We are all susceptible to gas-lighters."

Dr. Fraser explains that this conditioning starts long before we ever set foot in a doctor's office. From an early age, around four or five, our brains get wired by standard educational systems to raise our hands, sit quietly, and defer to the authority figure in the room. We are punished for being distracted when our sensory systems or other physical sensations make it impossible to focus on anything outside ourselves. We unconsciously carry that conditioning straight into adulthood and directly into the doctor's office.

Because physicians hold such immense societal authority, Dr. Fraser notes that we tend to be deferential unquestioningly. Dr. Jerrod Brown discussed how individuals with FASD often experience heightened suggestibility and difficulty asserting boundaries under pressure. We naturally want to avoid conflict, which makes us especially vulnerable to power dynamics. When you mix a doctor's authority with a neurodivergent patient's natural desire to please, it creates a perfect storm in which our lived experiences are completely swept under the rug.

But whether the gaslighting is malicious or just a simple human mistake, the damage to the patient feels the same. To protect ourselves from this pattern, Dr. Fraser suggests that patients learn to wear "progressive lenses" when dealing with healthcare systems. Wearing these lenses means seeing the helpful, caring side of professionals while also staying aware of systemic and ego-driven biases in the background. If we are unsure, we can request copies of our chart notes to see what is being reported after a visit. We can learn to stand up for ourselves, understanding that professionals are human. They can make mistakes, work within flawed systems, and often remain unaware of the complex, multifaceted realities of neurodivergence.

When our lived experiences are repeatedly dismissed by the very professionals who are supposed to help us, the trauma builds up layer by layer. Jessica Birch, a passionate Australian advocate living with FASD, powerfully summarized the devastating physical and emotional effects of this pattern during her interview for my first book:

"The amount of gaslighting, dismissals, snobbery, and diminishing of serious symptoms I experienced throughout my journey to diagnosis... made me very ill and essentially prolonged unnecessary suffering. The gaslighting needs to stop, and women need to know exactly what alcohol does to the developing child."

A Message to the Reader

Dear reader, if you've spent years collecting a jumble of partial diagnoses that never quite fit, or if you're living in the frustrating, ambiguous space of having "no diagnosis" at all because standard clinical guidelines require a history you can't provide, please hear me: Your struggles are deeply valid. You are not imagining this, and you are not broken. Your strength is remarkable; otherwise, you wouldn't still be reading and gathering new information.

The Way Forward

Ultimately, the diagnostic desert is not a place you are meant to inhabit, but it is a landscape we commonly traverse, so let's navigate it with precision. While a formal diagnosis remains the clinical goal, we no longer need to wait in limbo to understand our own needs. By shifting to a whole-body, 4D view, we can shed the weight of ineffective treatments and describe our reality more accurately.

The landscape of neurodivergence is changing. Conditions like ADHD and Autism, once deeply stigmatized, have moved toward broader societal acceptance as our understanding of neurodiversity has grown. However, the stigma surrounding FASD remains distinct and pervasive, rooted in outdated cultural judgments rather than in the full biological experiences we live with!

The power of the 4D Framework lies in its ability to bridge the gap between your lived experience and a provider's clinical understanding. By organizing your daily needs into the four dimensions (Neuroprint/Physical (D1), Metabolism/Energy (D2), Environment (D3), and Time (D4)), you create a clear, functional portrait of how your body and brain manage the world's demands. By presenting this level of detail, you transform a typical clinical encounter into a targeted collaboration focused on practical accommodations and a better daily quality of life, taking your whole-body functioning, rather than just surface behaviors, into account.

Pivot Points: Putting Chapter 3 Into Practice

- **For the Professional** — Review your diagnostic intake workflow. Identify one diagnostic label you frequently use that may be a catch-all, and evaluate whether a shift to a neurophysiological lens would provide more effective, long-term support for the patient. Focus on functional and adaptive assessment tools rather than waiting for written parental confirmation of exposure, and actively assess for unintegrated primitive reflexes, and help patients and families understand and monitor their lifelong predisposition to the 428 potential somatic co-morbidities that can emerge across any physical system depending on the timing of prenatal exposure.
- **For the Caregiver** — Reflect on the period before you understood the body culture of your loved one. How did believing in the labels of laziness or defiance affect you as their guide? How does this 4D Framework apply to your daily routine with them? What 3 stress signs (e.g., shallow breathing, dilated pupils, physical rigidity) and 3 strengths (e.g., creative problem solving, intense focus, artistic talent) does your loved one show

that can help you pivot when the allostatic load alarm goes off, and the background noise becomes overwhelming? Where and how does their reset happen?

- **For Individuals Living with FASD** — For those of us living with FASD, resilience is a daily, courageous act of navigating a world not built for our brains. I invite you to reflect on your own beautiful journey through the 4D Perspective. Are you honoring your unique **D1** needs and fiercely protecting your **D2** reserves from the sheer exhaustion of masking? I invite you to confidently seek **D3** workarounds (like visual calendars, noise-reducing headphones, or a quiet nesting spot for recovery) that let your unique nature flourish safely within your own **D4** Time. I invite you to celebrate your everyday victories and remember Josh Bechtel's wisdom that "half a loaf is better than none." I invite you to connect with your tribe, drop the mask, and embrace the truth that your tenacity is actively changing the world.

Up Next

We have explored the diagnostic mirage and unpacked the limitations of traditional desert field guides. We've seen how the wrong map (or no map at all) renders individuals trapped in a system that overlooks, dismisses, and under serves their biological reality. Even when a diagnosis is secured, the real work of integrating its unique implications into daily home, school, and work settings requires applying 4D principles. How do our diverse neuroprints survive the standard environments we deal with daily? In Chapter 4, we move from the clinical office to the classroom to explore the "quirky kid" years and the real need for habilitative support in early learning environments.

Sources and Resources

- **Neuro-Informed ADHD Subtypes:** Amen, D. G. (2001). *Healing ADD: The Breakthrough Program That Allows You to See and Heal the 6 Types of ADD*. Putnam. This clinical resource explores six distinct subtypes of ADHD and highlights how unique biological wiring requires tailored, sensory-based, and holistic supports rather than standard, rote stimulant prescriptions.

Chapter 3
Podcast Guests

- **Carl Young** – Episode 104 *(Understanding Neurodiversity: Beyond FASD with Carl Young)*
- **Elizabeth Kriston** – Episode 17 *(Diagnosing ND-PAE with Liz Kriston, LSLP)*
- **Dr. Jennifer Fraser** – Episode 116 *(Bullying & Medical Gaslighting with Dr. Jennifer Fraser)*
- **Dr. Jerrod Brown** – Episode 34 *(Understanding Suggestibility with Jerrod Brown)*
- **Jody Allen Crowe** – Episode 64 *(6 Stages of FASD with Jody Allen Crowe)*

- **Dr. Kathryn Page** – Episode 18 (*Intellectual versus Adaptive Functioning with Dr. Kathryn Page*), and Episode 83 *(Navigating Neurodiversity with Dr. Kathryn Page)*
- **Kokeb McDonald** – Episode 99 *(The Hidden Power of Reflexes: with Occupational Therapist Kokeb McDonald)*
- **Dr. Ken Jones** – Episode 27 *(A 50-Year Look back and Hope for the Future with Dr. Kenneth Lyons Jones)*, and Episode 55 *(Unmasking FASD: Insights from Dr. Kenneth Lyons Jones)*
- **Dr. Paul Connor** – Episode 13 *(FASD Diagnosis for Adults: Overcoming Inaccessibility)*

— Part 2 —

FASD ACROSS THE LIFESPAN

— CHAPTER 4 —

Childhood & School: Learning to Fight Our Biology

"Heightened sensory sensitivities
may persist into early childhood,
along with delays or difficulties in inhibiting reflexes
and other gross and fine motor and language differences."

Wildflower Seedlings: Rethinking the "Quirky Kid" and Early Milestones

Reflecting on early childhood with Fetal Alcohol Spectrum Disorder (FASD), we see a mix of unique and sometimes puzzling traits. At home, these children are affectionately called the "quirky kids." They may have intense passions for specific interests or objects that other children are not particularly drawn to (tools, rocks, or other nature items), boundless physical energy, or deeper empathy for animals and living things in nature.

For many families with young children, sleep, feeding, and daily functioning can be challenging, even as the child grows physically. Parents may struggle with differences in their young child's ability to sleep, feed and function smoothly adapting to seemingly routine environments and changes to settings (going from the home to the car, to a store, then back home, for example) finding themselves handling meltdowns that become major episodes of shrieking, stimming, aggression and other rigid responses which go on longer, are stronger, and are more intense than simple tantrums they are told to expect (a tantrum can last up to 20 min, whereas these episodes can persist for up to an hour or longer which is atypical for younger children). The children may have sensory sensitivities affecting their mouths, skin, scalp, and extremities causing a host of stimming responses or aversive reactions towards food, clothing, and routine patterns of affection in the parent-child relationship (some children lick, suck on, or strike their family members despite coaching otherwise, for example, while others are clingy as barnacles and protest any time that they are not held in a certain way).

Heightened sensory sensitivities may persist into early childhood, along with delays or difficulties in inhibiting reflexes and other gross and fine motor and language differences. This changes how the child's early self-help skills emerge; for example, learning to use a spoon or other utensils may be shunned, and the child defaults back to eating with their hands. When they are still doing so by age 6, despite the family trying to teach courteous table manners and the ability to repeat a rule such as "use your napkin, not your arm, to wipe your mouth," adults are perplexed about what to do. Parents try to teach routines but are unsure how to adapt the home environment for a more consistent outcome.

Parents naturally want to adapt the home environment to support their child; they may flex schedules, remove tags from clothing, change from direct overhead to indirect lighting sources, use white noise machines, and develop particular routines of physical affection involving massage or rhythmic movement like bobbing or swinging, or other kinds of care to help cushion the child's intense reactions. Dr. Emily Hargrove noted that her parents did not wait for a diagnosis before meeting her needs as a young child. "So, my parents relied on the grace of God, and all of the things they were already doing without realizing how beneficial they were."

Jody Crowe connects these early years to Stages 1 and 2 in his developmental mapping (see chapter 3). Here, neurodevelopmental differences are present yet managed by the family. Natalie Vecchione notes that parents instinctively try to adjust routines before seeking a formal diagnosis to keep the family system stable. Emily Hargrove described her parents as providing enriching environments and activities, including piano, martial arts, and gymnastics lessons, which helped build her brain's plasticity. My own mother was highly intuitive; her persistent demands for an appointment with my pediatrician wore him down, and he gratefully admitted to her that if she had not gotten me in to see him when she did, my as-yet-undiagnosed diabetes would have killed me. However, most parents feel unsupported and unsure how to help their children. As a retired social worker, I found that almost all of the foster and adoptive parents I worked with across a 25-year career reported to me that counseling always made their children's behavior worse.

Crossing the Threshold: The Widening Developmental Gap

While parents struggle to manage the unevenness of their child's abilities and delays at home, this mismatch worsens when their child is involved in more structured environments such as schools, faith communities, and recreational programs, where expectations of "good behavior" rise sharply. The expected behavior is believed to reflect parenting that has ‘provided, nurtured and protected’ enough to teach children the basics of self-regulation and social reciprocity. Instead, the child lives within a body culture that is stressed beyond their ability to regulate or communicate, even if they have learned how to talk. Outside the home, their wonderfully complex neurodivergent profile is forced into a painful conformity-driven mold, highlighting the gap between their chronological age and developmental stage. As the gaps widen and struggles intensify, families need a roadmap for revising their expected developmental timeline.

During one of my earliest podcast episodes, fellow FASD podcaster Natalie Vecchione mused, “I like to call myself the accidental advocate because I was just a mom and, you know, we struggled with so many of the symptoms and characteristics of our son’s FASD... nobody really connected the dots until just before his second birthday.” She went on to explain, “Sensory issues were what we thought when we brought him home. We were like, ‘Oh, these are his cute little quirks.’ They were quirks, but then they became impactful because they were impairing him.” She observed that without proper accommodation and a complete shift in viewpoint, this developmental gap grows exponentially, leaving our children behind on the wrong side of society’s expectations and facing bullying and teasing from peers. Society expects that because a child is seven years old chronologically, they should have the cognitive functioning, emotional regulation, and social skills of a typical seven-year-old. However, neurologically, that same child might have the emotional processing of a three-year-old, the receptive language skills of a four-year-old, and the concentration and intellect of a bright, highly focused 7-year-old in specific areas. The wide range of abilities perplexes the adults who guide their learning activities.

By adjusting the diet of sensory factors at home, parents may prolong the child's ability to meter energy out to meet the daily demands their body must manage. The tragedy of the school system is that it fundamentally fails to account for these dimensions, treating the child's need for regulation as 'non-conformity' rather than a biological necessity.

This mismatch places children in Crowe's Stage 3 (elementary) and Stage 4 (middle school/adolescence) as requirements rise. At the same time, neurological functions remain uneven, a challenge that educator Deb Evenson has discussed for decades. In a joint episode with Deb Evenson, Dr. Kathryn Page discusses how an unaccommodated FASD profile can appear "cunning, baffling, and powerful" to outsiders. Early childhood learning is concrete and play-based, but by 4th grade, elementary school education includes abstract information and a faster pace. Without a tailored plan, the PAE-affected child has difficulty keeping up under new pressures, and their random fit within surroundings leaves them dragging on at the edge of collapse.

Nury van Beers shares how undiagnosed FASD in a strict school caused exhaustion from constant sensory overload. When a child spends most of their energy filtering stimuli that compel movement while forced to stay still, there's little stamina left for academics. By mid-morning, their nervous systems are over-saturated and fatigued; teachers misinterpret zoning out or fidgeting as inattention or discourtesy toward peers. They are seen as 'acting out' for attention or deliberately picking power struggles with staff when they can no longer inhibit motor activity, fly out of their seat, or touch other students.

Educational Gaslighting and the Load on Neurobiology

When executive processing systems are overwhelmed, the brain triggers cognitive rigidity. Eileen Devine clarifies that this is a physiological state, not stubbornness or a power struggle. "Cognitive rigidity is not a choice; it is a protective response," she notes.

When a neurodivergent child under excessive, prolonged load finally becomes overwhelmed, unsafe, or unable to process more changing demands, higher-level cognitive functions in their brain shut down. The reflex system kicks in. When they act extremely rigidly, perseveration has taken over. Their specific routine, rule, or practice is all that gives order against the crushing cascade that has depleted their reserves. This is not a cognitive decision; it reflects the body's neurophysiological default setting in a low-battery state. We can see it as a warning that they are running on empty. Sadly, standard educational practices respond to this rigidity with increased behavioral pressure, insisting that the child comply and adapt immediately. Eileen reframes this entirely, calling attention to the basic human need essential to supporting a child in this neurological freeze or fight reflexes: "As human beings, we have a biological imperative for people to be with us in our distress. We don't necessarily need the solution or for things to be fixed, or to be left alone until we can reboot."

If educators ignore this biological imperative and punish a child's rigidity, they are working against what the body needs. Enter what Dr. Jennifer Fraser calls institutional educational gaslighting. When an authority figure repeatedly tells a child an environment is safe when it feels dangerous, or insists a task is easy when it is neurologically impossible in that moment, the conflict piles onto the fundamental overload the child is already enduring. This challenges their trust in their own perceptions, as if they are expected to agree with an authority figure rather than their own bodily information.

Dr. Fraser's groundbreaking neuroimaging research reveals a disturbing biological truth: chronic gaslighting, emotional abuse, and systemic shaming physically change the structure of the developing brain, actively shrinking the hippocampus (central to memory and learning) while over-activating and enlarging the amygdala (a central part of the alarm system). By forcing a neurologically altered child into a conformity-driven box, the school system isn't teaching them a lesson; it is actively damaging their neurobiology, trapping them in a perpetual state of survival-driven hyper-vigilance.

The Anatomy of a School Crisis: Petal Closure and Anosognosia

Throughout this childhood and school journey, we use the term "petal closure" (often experienced as an acute somatic shutdown or "bristle attack") to describe the intense, often overwhelming episodes of dysregulation. This phrase avoids traditional, pathologizing words like "tantrum" or "meltdown." To understand this, we look to the national flower of Iceland, the beautiful, eight-petaled **Holtasóley (Mountain Avens, *Dryas octopetala*)**.

In a classroom, we constantly ask young children to pay attention and "track" the teacher. For a child with FASD, this constant tracking and filtering of background sensory noise is an exhausting, high-cost metabolic task—much like a solar-tracking wildflower absorbing every bit of sun to fuel its core. When a sudden, overwhelming sensory or emotional load sweeps through a classroom, the child undergoes an involuntary physiological reflex.

"Our quiet shutdowns are not stubbornness; they are the automatic, involuntary act of petal closure used to protect our sensitive biological core."
(For the full biological profile of this wildflower, see Appendix: The Wildflower Field Guide).

This is the biological reality of a neurodivergent nervous system under severe stress. In her clinical art therapy sessions, Antonia Rathbun-Lindsey observed that children can more easily show than say what distresses them, using visual symbols—like a dark, choking cloud or a tightly folded bud —to represent how worn down they feel. When we see a "petal closure" in a school setting, we are not looking at a willful act of defiance; we are looking at a D2 (Metabolism/Energy) crisis. The child is running low on fuel, and the petal closure is the nervous system's involuntary way of saying, "I am over-taxed and need an immediate energy reset." If we viewed behavior through this 4D lens, we would stop asking how to discipline the shutdown and start asking how to clear the sensory environment and allow a reset.

When a child with an FASD is placed in a high-stimulus environment—such as a crowded school hallway, a chaotic classroom transition, or a loud assembly—their sympathetic nervous system registers stress that can quickly escalate into panic. It shifts into fight-or-flight long before the reasoning system can organize or speak to identify the threat. While this micro-somatic shift (the microscopic spike in cortisol and adrenaline) is invisible to the human eye, it is a physical reality that begins minutes before a visible shutdown or petal closure occurs. As we will explore in our intervention roadmap, this chemical bracing is so real that a trained service dog can smell the shift before anyone in the classroom even knows a crisis is brewing.

The systemic misreading intensifies after a petal closure has occurred. When the child finally calms down, a principal or teacher will frequently ask them to explain their behavior, posing questions like, "Why did you do that?" or "Don't you see what you did wrong?" Barb Clark shares a vital neurological concept that every parent, provider, or educator must understand to avoid misinterpreting this reaction: anosognosia. Anosognosia, a condition caused by physical damage to the networks involving the right parietal lobe, is a neurological error of self-appraisal; the person cannot recognize an obvious gap in their thinking or actions. A child with anosognosia has an impaired grasp of their own thought stream or actions; for example, caught with their hands still on a cookie or toy, they might say "She took it. I never saw it. The dog did it," (when none of these statements match or fit the fact of their hand holding the object). When asked to look at what is still in their hand while blurting conflicting statements, the child cannot account for their mindblindness.

The child, caught in the act while looking a teacher in the eye and saying, "I didn't do that; they made me; I wasn't even there," is not showing deliberate intent to lie or manipulate the adult. They don't have denial. They cannot accurately account for where the mismatch occurred between others' expectations and their reactions. Spikes in adrenal cortisol (the stress hormone) from petal closure wiped their short-term working memory clean. They do not know why they do not know what went wrong! Furthermore, they are expected to explain where they made an error in the chain of events. As a result, their memory fills in the blanks with plausible explanations that do not match one another, a neurological symptom called confabulation.

The Playground and Neighborhood Ecosystem: Suggestibility, Acquiescence, and Victimization

The structural and social vulnerability of a child with an FASD goes beyond the classroom and does not end at the boundary of school property; risk on the playground is pronounced and spills into neighborhood streets. School and neighborhood peer groups form a complex social hierarchy based on a blend of social skills, rapid interpretation of nonverbal cues, and future-oriented risk assessment. Because an FASD profile can commonly include social naivety and disconnection between action and consequence, the children may be vulnerable targets within their communities.

Dr. Jerrod Brown's extensive clinical research into vulnerability and victimization highlights how underlying executive functioning deficits specifically distort a child's sense of time, boundaries, and peer hierarchy. On an unmonitored playground, a child with FASD cannot map out the shifting social boundaries or subtle power structures of peer groups in real time. This disorientation triggers three chilling vulnerabilities in social and recreational spaces: suggestibility, acquiescence, and credulity. Due to their underlying neurobiology, these children exhibit a high degree of suggestibility, making them easy to influence, for the better as well as the worse, depending on the stage and type of peer influences.

Dr. Brown explains the particular operational danger of acquiescence in peer exchanges: "When we talk about acquiescence, it's that tendency for an individual to answer 'yes' or agree to things, especially when they feel cornered, anxious, or when an authority figure or a dominant peer is pushing them. They will agree to things merely to escape the immediate distress of the social interaction, completely unaware of blame or legal consequences downstream."

Credulity worsens this, making the child naturally inclined to believe whatever a peer tells them and ignore logical counter-evidence or a realistic assessment of danger. The desire to have social acceptance and positive participation is readily exploited, especially in adolescent culture.

Neighborhood peers and predatory individuals quickly recognize this vulnerability on the street. All too often, on the walk home, a group of kids will intercept a child with FASD, using their suggestibility as a tool. They might whisper, "Hey, it would be funny if you break that tree branch in Mrs. Smith's yard," "Go steal that soda from the corner market," or "Carry this backpack home for me." The child, desperately seeking connection, validation, and a feeling of belonging with the neighborhood group, complies immediately. They love humor, want positive social interaction, and respond, completely unaware of the impending consequences or that others are actively exploiting them as targets of humiliation.

When the property owner calls the police or a store manager intervenes, the instigators scatter instantly, disappearing down side streets. The neurodivergent child is left standing alone on the sidewalk, holding both the blame and the evidence. Because they cannot process the intense panic of an interrogation quickly enough, their people-pleasing reflex kicks in under the pressure of adult questioning. They will agree to whatever narrative the authorities or angry neighbors feed them, leading directly to police contact or juvenile justice involvement before they even reach their own front porch.

Jody Allen Crowe stresses the tragic predictability of this exact path when the systems around them ignore a child's prenatal exposure history. Jody points out that when we fail to recognize the biological basis of prenatal exposure early on, we condemn the individual to a predictable course of secondary disabilities and interaction with institutions. Without an early, brain-compatible roadmap of strategies to help the vulnerable child, the natural outcome of this systemic neglect is entanglement within the juvenile justice system.

As RJ Formanek tragically summarizes: "What they saw was the [behavioral] explosion... but they'd never see me." These lived experiences demonstrate an anguishing reality: when a child's invisible brain injury goes unsupported, and they are continuously scapegoated for their gaps in adaptive coping skills and defensive, reflexive behaviors, trauma and maladaptive habits accrue that can haunt them long into adulthood.

Rethinking Support

Dear reader, if we want our children to survive and truly thrive during their childhood and school years, we need to completely dismantle the rigid behavioral box and replace it with a compatible map of environmental support for children with neurophysiological differences. This requires a multi-layered intervention framework that closes gaps among institutional policy, somatic physiology, and emotional expression.

First, it would help to transform how we handle the Individualized Education Program (IEP) process. Educational advocate Kelly Rain Collin encourages families and professionals to move beyond the standard, bureaucratic, performance-driven approach of IEP meetings. School districts are well-known for walking into an IEP meeting and saying, "This is how we always do things; this is our standard protocol."

Instead, Kelly Rain Collin urges families and professionals to halt the behavioral conveyor belt and collaborate on what we can do differently. School systems must adapt to the child's neurobehavioral needs, shifting the focus from a standard behavioral modification contract to what can support the student's brain-based needs. This requires a profound paradigm shift from "trying harder" to "working differently."

Similarly, pioneering educator Deb Evensen has argued for decades that taking a neurobehavioral approach in classrooms makes everyone's job easier, not harder. In her collaboration with Jodee Kulp, she co-created the "13 Beams of Moonlight" framework, a beautiful set of principles and strategies for supporting students in remote Alaska communities. This framework serves as a practical, brain-compatible guide for educators, encouraging them to replace rigid behavior charts and public tracking systems with predictable, visual, and relationship-based supports.

When we shift our focus to the physical environment, we stop expecting a vulnerable nervous system to manually override its own biological baseline. By implementing simple, reliable environmental workarounds, we can take the pressure off the child's D2 (Metabolism/Energy) battery, preserving their limited spoons for learning and self-regulation. In the language of the 4D Model, an accommodated classroom is not a luxury or a special favor; it is a permanent ramp, a somatic necessity for a brain affected by prenatal alcohol exposure.

Second, we can look beyond traditional, human-centered interventions and introduce external somatic regulators that regulate a child's nervous system before a petal closure occurs. Jodee Kulp, who trained the very first FASD Service Dog in her Expanding Mindz with Canines program, also uses animals, primarily dogs, to build executive function skills, self-care, and parasympathetic regulation in the animal's owner. She became an animal behaviorist to quickly gain a broad understanding of how to work with highly reactive minds, because her daughter with PAE was a concrete learner with a passion for animals. This has proven to be a tremendous strength for many people with FASD!

A decade later, Allison McCormick became the second FASD Service Dog trainer of note. FASD Dogs in Kansas became the third notable source for this specialized support. Allison McCormick's clinical work with specialized FASD service dogs tackled some of the initial challenges Jodee had encountered and offered a brilliant neurobiological blueprint for this physiological scaffolding. As an experienced social worker and passionate expert in canine intervention, Allison shows that these dogs do not rely on logic, behavioral token economies, or verbal lectures; they work through pure biological co-regulation, engaging their human counterpart in beneficial regulatory and communication interactions with every practice.

When a child with FASD is placed in a high-stimulus environment, such as a crowded school hallway, a chaotic classroom transition, or a loud assembly, their sympathetic nervous system registers stress that closes into panic. It shifts into fight-or-flight long before the reasoning system can organize or speak to identify and name the environmental factors that heighten the threat. Allison explains that a highly trained service dog can actually smell the chemical shift, the sudden, microscopic spike in cortisol and adrenaline, or detect the micro-somatic bracing of an impending petal closure before the child, teacher, or parent is even aware that a child's crisis is brewing. (I can attest to the sensitivity of a dog's amazing scent work: Tzaylie, my diabetic alert dog, was routinely 45 minutes faster at detecting impending low blood sugar crises than the state-of-the-art technology when I got her in 2012. There were 54 times from when she was placed until she retired, which would have been fatal events had I waited for my body to "feel" the symptoms she sensed and intervened on.)

An FASD dog executes specific, trained physical interventions in response to the biochemical data generated by their human. By leaning their full body weight against the child, providing deep-pressure therapy across the child's lap, or placing its body as a buffer to block a crowding peer group, the dog acts as a grounding anchor and protector. This intense, tactile somatic feedback registers as an immediate physical "brake" to the child's accelerating nervous system by lowering their heart rate, stabilizing their breathing, and halting the physiological cascade that leads to a full neurological meltdown.

A service dog eliminates this barrier by providing pure, non-verbal somatic safety. With a working dog, there is no spoken language to interpret, no complicated emotional state to manage, and no fear of disappointment or judgment. The dog simply offers a calm, steady, unwavering mammalian nervous system for the dysregulated child to latch onto.

This sharply contrasts with traditional school "calm-down corners," "time-outs," or behavioral restraint rooms, which often feel punitive, isolating, and laden with the transactional demand to "fix" oneself before being allowed back into inclusion within the group. Animal-assisted co-regulation does not ask the child to change or perform to belong; instead, it actively surrounds them with an external nervous-system scaffold of calm presence, restoring a sense of biological safety and belonging. One can be both authentic and attuned to another being. For parents and teachers willing to view this through a neurological lens, the working dog offers powerful proof of what is possible when we stop punishing a child's distress and begin scaffolding to support their neurophysiology.

Finally, it can be helpful to use non-verbal channels for sensory and emotional organization and expression, such as the Expressive Media Continuum, as explained by Antonia Lindsey. When a child is overwhelmed by the sensory waterfall of school, asking them to label and express their feelings verbally adds further demand, instead of relieving the load. Counselors, teachers, and parents have been taught to name emotions, hoping insight will relieve symptoms. Instead, visual communication makes visible what lies beyond words: where the load builds in their bodies and what the physical distress feels like. That provides the person with a visual map to the common stuck point: where and when the threshold is too high, while giving their body a way to show what gets stuck and find a way to cope. What matters most is the bodily information, as each neuroprint is very individual. The emotional labels for a cluster of specific interoceptive signals are secondary. This framework teaches us to carefully match art and expressive materials to the child's internal state of regulation, which can improve even without specific emotion names.

The Masking Tax

As our children go through the social challenges of school years, they start to notice that their natural ways of processing information, sensory needs, unique cognitive profiles, and difficulty understanding linear social cues are often seen as "other" or "wrong." To get by, they live 'as if,' coping through a survival tactic called the "Mask of Normalcy."

This is the exhausting, constant effort to "perform" neurotypically by sitting still, monitoring voice volume, and mimicking peers' social cues, all while the brain is already overworking to manage basic regulation. This is not "fitting in"; it is a high-stakes neurocognitive performance. The "tax" is paid through deep, energetic exhaustion. When these children return home to the safety of their families, the "mask" drops, and they are left completely drained of the neurophysiological battery for further cognitive and emotional tasks, often leading caregivers to mistakenly see their meltdowns or other signs of stress collapse as an attack when, in fact, they have simply run out of the energy to sustain performance, leaving home the only safe place to explode or implode.

By replacing punitive responses with neurodiversity maps, we are not only helping them survive school; we are also laying the groundwork for them to navigate their autonomy. We are moving from a system that demands performance to one that provides support across the unique, individualized developmental timeline.

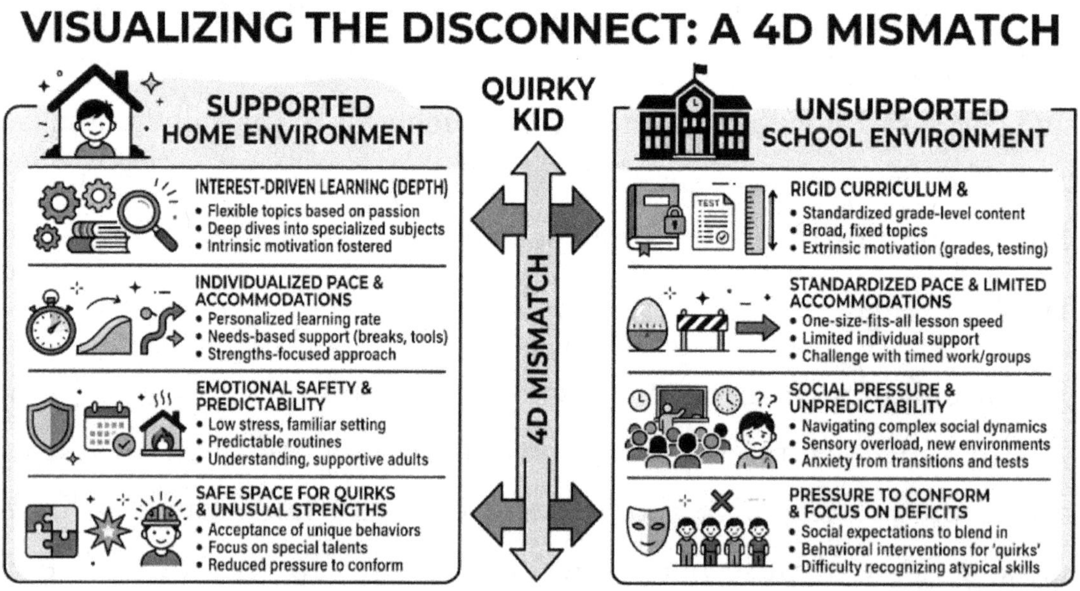

4D Living with FASD, Patricia Kasper, MA, ©2026

Pivot Points: Putting Chapter 4 into Practice

- **For the Professional** — We assess our protocol for "behavioral crises." Instead of asking "Why did you do that?" (which ignores the child's D1 and D2), what signs did we observe when the child's energy was depleted? We can replace "accountability" with a "regulation-first" protocol that respects their battery life.
- **For the Caregiver** — Use the 4D lens to observe a child's "quirks." Which ones are actually D1 strengths? Which ones are D3 reactions? When faced with a "petal closure" like a folding Holtasóley, pause and identify if it's a failure of D3 (a mismatch of input) or a depleted D2.
- **For those living with FASD** — Identify one environment (school, work, or society) that acts as a "sensory waterfall," overwhelming mental and/or physical energy. This doesn't mean you are "bad at" school (or work or community role). You have different environmental needs: in D2, your energy battery gets overtaxed. Build one D3 accommodation into your day (such as noise-canceling headphones, a specific seat, or scheduled sensory or movement breaks) to refuel.

Up Next

We've seen how the system breaks down when it forces a neurodivergent person to comply with a one-size-fits-all map. But what happens when the scaffolding is removed? In Chapter 5, we move from the playground to the cliff to adulthood, when the support structures vanish, the stakes of the "real world" skyrocket, and the transition from childhood reliance to adult independence becomes a matter of survival.

Chapter 4
Podcast Guests

- **Allison McCormick** - Episode 89 *(FASD & Trauma: How Social Services Fail & Dogs Help, with Alison McCormick)*
- **Antonia Rathbun-Lindsey** - Episode 43 (*Parenting Your Porcupine, Part 1, with Antonia Lindsey)* and Episode 131 *(Unlocking Emotions Through Art: A Therapist's Perspective with Antonia Rathbun Lindsey)*
- **Barb Clark** - Episode 118 *(Denial, Anosognosia & Delayed Remorse with Barb Clark)*
- **Deb Evensen** - Episode 14 (*Deb Evensen: Creator of Eight Keys for Adults with FASD*)
- **Eileen Devine** - Episode 112 *(Understanding Cognitive Rigidity in FASD with Eileen Devine)*
- **Dr. Emily Hargrove** - Episode 41 (*The Superpower Within: FASD and Embracing Inner Strengths with Emily Hargrove*)
- **Dr. Jennifer Fraser** - Episode 116 *(Bullying & Medical Gaslighting with Dr. Jennifer Fraser)*
- **Dr. Jerrod Brown** - Episode 22 (*Confabulation: What it is and How to Help with Dr. Jerrod Brown)* and Episode 102 *(Safety First: Addressing Vulnerability & Victimization in the FASD Community with Dr. Jerrod Brown)*

- **Jodee Kulp** - Episode 123 *(The Neurobiology of Migraines in FASD: What You Need to Know)*
- **Jody Allen Crowe** - Episode 64 *(5 Stages of FASD With Jody Allen Crowe)*
- **Dr. Kathryn Page** - Episode 14 (*Deb Evensen: Creator of Eight Keys for Adults with FASD*)
- **Kelly Rain Collin** - Episode 36 (*FASD and Education: Beyond Diagnosis in IEP Meetings with Kelly Rain Collin*)
- **Natalie Vecchione** - Episode 3 (*Our Candid Conversation with Natalie Vecchione*)
- **Nury van Beers** - Episode 15 (*FASD and Motherhood: Nury van Beers of the ALC*)
- **RJ Formanek** - Episode 44 (*From Misunderstood to Mentor with RJ Formanek*)

— CHAPTER 5 —

Teen & Transitional Years: Who Needs a Parachute

"A person may be eighteen chronologically, but have a developmental processing age of eight under stress"

If the school years often feel like navigating a sensory waterfall without an umbrella, the transition into the teen years and young adulthood can feel like finding that umbrella, only for a tornado to fly in. This transition tornado spins the individual, their family caregivers, and the professionals supporting them in its dizzying circle. The coming-of-age years are notoriously tumultuous, filled with angst, identity exploration, and a search for belonging. However, for those living with FASD, this period is exponentially more complex, as the developmental stage is rarely in sync with chronological age. To safely navigate this whirlwind, the self-advocate, the caregiver, and the professional must work closely together, shifting away from the unrealistic demand for immediate, isolated independence to build a lasting network of interdependence.

Asynchronous Growth:
The Airport Concourse and the Moving Walkway

To understand why the transitional years feel so incredibly chaotic, we must first throw away the linear growth chart. Standard societal systems are built upon the rigid assumption that human development is a uniform, synchronized march. We expect that when an individual's eighteenth or twenty-first birthday arrives, their cognitive, emotional, and social capacities will automatically catch up with their physical size. We act as if adulthood is a smooth, predictable runway where the plane is now ready for takeoff.

But for a brain impacted by prenatal alcohol exposure, development follows a deeply asynchronous growth timeline. A person may be eighteen chronologically, but have a developmental processing age of eight under stress, and an executive planning capacity of ten. Their physical body and chronological age zoom ahead, while their emotional processing and executive functioning amble along at their own organic pace.

This physical mismatch resembles a busy airport: developmental maturity ambles along the broad concourse, while the body and chronological age zoom ahead on the motorized walkway.

Society expects the young adult to be standing at the far end of the concourse, fully prepared to navigate the high-stakes demands of independent living, employment, and legal contracts. But neurologically, they are still walking the long floor, paced by a brain that simply needs more time to filter, organize, and retrieve information. Society has no clue that a young person's whole being is not on the motorized walkway. We do, however, lurch with the sudden change of pace when the walkway dumps us onto unmoving pavement. We quickly take stock, readjust, and move along. Our community's youth struggle to readjust because many aspects of them are still catching up, leading instead to a rapid depletion of their D2.

This asynchronous timeline is not a moral failure or a lazy refusal to "grow up." It is a physical, biological reality. The "tornado" of the teen years occurs because we, as a society, prematurely tear down the protective scaffolding of childhood before the individual has had the opportunity to design their own supportive, neurobehavioral workarounds.

The Transitional Age Youth Chasm: When Systems Misread Asynchronous Development

During my twenty-five-year career as a social worker, I lived on the front lines of this structural disconnect, witnessing firsthand the human cost of forcing independence on asynchronous timelines. My colleagues and I would take week-long shifts covering on-call duties, managing not only our regular caseloads but also a Transitional-Age Youth (TAY) housing program designed for supervised apartment living.

During daylight hours, these young adults—all eighteen to twenty-one years old—would meet with their assigned case managers to work on "independent living skills," such as budgeting, grocery shopping, and household chores. But during the evening and the wee-morning hours, the on-call phone would ring incessantly.

The calls would drive the staff absolutely crazy because the crises seemed so elementary, so basic: "I'm locked out of my apartment." "I need a ride." "I got into a fight with my roommate over who used the peanut butter."

Under the traditional behavioral paradigm, the staff, including myself at the time, defaulted to frustration. We viewed these midnight crises as attention-seeking behavior, laziness, or a stubborn refusal to use the tools we had repeatedly taught them during the day. (As a confession of an old social worker, adding a ninety-mile round-trip midnight commute to help a young adult open a locked door did nothing for my degree of burnout or my mood at the time.)

But we were asking the wrong questions because we were operating from an incomplete, conformity-driven map. We failed to connect the dots and realize the why: the young adult was calling us with the problem-solving skills of an eleven-year-old because, developmentally, that is exactly who they were in that high-stress moment.

During the day, in a structured, quiet, one-on-one meeting with a case manager, the young adult could access their cognitive pathways and repeat the rules of apartment living perfectly. But after the staff went home at the end of the day, and the relational pressure of roommates intensified, or the sensory noise of the neighborhood escalated, their lower brainstem registered threat. Under the weight of this allostatic load, their prefrontal cortex went completely offline, and their short-term working memory was wiped clean.

They did not call us at 2:00 AM to be manipulative. They called because their metabolic battery was empty, their cognitive GPS was broken, and they had no biological capacity to retrieve the abstract "independent" rules they had practiced hours earlier. They were not refusing to comply with the program's rules; they were physically incapable of executing them in a state of neurophysiological panic.

When our macro-systems demand total, isolated self-sufficiency at age eighteen, they are effectively abandoning highly trusting, neurodivergent young adults to navigate a hostile world entirely on their own, setting them up for a predictable cycle of eviction, exploitation, and systemic collapse.

The Forensic Pipeline: Suggestibility, Acquiescence, and Interrogation

The vulnerabilities of asynchronous development do not end at the boundaries of the housing program; they spill directly onto neighborhood streets and playgrounds. Because young adults with FASD experience high levels of suggestibility, acquiescence, and credulity, they are highly vulnerable to peer manipulation and systemic exploitation.

On an unmonitored playground or a street corner, a teenager with FASD cannot map out the shifting social boundaries or subtle power structures of peer groups in real time. Desperately seeking connection, validation, and a feeling of belonging, their people-pleasing reflex kicks in. If a dominant peer or a predatory neighborhood group whispers, "Hey, go carry this backpack home for me," or "Go take that soda from the corner store," they comply immediately. They respond, completely unaware of the impending consequences or that they are being actively exploited as the "fall person" for other people's bad decisions.

When the property owner calls the police, the instigators scatter instantly, disappearing down side streets. The neurodivergent youth is left standing alone on the sidewalk, holding both the blame and the evidence. Because their brain cannot process the intense panic of an interrogation quickly enough, they are thrust into a forensic pipeline they have no biological baseline to navigate.

To map out the internal mechanics of this crisis, we must look to the forensic research of Dr. Jerrod Brown. Dr. Brown has meticulously documented the profound intersections of neurodevelopmental disorders, memory distrust, and the dangerous phenomenon of psychological suggestibility within legal settings.

Suggestibility is a direct, physiological vulnerability rooted in the cognitive architecture of FASD. Dr. Brown's research highlights that when a neurodivergent individual is placed into a high-stress, sensory-overloading environment like a police interrogation room, their primitive survival brain immediately overrides their logical processing.

Excerpts from Dr. Brown's interviews clarify the particular operational danger of acquiescence in peer and police exchanges: "When we talk about acquiescence, it's that tendency for an individual to answer 'yes' or agree to things, especially when they feel cornered, anxious, or when an authority figure or a dominant peer is pushing them. They will agree to things merely to escape the immediate distress of the social interaction, completely unaware of blame or legal consequences downstream."

If a detective, trained to use aggressive, leading questions, repeatedly insists, "We know you broke into the store, just sign this paper so we can let you go home," the youth's executive control completely fractures. Under the room's crushing pressure, their brain distrusts its own internal, fragmented memory. To please the authority figure and escape the room's immediate sensory nightmare, they agree to whatever narrative the detective feeds them, leading directly to a signed false confession to a crime they never committed.

The Legal Gauntlet: Conformity and the Illusion of Understanding

Once caught in the legal system, the vulnerability of the FASD profile escalates exponentially. Retired attorney David Boulding delivers a devastating critique of the modern judicial machine, pointing out that our entire legal framework rests on the false assumption of conformity. David notes the systemic absurdity that contemporary courts judge brain accountability using legal rules originally written in 1854, long before modern neuroimaging exposed the physical realities of prenatal alcohol exposure.

One of the most dangerous pitfalls David maps out is the systemic confusion between verbal fluency (expressive output) and conceptual comprehension (deep cognitive processing). Because individuals living with FASD often possess highly expressive verbal skills and an eager-to-please posture, they can mimic the language of accountability perfectly. They can nod their heads, look a judge in the eye, and repeat the exact terms of a complex probation order or a bail agreement.

But repeating the words is a surface-level cognitive reflex; executing them across a linear timeline requires executive-functioning capacity that may be deeply fragmented. David describes a tragic scene that happens daily in courtrooms across the globe: A young adult stands before a judge, smiling, nodding, and agreeing to their probation terms to maintain attachment and please the court. But the moment they step away, they turn to their attorney and ask, "So, when do I go to jail?"

They did not comprehend a single phrase spoken from the bench. Yet, because they nodded, the legal system presumes they understood.

When they later fail to meet these complex conditions—missing a court date, losing a mandatory check-in form, or getting lost trying to find a probation office hidden in the basement—the court misinterprets this competency deficit as willful contempt. The legal gears lock shut, not because a violent crime was committed, but because their memory and processing speed hit a systemic wall they had no capacity to climb.

To protect our youth from these systemic chasms, we must replace abstract, verbal rules with concrete, physical, and somatic workarounds. David Boulding advocates for two highly practical, real-world interventions:

1. **The Tactical Boundary (The Jail Tour)** Because abstract verbal warnings about "getting arrested" or "going to jail" carry zero meaning for a brain that struggles to connect cause and effect, David suggests a powerful, tactile intervention. Parents and advocates can proactively arrange a physical tour of a local jail cell. Allowing the youth to touch the cold iron bars, hear the heavy slam of the door, and see the concrete floor replaces an abstract concept with an unerasable sensory boundary. This provides the concrete reality their brain needs to understand the weight of the legal system and retrieve that memory in high-risk moments.
2. **The Somatic Circuit-Breaker (The 5-Breath Apple Bite)** When young adults are caught in a transition tornado, task paralysis, or moments of sensory overload, they need an immediate physiological reset to prevent a complete system crash. David Boulding shares an emergency somatic regulatory technique: Sit up tall, place your hands flat on your thighs, close

your eyes, open your mouth wide as if you are about to bite a whole apple, and take five slow, deep breaths. This mechanical posture manually forces the nervous system to disengage from its fight-or-flight panic loop, lowers the heart rate, and pushes much-needed oxygen back into the frontal lobes, delaying impulsive reactions just long enough for the brain to recognize a bad idea.

Beyond Independence: The Supple Strength of the Arctic Riverbeauty

Dear reader, if we look across these massive macro-systems, the truth is undeniable: our societal safety nets are locked into permanent, structural blindness. They are continuously demanding typical cognitive performance from brains with physical neurological differences, and they relentlessly punish those who predictably cannot comply.

The path to young adulthood is not a linear progression, and success for the FASD community will never come from forcing individuals to navigate these hostile, punitive institutions alone. We must abandon the myth of forced, total independence. True survival and success will come only when we replace the demand for isolated self-sufficiency with the protective safety net of interdependence.

To understand what true, life-saving interdependence looks like in the real world, we look to the Eyrarós (Arctic Riverbeauty, *Chamerion latifolium*). When a roaring glacial flood sweeps through its riverbed channel, the Eyrarós does not attempt to stand rigid or fight the freezing current. If it tried to stand rigid, it would instantly snap and be washed away. Instead, the Eyrarós lies completely flat against the gravel, allowing the torrent of water and debris to wash entirely over its supple stems without breaking, relying on the neighboring root systems of its tribe to anchor it. Once the flood passes, the flower stands right back up and continues to bloom.

"When the demands of society flood like a glacial torrent, our young adults do not have to stand rigid and snap—they are permitted to lay low, protect their metabolic battery, and lean on the supportive root systems of their tribe." (For the full biological profile of this wildflower, see Appendix D: The Wildflower Field Guide).

We can build this Eyrarós scaffolding into the very architecture of our transition plans by implementing three vital, interdependent workarounds:

1. **The Translation Support Partner:** We can introduce an educated third party—such as a parent, spouse, or transition coach—into the relationship between the young adult and complex systems (such as primary care physicians, employers, or probation officers). This partner serves as a crucial, non-judgmental bridge, ensuring the individual truly understands expectations, translating jargon, and acting as an external memory bank.
2. **The Strategic Pause (The Self-Advocacy Card):** Co-designing a simple "pause button"—a physical card carried in a wallet or saved as a phone lock screen—that a young adult can choose to present when pressed to sign documents or agree to plans in high-pressure moments. This shifts the cognitive load and

the burden of explanation off their shoulders: "I do not make decisions or sign documents on the spot. My policy is to review all paperwork with my support team and respond tomorrow."

3. **The "Never Too Late" Cushion:** We can connect our young adults with peer-led, neuro-informed communities—such as the Flying with Broken Wings community—and integrate Shannon Butts' somatic "Anchor" program. By teaching simple regulation tools like rhythmic breathing, grounding, and body-based movement, we help our young adults monitor their physical thresholds, protect their metabolic batteries (D2), and find a safe, unmasked sanctuary where they can exist without the exhausting tax of performance.

By proactively providing this robust neurobehavioral scaffolding and honoring differing developmental timelines, we can finally transform hostile bureaucracies into networks of true, life-saving interdependence. We are moving from a system that demands performance to one that provides shelter, ensuring that our wildflower seedlings have the space, the soil, and the support to safely rise, adapt, and bloom beautifully in their own season.

Pivot Points:
Putting Chapter 5 into Practice

- **For the Professional** — Instead of asking, "Why aren't they more responsible?" we can ask, "What environmental workarounds are missing that would make this task sustainable?" Your job is not to help your clients to "grow up" to meet a chronological milestone; it is to help them design a supportive, interdependent scaffold that respects their metabolic battery limit.

- **For the Caregiver** — The "tornado" of the teen years stems from the gap between a teen's chronological age and their social and emotional maturity. See "beyond the behavior" to identify how the four dimensions are playing out for your loved one. Build a multi-person respite network so you are not on call twenty-four hours a day, preserving your energy to remain a steady, co-regulating presence.
- **For those living with FASD** — The world calls you "high functioning" or "low functioning" based on whether you can pass as neurotypical. Ignore their labels. Like a wildflower, you are resilient. You have a specific, beautiful neuroprint. Identify your somatic anchors—the trusted people, tools, and environments that keep you regulated—and treat them as essential equipment. You do not have to stand alone to be worthy of respect; your strength lies in your connection to the tribe.

Up Next

We have weathered the 'tornado' of the transition years, recognizing that the cliff many face is not a personal failure, but a mismatch between having neurodivergence and a system that demands neurotypical consistency. We have seen how applying the 4D lens allows us to stop pathologizing execution errors and start designing the scaffolding necessary for survival. But the arc of life extends far beyond the initial leap into adulthood. How do we sustain this effort as we age? In Chapter 6, we turn our attention to the 'Longitudinal Self', exploring what it means to build a life of purpose and regulation through the middle years and beyond, ensuring that our 4D reality is not just survived, but authentically lived.

Chapter 5
Podcast Guests

- **David Boulding** - Episode 31 *(David Boulding: the Intersection of FASD and both the Law & Sex)*
- **Dr. Emily Hargrove** - Episode 41 *(The Superpower Within: FASD and Embracing Inner Strengths with Emily Hargrove)*
- **Dr. Jerrod Brown** - Episode 22 *(Confabulation: What is is & How to help, with Dr. Jerrod Brown)*, and Episode 102 *(The Neurobiology of Migraines in FASD: What You Need to Know)*
- **Shannon Butts** - Episode 113 *(Empowering Change: Shannon's Insights on FASD and Mental Health)*
- **Tami Eller** - Episode 115 *(The Spectrum of Experience: Moving Past Labels in FASD with Tami Eller)*

— Chapter 6 —

Living (and Aging): With FASD

"Aging is not an exit from FASD,

only a continuation of the same journey."

FASD is a permanent, physical, neurodevelopmental condition that shapes the entire life-arc, yet healthcare, educational, and social systems stubbornly treat it as a temporary pediatric stage. This systemic blind spot is dangerous: when society treats adulthood as a standardized milestone at age eighteen or twenty-one, it forces individuals with lifelong neurophysiological differences to navigate a world without structural scaffolding, ignoring the reality that challenges often intensify as we age. Aging is not an exit from FASD, only a continuation of the same journey requiring evolving support across the lifespan. CJ Lutke describes this pain: "People tend to think that once someone has become an adult, all those struggles magically disappear. You're supposed to understand everything and be able to function in society. Where are all the adults with FASD (in the minds of the general public)? Only these pitiful children. No one stops to think that those same children have grown up."

During my conversation with CJ Lutke for my first book, I addressed this misconception: "I never outgrew my 'juvenile' diabetes. I stopped being a juvenile decades ago, but I'm still diabetic. You can't outgrow FASD, either."

We do not expect a person in a wheelchair to outgrow the need for a ramp. It is equally wrong to expect individuals with neurophysiological differences to outgrow their need for environmental support.

The 4D Framework: The Lifelong Reality

The 4D Framework helps us understand the FASD neurotype across the lifespan.

- **Neuroprint/Physical (D1):** Our neuroprint, our unique neurophysiological makeup, is permanent. It is not erased as we age. Are we managing our challenges over time? Do we adjust our workarounds as our functioning changes? Where can we use our strengths to our best advantage?
- **Metabolism/Energy (D2):** Aging changes our capacity. A task that was manageable in our twenties may cause a system crash in our forties or fifties. Are we adjusting our energy budget to reflect our current physical reality? Are we following good sleep habits to ensure we get the rest we need?
- **Environment (D3):** What accommodations do we need now? Are our current tools still effective, or do we need to adjust our routine or environment to match our current needs?

- **Time (D4):** Life is a continuous journey. Do our long-term plans account for our unique energy needs, or do they still reflect what we believe to be "normal" for our culture or society? As we age, do we focus on our bodies' diminished capacity or on our resilience, coping skills, and unique gifts? The challenges remain regardless of age, demanding that we align our expectations with our bodies' natural timelines rather than the artificial milestones of a neurotypical society.

The Whole-Body Reality: The 428 Co-morbidities

Fetal Alcohol Spectrum Disorder is not just a neurodevelopmental profile; it is a comprehensive medical condition affecting the whole body. Because alcohol acts as a solvent and a potent teratogen, it affects cell replication and organ tissue development in any biological system that is actively forming or being programmed at the time of exposure. While the brain remains under construction throughout all nine months of gestation, other organ systems, including the vascular network, skeletal system, endocrine glands, kidneys, and gastrointestinal tract, have specific periods of peak vulnerability. As self-advocate Alice Foote famously observed, "FASD hasn't got just a face... it has more internal organs than it has a face." When we follow the 4D life-arc into midlife and beyond, we see that the 428 physical co-occurring conditions documented by the Adult Leadership Collaboration (ALC) are not isolated medical anomalies. They represent the cumulative biological wear and tear of living in a body built on a fragile foundation, compounded by decades of unaccommodated allostatic stress.

Systemic Prenatal Exposure

↓

428 Physical Comorbidities → • Autoimmune
• Joint Degeneration
• Vascular Shift

↓

\+ Decades of Unaccommodated Allostatic Load

↓

The Midlife Friction Point → Cognitive Bloom vs. Physical Burnout

1. The Autoimmune and Inflammatory Load In adulthood, the immune system often becomes a major friction point. As neuroscientist Dr. Tamara Bodnar notes, adults prenatally exposed to alcohol demonstrate elevated baseline levels of pro-inflammatory cytokines, chemical messengers that keep the immune system in a state of chronic, subclinical alarm. Rather than presenting as simple allergies, this chronic neuroinflammation frequently manifests in midlife as full-blown autoimmune and endocrine dysregulation:

- **Systemic Autoimmune Conditions:** High rates of lupus, rheumatoid arthritis, fibromyalgia, and chronic fatigue syndrome. As self-advocate Carl Young shares, managing multiple autoimmune conditions, including rare connective tissue disorders like mesenteric panniculitis, means his body has been "fighting a war since before I was born."
- **Endocrine and Organ Vulnerability:** Early-onset Type 1 Diabetes, thyroid dysregulation, and non-alcoholic fatty liver disease (such as the Stage 3 fatty liver Mary Byrnes manages despite never drinking alcohol). Carl Young shared the double

standard and social stigma he faces managing stage four cirrhosis of the liver as a non-drinker: "When I tell people I have stage four cirrhosis, they say, 'Well, you need to quit drinking.' My response is, 'Maybe I need to start drinking, because I'm not a drinker!' Our bodies respond atypically to exposure, yet we are constantly subjected to pejorative, uninformed judgments by a medical community that views our health crises through the lens of behavioral blame."

2. Accelerated Structural and Joint Degeneration

The physical mechanics of aging with FASD frequently reveal premature wear on the musculoskeletal system. Skeletal anomalies, altered muscle tone, and unintegrated primitive reflexes force the body to exert twice the physical energy to maintain posture, balance, and gait. Over time, this mechanical inefficiency accelerates joint breakdown:

- **Early Joint Replacements:** Adults in their 30s, 40s, and 50s frequently undergo major hip, knee, or shoulder replacements (surgeries typically reserved for individuals decades older). Advocates Carl Young and Barb Clark both describe undergoing multiple joint surgeries and replacements in midlife despite never engaging in heavy construction or high-impact athletic careers. During our August panel discussion, Barb Clark and I compared notes on our extensive spinal surgeries. My lowest five vertebrae are fused, and I described the daily mechanical limit: "I can't reach my feet anymore. That's a bit of a drag," finding functional relief in Skechers with built-in shoehorns. Barb Clark, who underwent spinal decompression and fusion four years ago, described how chronic somatic pain persists as a constant background hum: "My husband will see me grimacing and say, 'I thought you had surgery.' And I'm like, 'You just don't understand pain, buddy. It's there all the time.'"

- **Spinal and Connective Degeneration:** High prevalence of early-onset degenerative disc disease, severe scoliosis, and radioulnar synostosis, which severely restrict adult mobility and daily stamina. In addition to her work that found elevated rates of inflammation (itself a predictor of challenging health outcomes) in adults living with FASD, Dr. Bodnar is also investigating the gut microbiome to understand these systemic links. She notes, "We're also starting to look at the gut microbiome because we know in other neurodevelopmental conditions, shifts in the microbiome are tied to health, other health outcomes, and brain changes, but actually we know nothing about this in FASD at all... We're looking in adults as well to ask: are there shifts in the microbiome? And it really appears like there are."

3. Premature Dental and Enamel Degeneration

Premature dental wear and enamelization challenges are another prominent whole-body friction point as we age. In our August panel on aging, Jodee Kulp highlighted how our dental health acts as a systemic early indicator: "Teeth tell a huge story. They tell a whole huge story for the rest of your organs and the rest of your body. So it often shows up in your teeth early."

This is not a failure of hygiene, but a biological reality. Carl Young recalled his dentist's confirmation of this organic structural breakdown: "You could brush your teeth all day long... but it won't save your teeth.

You're eventually going to need dentures." I recalled my own realization during FASCETS training, where instructors explained that prenatal exposure can disrupt dental development, leading to too many or too few teeth: "I have always been missing four teeth. They just were never there. My mom's older brother, coincidentally, had four too many." Living with an FASD is an expensive condition, with premature dental wear and systemic joint surgeries draining both our physical reserves and our financial battery over the lifespan.

The Overlooked Baseline: Interoception

A persistent hurdle in medical care is the "standard presentation" trap. PAE alters the neurological pathways of interoception, our body's internal sense of signals such as pain and temperature. We often don't present the "typical pain profile" the physician expects. PAE alters the neurological pathways of interoception, our body's internal sense of signals such as pain and temperature. We often don't present the typical pain profile physicians expect. When I broke my arm as a teenager, no one believed me because I was not crying, and X-rays were required before anyone took the injury seriously. This mismatch continues into adulthood, where doctors regularly misread our internal distress. Barb Clark notes: "Our pain tolerance is very different. I don't go to the doctor every day or every week, but when I go, I'm like, they need to really listen to me because something is going on if I'm sitting in their office." Unfortunately, this can lead us to ignore early signs and symptoms that could prompt more timely care for certain illnesses. Our bodies communicate in a different, individual biological language. We are not "fine" simply because we do not look like we are in pain. In our living experience panel discussion on aging well episode, Carl

Young shared an extraordinary example of how pain shifts our baseline biochemistry, even when our conscious minds cannot detect it: "My wife can tell when I'm in pain before I can usually, because she says I smell different. She says I have a different scent to my body when I'm in pain." This chemical shift is a biological reality that occurs long before our brains register interoceptive awareness, demonstrating why objective, non-verbal tracking is so vital.

Antonia Rathbun Lindsey shares that interoception also helps us know whether we are hungry, full, or thirsty. When a child with FASD feels a gnawing sensation in their stomach, caregivers often ask, "Are you hungry?" As a result, the child learns to label all stomach discomfort as hunger. However, that gnawing feeling is frequently anxiety. Apprehension and fear can cause a sensation as if the stomach 'drops,' tightens, or cramps. It can reflect stress, not a need for food. Actual hunger and fullness signals can get completely scrambled. When the brain does not accurately signal the physical need for food, an individual may only experience the somatic fallout of hunger as unexplained irritability, anger, or agitation. Conversely, the brain might never receive the signal that the stomach is full. A child might gorge on food until they vomit simply because they cannot feel satiation.

Finally, these internal sensory and gut differences directly impact bathroom habits. Chronic constipation, bedwetting (enuresis), and soiling (encopresis) are frequent, difficult challenges. They are physical symptoms tied directly to the neurodevelopmental profile of FASD. They are not a person's character, a behavioral choice, or a failure of parental potty-training efforts.

The Lifespan Tension: Cognitive Bloom vs. Somatic Burnout

FASD is a lifelong physical and neurological condition. Many adults discover their emotional maturity later in life. Mary Byrnes shared: "I'm more open now than I was in my twenties and thirties to trying new things... it is definitely part of the bloom for me." This delayed social and emotional maturation is a beautiful development, yet it stands in stark contrast to our physical trajectories. Our culture has internalized a rigid stereotype of adult autonomy that teaches us false benchmarks, assuming that independence and physical capacity increase in lockstep with age. But for the FASD neurotype, peak physical and neurological vitality often falls in our thirties and forties.

Just as this late cognitive maturity peaks, physical health may decline sharply, and many adults with FASD age faster than the general population. I recently realized that while I am in my early sixties, I move through the house like someone in their seventies. This is alarmingly common. Barb Clark notes: "At 57, again, from a brain-based perspective, I feel like I'm in my prime, right? But my body is not happy... There are many things that we can't do."

Carl Young experiences this physiological amplification. Despite not being a drinker, he battles liver disease, lupus, and autonomic dysfunction. He notes: "Every health outcome you can imagine in somebody with an FASD is amplified." His doctor confirmed: "Your body is aging exponentially faster than the general population... you're aging faster than I would consider typical for a 54-year-old man." We find our minds blooming while our bodies are burning out.

The Statistical Reality of Burnout

We are navigating an accelerated physiological breakdown that the current medical framework does not account for because most doctors do not realize how FASD impacts the body over the lifespan. Dr. Claire Coles reports that in their sample, "the probability of having cancer by the time you're thirty-five was five times higher in this group."

Nuances of the "Premature Aging" Theory

Dr. Coles notes that standard epigenetic clocks do not show simple "fast-forward" aging. Instead, we see a pattern of cumulative instability. Our bodies have spent decades on high alert to survive in a neurotypical world. Dr. Tamara Bodnar explains that this stress manifests as inflammation, which predicts and causes further health complications. We are exhausted by the biology of FASD plus the decades spent navigating neurotypical expectations. Beyond the biology of FASD, the grueling, decades-long performance of navigating neurotypical load and expectations acts as a direct driver of our accelerated physiological breakdown. Carl Young captures the disconnect: "My mind thinks I might be 25, and physically my body is like, you know, you are probably closer to 90." RJ Formanek laments this loss of the physical self, noting: "That is what is so frustrating: I have always been very athletic all of my life and it is hard for my brain to tell my 60-some-year-old body 'you cannot do that anymore.'" For many of us, this is not just a frustrating idea; it is a source of deep grief and anger at our bodies, which seem to function on a timeline our spirits don't share.

The sheer metabolic tax of the Mask of Normalcy compounds this tension. Jodee Kulp recounted a flabbergasting moment from her career when researchers at a New York conference projected her face onto a twelve-foot screen as a random example of an adult FASD profile (right before she was scheduled to speak). Standing at the podium to deliver an authoritative talk immediately after your own biology is projected to the room represents the absolute epitome of masking. While Jodee shrugged it off as "water off a duck's back," she admitted that public performance drains our metabolic reserves: "I'm just allowing my body just to be who I am at home with my family, not in a position where I have to go out and mask or camouflage, because when I have to do that, that's a lot of energy and a lot of hard work." When training a roomful of social workers recently, Carl Young explained the immense relief of unmasking: "The person who gets home 20 minutes after our session ends today is not the same person who is here now. It's like I'm taking off my Halloween costume."

We must acknowledge that no single, mandatory route to self-reconciliation exists; everyone needs to choose their own path around diagnosis. For some, a formal clinical label is a life-saving shield. For Mary Byrnes, obtaining her diagnosis in her late fifties was a physical necessity: "Had I not pursued the diagnosis, I may not be here. I would have liver failure. It's that simple." For others, like Barb Clark, receiving her diagnosis at age fifty-six was an emotional game-changer that dismantled a lifetime of guilt: "It has been giving me more grace with myself in certain areas. It's helping me to be like, 'Why do I feel guilty about this accommodation?' And still, every couple of months, I'll have a moment where I realize, 'Wait, this is me in so many ways.'"

But a formal paper is not a prerequisite for peace. Jodee Kulp, at seventy, delivered a defiant and liberating truth about her own choice to live without a clinical stamp: "Am I diagnosed? No. I did not go for diagnosis, and you know what? I'm seventy years old. I don't care."

Jodee's peace of mind comes from living "as if" the diagnosis is in place, using proactive 4D adjustments and somatic self-care without needing a clinician's signature to validate her reality.

A diagnosis changes nothing about our history; the biology was always there. But the shift in how we understand ourselves, our quirks, and our lifelong histories is a priceless source of grace and peace. We need that peace as we begin to wrestle with our bodies' limits and our own mortality. At fifty-six, I self-identified after recognizing my own story in the neurodevelopmental profiles, and at sixty, I was officially diagnosed with ND-PAE. Whether through a clinical chart or a quiet mirror of self-identification, discovering our Wildflower Nature allows us to lay down the exhausting, lifelong burden of "not trying hard enough." This self-understanding opens the door to profound emotional forgiveness—releasing the guilt of our past struggles. But to protect our bodies as we age, we must follow that emotional release with somatic grace: actively equipping our physical environments and pacing our energy so our aging nervous systems can rest safely.

The Sovereign Path:
Laying Down Our Weapons and Finding Grace

When we view the aging process through the 4D framework, we realize that rest and Dimension 3 environmental supports are not optional luxuries or passive gestures of self-forgiveness; they are medically necessary somatic equipping required to protect our long-term health.

As we look ahead and begin to wrestle with these physical limits, we are naturally brought face-to-face with the ultimate horizon of the lifespan. Aging with a prenatally altered nervous system forces us to confront our mortality not as a distant, abstract concept, but as a visceral physical reality. Yet, this confrontation does not have to be a source of terror. Instead, it can catalyze the deepest healing of our lives.

To prepare for our mortality, we must first lay down our weapons. For a lifetime, people on this spectrum have been fighting a war against our own biology, desperately trying to "perform" typical standards to prove our worth. Finding "sovereign peace" means declaring a unilateral ceasefire. It is the spiritual realization that you do not need a clinical signature or a systemic rubber stamp to be worthy of grace, space, and a peaceful resting place.

A large part of this journey is finding acceptance and peace about the decisions, reactions, or behaviors we have blamed ourselves for over years or decades. So many of us have carried a heavy, silent load of self-reproach, only to discover in our later years how prenatal alcohol exposure and our unique 4D neuroprints played into those very moments. Realizing that our struggles were rooted in a physical, neurodevelopmental baseline, not a failure of character or moral resolve, opens the door to profound relief.

With this shift in understanding comes reframing our past, self-understanding, self-forgiveness, self-acceptance, and, with that, peace. This journey of reconciliation is a vital part of the human path, holding across every culture and belief system. It is the sacred task that one conventionally faces in the twilight of life, during the process of dying. But if we can do this work ahead of time, if we can look back at our histories with compassionate, neurodevelopmental understanding and forgive ourselves today, then life becomes incredibly sweet indeed. We free up the precious metabolic energy we need to equip our environments actively, step into our creative power, and finally begin to bloom.

The Cognitive Bloom: Creativity as an Adaptive Anchor

While the physical burnout we've discussed is undeniable, a paradoxical cognitive phenomenon often emerges in our fifties and sixties: the "Cognitive Bloom." As we stop holding ourselves to neurotypical standards and finally step into our inherent purpose, people living with FASD often enter a period of unprecedented creative production. Mary Byrnes illustrates this beautifully: "I'm more open to trying new things now than I was in my twenties and thirties ... it is definitely part of the bloom for me, and it's why I'm so much more productive."

This late-life creative surge is not merely a hobby; it acts as a literal neurobiological shield against somatic burnout. When we stop trying to force typical performance and instead pivot to creative adaptive workarounds, such as Antonia Rathbun Lindsey's expressive art mediums, which help lower the defensive quills of our somatic porcupine and bypass the language centers of the brain, we stabilize our nervous systems. Shifting to creativity allows us to use our bodies' built-in parameters in new, surprising, and restorative ways. As Carl Young and Mary Byrnes show, this is the adaptive shift: we learn to dance with our hands when our legs fail, or capture the wilderness with a camera when our joints can no longer hike rough mountain trails. The closer you get to your inherent purpose, the easier things become. I use two related phrases throughout this book, one referring to our neurophysiology and the other to our cognitive assets. "Wildflower Nature" is the totality of who we are, how prenatal alcohol exposure has affected us as whole beings, and how we rise above those conditions across our entire lifespan. "Wildflower Intelligence" is the unexpected, beautiful flashes of brilliance, those creative, out-of-the-box strengths that we are exceptionally good at because we tend to be out-of-the-box thinkers.

The Dementia Connection & The Medical Silo

The ALC survey revealed that individuals with FASD are significantly more likely to face early-onset cognitive decline or dementia before age sixty-five. As neuroscientist Dr. Tamara Bodner notes, this is not necessarily classical, fast-forward Alzheimer's aging, as standard brain biomarkers like tau protein are not elevated. Rather, we are looking at neural damage driven by decades of cumulative, unaccommodated allostatic load and chronic baseline inflammation.

Unfortunately, what little training and infrastructure the medical establishment has for FASD remains almost exclusively pediatric-focused, leaving adults entirely stranded. Once we transition out of childhood, we are forced to navigate a standard medical system that is heavily fragmented and siloed. The cardiologist does not talk to the gastroenterologist, who does not talk to the neurologist. Because clinicians are trained in siloed specialties, they view an adult's scattered profile of failing body systems as unrelated anomalies rather than the cohesive, systemic fallout of a prenatally acquired neurodevelopmental injury. This structural blind spot is a dangerous vacuum that routinely gaslights and abandons the adult patient.

To survive this medical maze, we must reject the traditional "psychiatric trap" that blames our physical distress on psychological issues, and instead implement concrete lifespan workarounds.

Lifespan Scaffolding: Navigating the Medical Maze

To bridge these clinical gaps and protect our long-term health, we advocate for two vital, real-world scaffolding tools:

The **Anticipatory Wellness Card and Medical/Surgical History:** We cannot assume that all individuals on the spectrum experience atypical thresholds or responses to pain, but many of us do navigate unusual sensory responses or physical quirks. To bridge this communication gap, we can carry a small, portable Anticipatory Wellness Card in our wallets, with blank spaces for us to write our major medical and sensory details by hand.

The **Medical/Surgical History** and **HD Sunflower Badge**: Because many of us navigate atypical pain thresholds or sensory quirks, bridging the clinical communication gap is vital. We recommend typing a comprehensive medical and surgical history on your computer to print and hand directly to new doctors, surgical centers, or urgent care staff. For public and travel settings, wearing an official Hidden Disabilities Sunflower badge (hdsunflower.com) discreetly signals that you may need extra patience, time, or sensory understanding.

Saving this document on a computer lets us update it easily, print a copy, and bring it to the clinic. Completing standard clipboard paperwork by hand in a waiting room can easily take an hour and risks memory glitches under stress; printing a single neat page is far easier, and doctors absolutely love it. Keeping this file saved on our own devices allows us to maintain a dynamic, personalized clinical record that evolves alongside us.

The Clinical FASD Case Coordinator: We advocate for the systemic recognition and funding of a dedicated Clinical Case Coordinator.

While the career training paths and policy funding structures are systemic matters beyond our immediate hands, we clearly identify the profound benefit of this role: a specialized, neuro-informed advocate who holds the patient's full clinical history. The Case Coordinator acts as a professional bridge across specialties, ensuring the primary care physician, neurologists, and gastroenterologists communicate actively within the care team and ground all treatment decisions in the patient's unique neuroprint.

By establishing these proactive tools, we can extend grace, anticipatory medical accommodations, and genuine support to ensure our later years are defined by dignity rather than systemic neglect.

We live in the shadow of statistics designed to measure us against a monotone ideal, not to see us. For too long, the narrative has been one of premature death and catastrophic expectations. We are fiercely moving beyond that false thirty-four-year lifespan myth.

To anchor this journey of aging, we look to North Dakota's native wildflower: the **Wild Prairie Rose (*Rosa arkansana*)**.

"Our growth follows its own unique timeline, and our deep roots are built to survive the coldest prairie blizzards." *(For the full biological profile of this wildflower, see Appendix D: The Wildflower Field Guide).*

The Wild Prairie Rose is an exceptionally tough Great Plains survivor that beautifully illustrates the complete, decades-long integration of the 4D lifespan:

1. **Neuroprint/Physical (D1):** It carries sharp, protective thorns (bristles), offering a beautiful illustration of somatic boundaries and protective defenses.
2. **Metabolism/Energy (D2):** It is a perennial that conserves its energy during sub-zero plains blizzards by shedding its leaves and retreating its resources deep underground to survive on an empty battery.
3. **Environment (D3):** It thrives in heavy clay soils, intense prairie droughts, and windswept plains where cultivated, greenhouse-bred tea roses would instantly die.
4. **Time/Lifespan (D4):** Its roots can tunnel up to several feet deep, allowing it to sprout back even after a sweeping prairie fire.

This is the ultimate representation of our Wildflower Nature. As Jodee Kulp beautifully observed during our panel discussion on aging well with FASD, "The prairie has been burned, and out of the prairie comes the wildflowers. Brilliant." Like the Wild Prairie Rose, we are not fragile; we are tenacious, beautiful, and unpredictable. Our deep root systems are anchored in decades of lived experience, built to survive the coldest winters and designed to sprout back and bloom across our entire lifespan. Every day we exist, every day we show up, and every day we advocate for ourselves, we prove that our lives have value and purpose. We are not the statistics. We are the wildflowers.

Pivot Points: Putting Chapter 6 into Practice

- **For the Professional** — I invite you to step away from the traditional hunt for "rehabilitation" or "cures" and instead transition toward a sustainable model of lifespan management. We might consider how support naturally evolves alongside the individual, recognizing that their metabolic needs will shift as they age, and that creativity offers powerful benefits by utilizing the body's built-in parameters in new, surprising, and restorative ways. I encourage you to help clients shift from the exhaustion of "oh no" to the liberating "aha" of changing their workarounds—celebrating how we can adapt, such as dancing with our hands when our legs fail or capturing the beauty of the wilderness with a camera when our joints can no longer hike the rough trails.
- **For the Caregiver** — You are invited to gently observe the whole-body comorbidity load of your loved one, treating sleep glitches, joint stiffness, and gastrointestinal flares as raw

biological realities rather than behavioral choices. I encourage you to support their adaptive transitions over time and help them co-create their own custom "Anticipatory Lifespan Guide." In doing so, we can actively protect their long-term health and preserve your own precious metabolic battery from unnecessary depletion.

For Individuals Living with FASD — I invite you to set down the heavy, exhausting weight of society's expectations and gently banish the S-word from your vocabulary. You are invited to honor your body and mind as they operate on their own beautiful, unique timeline. I encourage you to protect your daily metabolic battery, so you have the fuel to nourish your creative wildflower bloom. What if we took time today to celebrate your tenacity, trust your wildflower ways, and connect with your tribe? Aging with FASD is not merely surviving a broken system or navigating life with a fragile body; it is a profound, ongoing act of defiance, self-grace, and brilliant creativity. Every day we exist, every day we show up, and every day we advocate for ourselves, we prove that our lives have value and purpose.

Up Next

Having journeyed through the lifelong, whole-body reality of FASD, we now turn to Part 3, *What People with FASD Wish You Knew*. We shift from mapping the challenges to illustrating solutions. We begin in Chapter 7 by exploring the absolute necessity of Environmental Support. It is time to focus on adapting our conditions so that we who live with FASD can thrive.

Chapter 6
Podcast Guests

- **Alice Foote** – Episode 125 *(FASD and Masking with Alice Foote)*
- **Barb Clark** – Episode 138 *(Aging with FASD: Cognitive Bloom, Physical Burnout & Whole-Body Health Panel Discussion)*
- **Carl Young** – Episodes 129 *(Aging with FASD: Insights, Challenges, and Hope with Carl Young)*, 138 *(Aging with FASD: Cognitive Bloom, Physical Burnout & Whole-Body Health Panel Discussion)*
- **CJ Lutke** – previously interviewed for my first book, *Sip by Sip: Candid Conversations with Adults Living with FASD.*
- **Dr. Claire Coles** – Episode 132 *(FASD Across the Lifespan: A Longitudinal Perspective with Dr. Claire Coles)*
- **Dr. Jeff Wozniak** – Episode 95 *(Bridging Research & Reality: Dr. Jeffrey Wozniak speaks on FASD and Neurodevelopment)*
- **Dr. Ken Jones** – Episode 55 *(Unmasking FASD: Insights from Dr. Kenneth Lyons Jones)*
- **Dr. Tamara Bodnar** – Episode 134 *(Beyond the Brain: FASD, Aging, and Autoimmune Health with Dr. Tamara Bodner)*
- **Jodee Kulp** – Episode 138 *(Aging with FASD: Cognitive Bloom, Physical Burnout & Whole-Body Health Panel Discussion)*
- **Dr. Kathy Page** – Episode 138 *(Aging with FASD: Cognitive Bloom, Physical Burnout & Whole-Body Health Panel Discussion)*

- **Mary Byrnes** – Episode 127 *(Harrison's Hope: Building a Lifespan Support System with Mary Byrnes)*
- **RJ Formanek** – Episode 44 *(From Misunderstood to Mentor with RJ Formanek)*

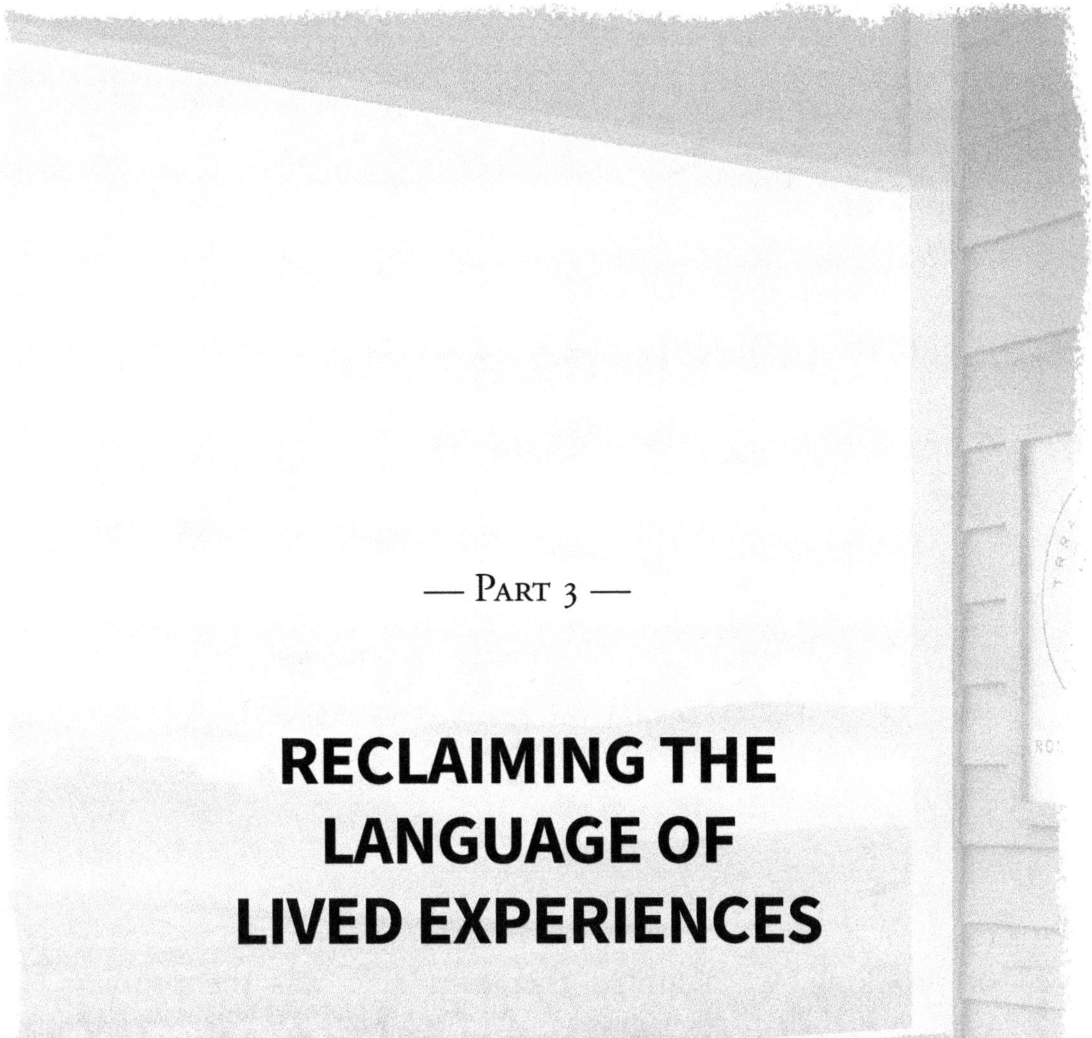

— Part 3 —

RECLAIMING THE LANGUAGE OF LIVED EXPERIENCES

— Chapter 7 —

Changing the Room

"For decades, the systemic observer
—the judge, the educator, the clinician—
has stood outside this box, focusing exclusively
on the visible 'wave' of behavior."
—Patricia Kasper

For too long, we assumed the individual was the problem. We believed that hard work, incentives, and discipline would help the person living with FASD "match" the world. We spent decades trying to change human behavior through charts, conformity training, and the pursuit of a uniform ideal called normalcy. We now know that the whole logic of that lens is an industrial formula mismatched with biological reality. When we demand that people adapt to environments hostile to their needs, we do not facilitate growth. We simply document a failed approach towards humankind, as we are not machines.

Instead, we shift our perspective. The environment actively participates in our regulation. When the world becomes too loud, bright, fast, or cluttered, it triggers what Antonia Rathbun Lindsey calls a "waterfall" effect—a rush of sensory input that derails energy otherwise available for executive functioning.

We move toward a neuro-informed framework by viewing the space we occupy as dynamic, operating through a 4D framework. By adjusting the Micro, Mezzo, and Macro layers, we manage D3, protect D2, and honor D1.

Our goal is to optimize alignment. Just as every person possesses a unique fingerprint, every individual has a unique neuroprint—a specific, irregular landscape of sensory processing, executive functioning, neurological responsiveness, and creative capacity that is uniquely theirs. This chapter focuses on improving environmental support in the Micro (immediate space), the Mezzo (relational space), and the Macro (public systems), for that unique neuroprint.

As Morgane Borzée reminds us, we can view bodily sensations as data rather than as bad behavior or a lack of conformity. A space full of competing sensory information loads the nervous system. Some people need more input; others need less. Mary Byrnes emphasizes using specific sensory objects to anchor communication and maintain focus. These are not crutches; they are essential tools for a brain that needs external support, a sensory trail to follow, which organizes internal experience.

Jodee Kulp has long taught that small adjustments to sound, lighting, and layout may prevent, or at least forestall, the frequency of regulatory collapse caregivers work so hard to avoid in their loved ones. We encourage adjustments to daily environments to meet regulatory demands. What to reduce, and conversely what to boost, is like a flavor palette for the body's sensory system, much like our taste and texture preferences affect our attraction to certain foods. Explore how to adjust your space to match your daily regulatory regimen.

I encourage you to do an environmental audit. As you walk through your home or workspace, gather data on what you see, hear, smell, and feel. Note what works for your neurotype and what does not. Consider how you might adapt these spaces for your own biological safety and your style of handling things.

The goal is to build our own safe foundation, setting, and habits so we can spend our energy living and sharing our gifts with others, rather than struggling to survive noxious environments that wear us down. This shift is the most effective intervention available. It costs us nothing but the willingness to recognize our physical cues, map what feels better to our bodies, and adjust how we set up our home and workspace so they work best for our unique neurophysiology. A detailed discussion of managing our stress and strengths map, and of creating an Individual Environmental Plan, can be found in Deb Evensen's *13 Beams of Moonlight* and Antonia Rathbun Lindsey's *Parenting Your Porcupine*.

The Micro-Environment

To begin a functional audit of our environment, we start with the Micro-Environment. This is the immediate, sensory radius surrounding the individual. It encompasses the desk, the bedroom, the "nest," and the sensory inputs that touch the nervous system when we retreat from shared settings where we eat, socialize, or engage with others.

When we examine a unique neuroprint, we observe an information-processing system with a specific filter. One person's neuroprint may be overwhelmed by a heavy sensory load. For another, their need for stimulation may be underfed. Because each micro-environment must be uniquely crafted, we pay careful attention to our own energy variability throughout the day.

As Morgane Borzée suggests, we can see immediate sensory feedback as primary data. If the body reacts with an alarm response or strong aversion, that is the right response for your sensory profile. When we adjust the Micro-Environment, we are adjusting the sensory load to optimize our capacity, given how our individual body battery handles the day's demands.

Think of this as energy management. By curating the Micro-Environment, you reduce the D2 drain. One person's sensory noise can be another's music for smooth management. Removing sensory pollution, which saps our personal system, helps us keep our battery charged longer, reducing the risk of crashes or collapse over the course of the day or week.

The "Neuroprint" Audit

We can treat your immediate physical space as a lab. We can conduct a sensory audit of the space where we spend most of our time. Walking through it, we consider the volume of belongings, the kind of reactions our bodies have, and how our surroundings align, or clash, with our specific sensory appetite:

- **Visual Noise:** Are there too many competing stimuli? As Mary Byrnes illustrates, the brain can anchor on a single sensory item that provides focus—experiment with removing clutter in favor of a few specific functional grounding objects.
- **Tactile Anchors:** Does the space provide tactile regulation? A

super-soft blanket to swaddle in, a weighted object, a textured mat, or a heating or cooling mat to serve as a physiological tether.

- **The "Nest" Protocol:** Introduced by Antonia Rathbun Lindsey and explored in podcast with AJ Locashio, where someone spends the most time has to be a retreat—a nest where the nervous system can reset, with zero requirement for social performance.

A visceral example is the "nest," as described by AJ Locashio. A "nest" is not a childhood accommodation; it is a necessity for the dysregulated nervous system, regardless of age. When the brain enters a survival state, the environment must provide safety so the organism can regroup. It helps an overwhelmed nervous system reset through rest, allowing the body to metabolize out the flood of stress hormones and return to neutral. A "nest" is a sanctuary. It helps an overwhelmed nervous system regulate. These spaces need to be tailored to a person's unique neurotype, whether that means retreating to a hammock, a bathtub for a soak, or a small, enclosed area like a nook filled with soft pillows so they can cocoon and reset. While AJ uses a closet for her nest, anyone with a trauma history of being enclosed in a closet will want something more open than a closet for their nest. One might gather a "recipe" of soothing supports to keep there: a washcloth, a favorite cup and bottled water, tissues, a blanket, a pillow, a weighted comfort object, a soothing aromatherapy scent (lavender or other preference) to make the space comfortable. The nest signals safety for the whole body.

Somatic Scaffolding: Nesting vs. Dosing

To support regulatory balance, we must treat environmental design as a primary intervention, organized under two distinct pillars of somatic scaffolding: nesting and dosing. Distinguishing between these two interventions is vital, as they serve entirely different physiological purposes for a sensitive neuroprint.

Dosing is about adjusting active external inputs in real-time to manage the sensory load of a shared setting. Think of dosing as wearing noise-canceling headphones on campus or dimming harsh overhead lights. It has nothing to do with creating a safe sanctuary; rather, it modulates sensory input so we can keep functioning in active, demanding spaces. Clinical art therapist Antonia Rathbun-Lindsey perfectly anchors this through the concept of "dosing" the environment, noting that "just as a doctor prescribes a specific dose of medication, we must carefully measure the sensory input we provide."

Nesting is the creation of a physical container—a safe sanctuary where the individual can completely disengage from all social demand and performance. If dosing is wearing headphones on campus, nesting is retreating to a dedicated "cry closet" or enclosed nook. The nest is a protective, enclosed envelope designed specifically to help an overwhelmed nervous system and a depleted D2 battery reset, allowing the body to metabolize stress hormones and return to neutral without the expectation of performance.

If an environmental setup suddenly stops working, or if a previously tolerated space becomes a trigger for meltdowns, it is not a behavioral regression or character flaw. It simply means the individual's sensory body culture has shifted. We must remain endlessly curious and flexible, continually re-dosing and redesigning our somatic scaffolds to meet the nervous system's evolving needs.

Environmental design is an architectural principle that helps us rethink how we interact within our wide range of habitats. The idea is to maximize harmony between people and the parameters of the ecosystem in which they participate. Needs change with society. As we move from the era of industrial monoculture to more individualized remote work environments, the shift from one-size-fits-all uniformity (cubicle culture) to respect for people's individual pacing and habits (remote work, parklike interior and exterior spaces) is already underway. However, many school and work settings have not yet caught up. This calls for closer examination of how we build, teach, and manage public spaces to accommodate the spectrum of human differences rather than forcing rigid conformity to a single "ideal" image of humanity, as well as human productivity (for example, always online like a computer, vs having cycles of growth, fruiting, harvest, and resting like a garden patch).

A Mandate for Environmental Design

Today, our medical, educational, and care facilities are built on the myth of uniformity, which is more myth than reality. We see institutions ignore sensory differences inherent in human variability, leading to failure and inaccessibility, then blame the people in need. Genuine equity requires redesigning our physical environment to accommodate diverse neurophysiology rather than forcing conformity. As we make changes at home for our loved ones, we can see how environmental design also applies to shared spaces.

The Mezzo-Environment (Relational Scaffolding)

The Mezzo-Environment is the relational scaffolding we build to maintain nervous system stability. It bridges the individual and the community through social interaction at the kitchen table, in the classroom, or at the workplace.

Relational scaffolds consist of rhythm, pace, and shared communication. They are bigger than words; they include tempo and tone, content, gestures, and facial expressions. These are the inputs that language and processing networks must decode and exchange to understand one another. Many people with FASD may read movements differently, depending on their own sensory filters, or need to move and avoid direct eye contact during intense emotional exchanges.

When we view the neuroprint as unique, we see the household or classroom as a place to co-regulate within an adaptable ecosystem. If the Mezzo-Environment is unpredictable or charged with urgency, fear, or pressure, our nervous system defaults to a high-alert state, scanning for the next threat signal and draining energy and functional bandwidth.

The Importance of Predictability

The most effective key in the Mezzo-Environment is predictability. Eileen Devine highlights how crucial this is. She explains that when an individual with a fragile nervous system exists in a world they cannot predict, their resistance does not reflect defiance. Instead, they are struggling to regulate an environment that feels unsafe. When the world is predictable, the brain does not have to spend its limited regulatory budget guessing what comes next. It can direct its capacity toward goals other than survival. This safeguards the D4. A predictable environment allows the individual to move from reactive survival toward building a stable sense of self.

As we audit this layer, we ask:

- Is there a consistent rhythm within our household or workplace interactions and daily schedule?
- Are expectations clear, or are they shifting targets that keep the nervous system off-balance, in a state of high-alert scanning?

Behavior as Communication

We often treat verbal requests as neutral. But for many, processing language is a taxing sensory activity. If the environment is unpredictable, individual reactions are not malicious; they reflect data about their nervous system. Morgane Borzée captures this framework: behavior signals are not a nuisance; they are a reflexive imperative. As she explains, "behavior is... wired for protection" and "body sensations are just data," pointing toward an "underlying unmet need." When we view these behaviors through the lens of a neuroprint, we stop asking, "Why are they reacting this way?" Instead, we ask, "What is stressful enough that a survival reflex kicks in?"

Dismantling the "Defiance" Myth

Perhaps the most damaging failure in the Mezzo-Environment is labeling survival as "willful defiance." Dr. Maude Champagne dismantles this narrative, offering a vital clarification: when individuals display difficult or aggressive behavior, it is rarely about ill intent. Reflex reactions are not planned choices! Maude points out that we must look beyond behavior at physiological drivers: "I think it's oversimplified to say that aggressive behaviors are always a communication issue... sensory, sleep, HPA pathway that's dysregulated, it's being in pain, feeling hot, feeling hungry. All these things are factors."

When we adopt this perspective, the Mezzo-Environment shifts from a battleground to a laboratory for resetting internal organization and rebooting the system. Calm precedes reconnection. A middle way exists between calming alone and reconnecting; techniques help us stay close without escalating. When distressed, we may want others to back off without abandoning us, and backing off means stopping the cascade of social demand. Not abandoning means we are not sent away or punished; we are allowed to slow down and restart once our system settles.

A Mandate for Relational Safety

The Mezzo-Environment shows that scaffolding skills and adaptive functioning are not a solo act. Our relational interactions also affect individual health and stamina. As you examine D2, your battery life in daily routines, consider: Does your household allow an emotional exit when the body alarm blares, without others escalating or imposing a consequence? For example, a brief written reminder rather than someone asking, "Haven't you done this YET?" When calm, we can tell others which phrase or visual code to offer us instead. We can design our relational environment to be as simple, respectful, straightforward, and safe as the physical "nest" we've built. It is important to show respect rather than compassion. It is a difference in vocal tone. Respect is calmer. Males often misread compassion as being talked to like a child, though females do not intend this. Conversely, blunt comments or commands common in all-male teamwork can come across as brusque in mixed company, where courtesy habits like 'please' or 'thank you' are conventional—finding what is short, sweet, and simple. At the same time, remaining supportive can ease friction in families and households.

The Macro-Environment (Systems)

The Macro-Environment is the public landscape: the schools, legal systems, healthcare providers, and workplaces that govern our lives. We look to the institutions that are supposed to serve us and find that these structures are often unnecessarily rigid and resistant to simple changes. It is hard not to personalize this as if we were unworthy individuals, but the gridlock usually stems from people confusing sameness with equality.

The Systemic Failure: Opaque Walls and Environmental Barriers

When we look at the Macro-Environment of public systems, such as courthouses, clinics, schools, and workplaces, the failure is primarily one of physical and structural inaccessibility. Most public spaces are designed with absolute blindness to biological variation. For example, retired attorney David Boulding highlights the sheer environmental inaccessibility of modern courthouses, which lack clear physical signs, tactile directions, and visual landmarks. A young adult is expected to navigate a complex, echoing labyrinth and find a probation office hidden in a windowless basement solely by following abstract, verbal directions. When they get lost or miss an appointment due to these structural barriers, the system misinterprets their processing gap as contempt. This is a design flaw of the space, not a behavioral failure of the person.

To understand why public institutions remain so resistant to structural accommodation, we can look to the paradox of Schrödinger's Cat. Systems behave as if the individuals they serve exist inside an opaque, solid metal box. For decades, the systemic observer—the judge, the educator, the clinician—has stood outside this box, focusing exclusively on the visible "wave" of behavior. They ignore the "particle" of neurobiology (the physical baseline, the unintegrated reflex, and the processing delays) locked inside.

Because they cannot see inside the box, they default to punitive, consequence-based demands to enforce conformity. But what if we made the box out of glass? When we demand systemic transparency, the false conflict between behavior and biology dissolves. We can see both the wave of action and the particle of neurophysiology, shifting the macro-system's focus from behavioral control to spatial safety and environmental accessibility.

The Weaponization of Ignorance

As Julie Harris (Civil Rights Advocate, Episode 132) reveals, many institutions treat individuals poorly simply because they assume individuals do not know their rights. Julie notes: "Some companies genuinely don't know the law... but many do, and they only treat you the way that they do because they know that you likely do not know your rights." The fundamental systemic error is treating a right as a favor and a disability as a deficit. It's like a system bullying a person and expecting them to be fine with being mistreated. The burden of resisting maltreatment then falls on the target of the harm, instead of the imposing entity correcting its conduct.

From Deficit to Civil Rights

A radical shift in how we perceive "accommodation" can stop this cycle of physiological wear and tear. Julie argues that we must dismantle the narrative that needing support signals weakness. Instead, we must reframe it as a fundamental right, as all people merit participation and give-and-take within our circle of affiliation. "We talk about how to frame the accommodation request without deficit-focused language... view their request as not a deficit, not a sign that they are less... It's just a request for something that they are entitled to anyway."

A Mandate for Environmental Redesign

We can no longer ask the individual to "fix" themselves to fit into a system designed for machines, which ignores human variation and creativity. The Macro-Environment must be redesigned based on equity, not conformity. This means:

- **Neuroprint-Informed Policy:** Shifting from "consequence-based" policies to "safety-based" policies that account for biological variation.
- **The "Interactive" Standard:** Replacing arbitrary rules with an active, collaborative process that recognizes and matches each person's best and most effective, individualized solutions for supporting success.
- **Equity of Tools:** Currently, human resources departments have legal teams to protect employers, but employees are left to navigate the law alone. We need to bridge this resource gap to ensure that rights are accessible.

Pivot Points: Putting Chapter 7 into Practice

- **For the Professional/Educator**— I invite you to audit your environment for the "regulatory tax" on students, clients (and staff). Instead of targeting the person's behavior, you can identify the D3 flaw. Move from a behavioral control goal to a D2 safety goal: How does this space preserve the individual's battery life?
- **For the Caregiver**— I invite you to audit your energy to stop wasting your bandwidth justifying needs to systems not built to respect them. Instead, consider re-focusing your efforts on the Micro and Mezzo layers of your environment, where you have the power to create a "nested" safety zone, your primary D3 with workarounds that can be applied to wider environments in incremental ways.
- **For those living with FASD** — Let's stop framing our need for accommodations as a special favor. We are not begging. We can exercise our civil rights to full participation based on our D1 reality. We can specify a workaround to help preserve our D2 reserves, our battery. Using our Individual Environmental Plan, we can identify where we are encountering a barrier in the next environment. We are not asking to be 'fixed.' We are asserting what equipment or routine change will help us bloom and contribute our best.

Up Next

We have mapped the environment's impact. We learned that the "problem" is not our differences as individuals; it is the gridlock of the spaces we occupy. By applying the Micro, Mezzo, and Macro lenses, we can shape our personal and shared spaces into landscapes of respect and better support. This takes energy, but it also gives us back agency. Now, let's focus on how we sustain ourselves over time, including advocating for others like us and those we love who have a unique neurophysiology. If we have been holding back the dam of disaster for loved ones for years, we stand on the Caregiver Cliff. In Chapter 8, we will examine caregiver burnout and depletion from chronic advocacy, learn to choose our battles, and protect our energy by refueling.

Chapter 7
Podcast Guests

- **AJ Locashio** - Episode 110 *(Understanding Emotional Regulation in Neurodivergent Individuals)* and Episode 120 *(Finding Calm in Chaos: Practical Strategies for Emotional Regulation with AJ Locashio)*
- **Antonia Rathbun Lindsey** - Episode 43 *(Parenting Your Porcupine, Part 1, with Antonia Rathbun Lindsey)*
- **David Boulding** – Episode 31 *(David Boulding: The Intersection of FASD and both the Law and Sex)*
- **Eileen Devine** - Episode 112 *(Understanding Cognitive Rigidity in FASD with Eileen Devine)*

- **Jodee Kulp** - Episode 123 *(The Neurobiology of Migraines in FASD: What You Need to Know)*
- **Julie Harris** - Episode 132 *(Challenging the System: How to Manage Workplace Discrimination with Julie Harris)*
- **Mary Byrnes** - Episode 127 *(Harrison's Hope: Building a Lifespan Support System with Mary Byrnes)*
- **Dr. Maude Champagne** - Episode 94 *(Understanding Aggression in FASD: A Conversation with Dr. Maude Champagne)*
- **Morgane Borzée** - Episode 122 *(The Neuroscience of Emotions: How Recognizing Our Animal Responses Can Change Our Relationships)*

— CHAPTER 8 —

Sustaining the Caregiver

"I hate the term independent.
I want it to be wiped out of our systems of care.
It's a bunch of bull poop. It's ridiculous... "
— Barb Clark

Exhaustion, Mortality, and the Interdependent Horizon Systemic Support Drop-Off

Moving through the world with a neuroprint that functions differently is challenging, but doing so without an accurate map can feel nearly impossible. Standard medical training is designed to provide a reliable guide, yet for millions of individuals living with Fetal Alcohol Spectrum Disorder (FASD), standard diagnostic tools simply do not fit their reality. The status of "no diagnosis" or misdiagnosis does not reflect a person's truth, but rather a flaw in our systemic maps.

Society treats the transition into adulthood as a standardized, linear event (a graduation into maturity that miraculously occurs at age eighteen or twenty-one). For individuals with a Fetal Alcohol Spectrum Disorder (FASD) neurotype, this chronological timeline is an institutional fiction that ignores the nature of human development. The Caregiver Cliff is the moment this biological reality hits the legalistic wall of adult eligibility. Throughout childhood, parental scaffolding acts as a protective buffer, absorbing the friction of an unaccommodating society. This lifelong mediation takes an immense, invisible toll on the caregiver's own nervous system and metabolic reserves. The parent is not merely raising a child; they are constantly absorbing societal bumps, legal friction, and school-system shocks to protect their loved one's fragile nervous system, gradually depleting their own daily battery over decades. When a chronological milestone abruptly cuts off systemic support, the family is forced to interface directly with adult systems that demand absolute autonomy, as if all growth stopped at a prescribed age.

Expecting a sudden leap into absolute autonomy misunderstands the lifespan dimension (D4). A neuro-informed support structure recognizes that we remain on a lifelong journey, and accommodations must evolve as we mature on our own unique timeframe.

The current system assumes a caregiver will simply become obsolete. As Jodee Kulp points out, this is a biological impossibility: "How can adult loved ones or caregivers of persons with alcohol related disorders disappear? FASD doesn't just disappear in adulthood! The need for connection to caregivers doesn't either." When systems abruptly withdraw accommodations, individuals are left stranded without a safety net. Jake Tjapkes describes the real-world outcome of this abrupt cutoff: "Where are they? What happened to them? Oh, they're in jail. They're in a homeless shelter."

We must stop fixating on chronological age as a measure of capability. Dr. Jerrod Brown advises, "If someone with FASD is 30 or 40 years old on paper, how do they function developmentally, socially, cognitively, emotionally? That's another thing to be aware of." Because systems prioritize chronological markers, providers often misinterpret developmental differences. Carl Young explains that when a professional evaluates an adult, they are often "seeing a behavior and not the challenge," which obscures the underlying hardware reality.

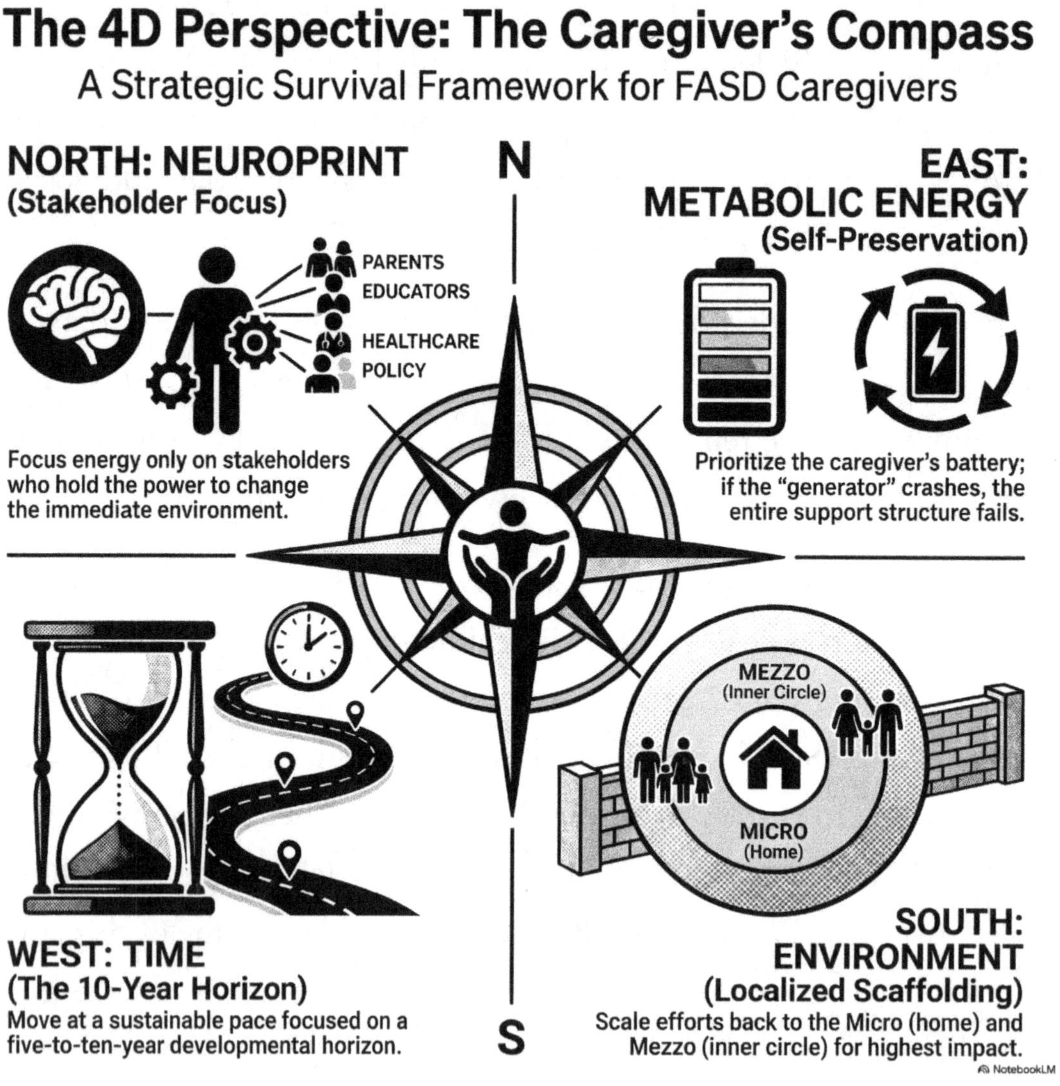

4D Living with FASD, Patricia Kasper, MA, ©2026

From Independence to Interdependence

The goal is not a sudden graduation into isolation. The goal is creating a stable community of support that allows our specific kind of intelligence to thrive at whatever age it blossoms.

True support normalizes interdependence. Barb Clark challenges the mainstream obsession with self-sufficiency: "I hate the term independent. I want it to be wiped out of our systems of care. It's a bunch of bull poop. It's ridiculous... We need to normalize that we all have people who provide support in our lives." Kenny LaJoy reframes this entirely: "Our society... would be nowhere if there were not an unspoken reliance on interdependence."

Instead of forcing individuals to climb a steep systemic cliff, we can design paths that last a lifetime. When we align our physical environments (D3) and relational rhythms, we create an interdependent safety net that honors our unique developmental timelines. Transitioning from frontline mediator to supportive consultant is a gradual, deliberate process.

The Transition from Buffer to Backup

Transitioning from a frontline environmental mediator to a supportive consultant is an act of radical self-preservation. Trying to carry the full load of buffering the outside world indefinitely sets up caregiver exhaustion. When a caregiver operates in a prolonged state of urgency, the physical and psychological toll is severe. Caregiver self-preservation is not abandonment; it is the core of a sustainable safety net. If the primary caregiver collapses under the weight of the advocacy tax, the entire support structure falls apart. Therefore, the gradual hand-off is a survival strategy.

This transition occurs across three distinct, practical phases, shifting the focus from parental mediation to supported interdependence:

The Phase	Caregiver's Role	Individual's Focus
Phase 1: Observer	Describe the solution. Narrate sensory adjustments aloud: "The lights are too bright; let's dim them. How is your breathing now that the light is softer?"	Map personal neurophysiology. Learn to recognize internal physical signs of stress or comfort.
Phase 2: Co-Pilot	Ask before acting. When a stress flare occurs, prompt with a direct question: "What is happening in your body right now? What would help?"	Identify environmental triggers. Communicate which inputs impact daily functioning using a script or simple visual cue.
Phase 3: Backup	Troubleshooting and consulting. Offer a view of the horizon and course correction on a structured schedule, setting clear boundaries to protect personal energy reserves.	Refine accommodations. Maintain a personalized list of environmental workarounds to share with the support team.

When a loved one enters a survival state, trying to reason, de-escalate, or impose consequences in the moment is a futile drain on the caregiver's metabolic battery. As Liz Kulp so vividly described, a neurodevelopmental rage is an unstoppable somatic launch sequence: "It starts at your feet and goes to your knees. By the time it's reached your knees, that rocket's taken off. We can't stop it. You just happen to be in front of us." Trying to stop a rocket that has already cleared the launch pad only depletes the caregiver's own energy reserves. A neuro-informed caregiver recognizes that the only effective intervention is preventative environmental design (D3) to calm the survival alarms before they ever trigger, preserving the caregiver's crucial daily battery.

Jodee Kulp captures the visceral reality of what happens when caregivers cannot step back into a backup role: "If I may not get to a bathroom for 12 hours, eat, or even get water because of heightened caring demands...

then that's when I find my FASD poking out in bristle attacks... plus, when so many bristle attacks are against you from people depending on you, eventually, I bristle back". No human being can remain on high alert indefinitely; physical rest and metabolic refueling are biological necessities.

The Neuroprint Passport as a Systemic Shield

To protect the caregiver's battery from the repetitive strain of explaining neurodevelopmental differences to every new provider, families can compile a typed, one-page Neuroprint Passport. This document is not a request for special favors; it is a clear statement of the individual's terms of service. It maps out specific triggers (such as unexpected schedule changes or complex verbal explanations) and non-verbal de-escalation strategies. Handing this passport directly to a clinician or educator establishes an immediate, objective baseline, ensuring that biological differences are never misinterpreted as behavioral choices.

High-Support Needs: Redefining Care

Dismantling the false ideal of absolute independence requires acknowledging that some individuals on the spectrum have high-support needs that extend beyond what a family home can provide. Securing qualified, specialized out-of-home care is a high-stakes journey often accompanied by profound grief, exhaustion, and worry. Caregivers face the realistic fear that institutional facilities remain blind to the FASD neurotype, relying on compliance models that exacerbate trauma.

A lack of lifelong systemic options intensifies this anxiety. Mary Byrnes highlights this clinical agony: "There is chronic anxiety and fear about how my loved one is going to manage after I pass away." Without systemic reform, aging parents are left terrified of the alternatives. As advocate Patrick Bross warns, caregivers fear their adult child will end up "in a small home, being taken advantage of".

Fostering Systemic Competence

Historically, institutional solutions have focused on offering more beds and residential placements rather than demanding neurophysiological competence. Physical containment has been prioritized over neurobehavioral literacy. This lack of specialized understanding is a critical systemic failure. Public facilities are often unequipped to handle complex neurodevelopmental conditions and rely on outdated compliance models that backfire.

True reform requires FASD-informed accreditation, with public funding contingent on verified clinical competency. Without this standard, facilities continue to use counterproductive methods. Dr. Jerrod Brown highlights this disconnect: "Some of the group homes use energy drinks or sugar-sweetened beverages as a reward for that person when they show 'good behavior,' proving they just don't understand that those kinds of things are a complete threat to someone's emotional, behavioral, and physical health."

Pivot Points: Putting Chapter 8 into Practice

- **For the Professional** — Recognize that the transition into adulthood is not an exit point for support, but a continuation of a lifelong, interdependent journey. View caregiver advocacy not as behavioral pushback, but as a vital clinical report that the environment (D3) is failing to support the individual's needs. Partner with families to design long-term, neuro-informed scaffolds that actively protect the aging caregiver from burnout. As social worker Debbie Michaud points out, we must reject the systemic fiction that "somehow somebody can transition out of their support."

- **For the Caregiver** — Shift your role from frontline environmental buffer to backup consultant to protect your own daily battery (D2). Caregiver self-preservation is a biological necessity, not a moral luxury. When chronic exhaustion sets in, treat it as a somatic warning that your metabolic reserves are depleted, and scale back your advocacy boundaries to prioritize your own physiological health.
- **For Individuals Living with FASD** — Reframe your need for support as a matter of civil rights and interdependent survival, rather than a special favor or personal deficit. Work with your family to compile a clear Neuroprint Passport to communicate your physical triggers and de-escalation needs to new providers, preserving your energy for your own creative goals.

Up Next

For decades, the therapeutic establishment has attempted to treat prenatally acquired brain injuries using traditional talk therapy. In Chapter 9, we examine how standard behavioral interventions often deepen the original injury, and how we can re-evaluate therapy using a 4D, neurobehavioral lens to support genuine healing.

Chapter 8
Podcast Guests

- **Barb Clark** - Episode 118 *(Anosognosia vs. Denial vs. Delayed Remorse)* and Episode 135 *(Panel on Aging Well with FASD)*
- **Carl Young** - Episode 129 *(Aging with FASD)* and Episode 135 *(Panel on Aging Well with FASD)*
- **Debbie Michaud** - Episode 138 *(Aging with FASD: Panel on Caregiving & Systemic Accreditations)*
- **Jake Tjapkes** - Episode 119 *(Lived Experience Series)*
- **Dr. Jerrod Brown** - Episode 102 *(Vulnerability & Victimization)*
- **Jodee Kulp** - Episode 100 *(Centennial Celebration with the Meliorists)* and Episode 135 *(Panel on Aging Well with FASD)*
- **Kenny LaJoy** - Episode 11 *(Reframing the Narrative)*
- **Mary Byrnes** - Episode 127 *(Harrison's Hope: Building a Lifespan Support System)* and Episode 135 *(Panel on Aging Well with FASD)*
- **Patrick Bross** - Episode 33 *(Lived Experience and Supported Interdependence)*

— Chapter 9 —

When Treatment Deepens the Injury

"Psychology focuses rather on what is happening in the mind, whereas neurology is concerned with what is happening in the brain... In essence, our hardware needs to be in the best shape possible for us to run well. We can't run Apple software on a Microsoft machine or vice versa."

— Antonia Rathbun Lindsey

The Systemic Mismatch

Throughout our exploration of Fetal Alcohol Spectrum Disorders, we have highlighted that this is a whole-body condition involving a structural profile of neurological injury. It is not just about specific regional damage; it is a fundamental change in neurophysiology that shapes how a person perceives, processes, and interacts with the world.

When we treat a structural neurological injury with traditional talk therapy, we try to fix a physical reality through a psychological conversation. Here is the problem, though: we do not talk people out of a physical, neurological profile any more than we can talk someone out of asthma or missing a thumb. We can talk about how to address those physical conditions, but telling us to just "buck up" and do everything the same way others do is nonsense. Further, it insults us by dismissing our previous efforts and instincts on how to cope, and basically demands that we mask and pretend to be like others while suffering. It is misguided, ineffective, and harmful because it misdirects us in how we spend precious energy and resources. Traditional approaches address a D1 reality by targeting only D3 interactions, most of which use the conversational logic of mindware to address "repair" of skills that are functions of physical neurology. When this fails, we blame the individual. If we want therapy that truly works, we must stop forcing psychological methods to handle physiological healing.

When individuals with an FASD face emotional distress, anxiety, or behavioral challenges, our institutional systems almost always steer them toward traditional talk therapies. Clinician Antonia Rathbun-Lindsey uses the term **"body culture"** referring to the ongoing personal experience of living in a body with unique characteristics of a chronic difference, disability, or medical condition; it is our functional norm, a physiological reality that others can only understand if we can explain how our condition, our diathesis, differs from what is typical, causing a distinct profile to how we function. (She likens it to trees; oaks, pines, and willows all have roots, trunks, and branches, but beyond that their habit relative to the surrounding elements looks quite different, though they are all trees that live in various landscapes).

Every hour spent in a therapy session that neglects the structural nature of FASD is not just wasted time; it drains D2. When an individual struggles to express their neurophysiological experience (shaped by differences in cognition, sensory, emotional, and language networks), and the therapist pushes for standard practices for stopping behavior, which are heavy on wording, labels, and self-appraisal to produce insight over time which is expected to shift actions, these networks can jam, overwhelmed by sensory, emotional, language, and cognitive input. This is why many leave mental health sessions feeling more exhausted than when they arrived. We are draining their metabolic energy in a process that too often offers little or no real benefit.

A Hardware Condition in a Software World

To understand why traditional therapeutic approaches so frequently fail the FASD community, we must return to our foundational analogy of hardware versus software. Treating a neurological brain injury with a purely psychological or behavioral approach is exactly like trying to fix a hardware problem by reinstalling the software.

Talk therapy, cognitive behavioral therapy, and traditional counseling are software patches. They rely heavily on a person's ability to utilize working memory, abstract reasoning, and cause-and-effect processing. But when the underlying physical brain structure (the hardware) is altered, trying to force compliance through these conversational tools is a biological impossibility.

Author's Note (Honoring Elias's Counsel): As we begin utilizing this *c*omputer analogy here and in Chapter 16, a vital distinction must be made. While comparing the brain stem to "hardware" and behavioral demands to "software" is a powerful tool to expose the mismatch of standard treatments, we must remember that a living nervous system is not a rigid metal circuit board. The human body is not static hardware running faulty software; it is an adaptive, dynamic organism that continually reorganizes and remodels itself through interaction with its environment. We use this mechanical comparison not to suggest that a person is locked in a fixed state of limitation, but to highlight the injustice of demanding cognitive overrides when the body actually requires physical, somatic, and environmental safety.

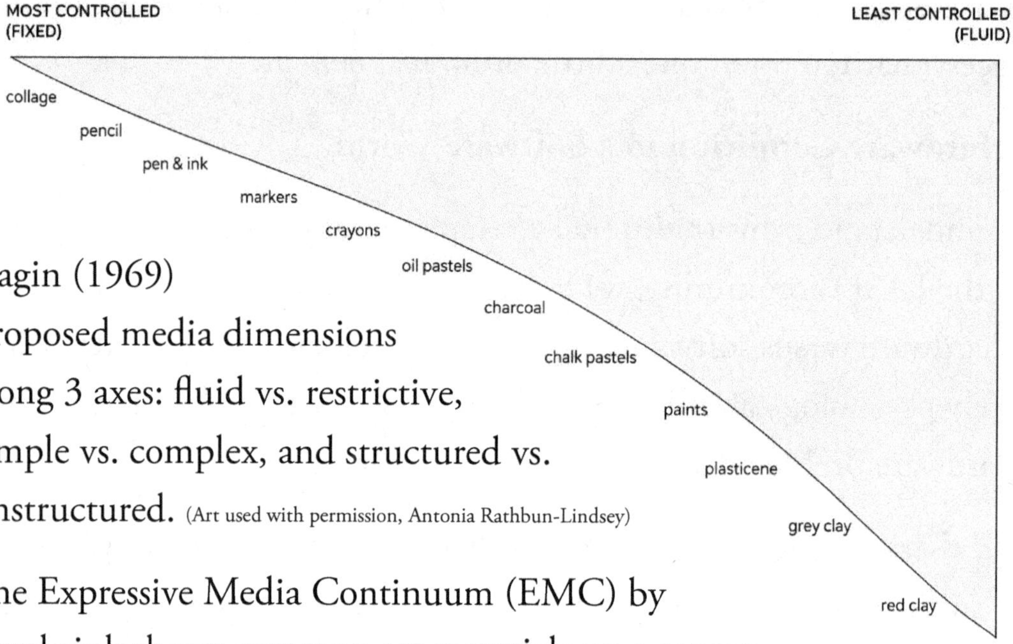

Kagin (1969)
proposed media dimensions along 3 axes: fluid vs. restrictive, simple vs. complex, and structured vs. unstructured. (Art used with permission, Antonia Rathbun-Lindsey)

The Expressive Media Continuum (EMC) by Lusebrink shows common art materials on a sensory spectrum from most to least controlled (fixed to fluid properties).

People with functional differences may have strong reactions to how changeable a material is. These can be positive or negative. Fluid media of paint & clay are highly expressive but harder to control. Wet, soft, mobile sensory properties may invite or repell, based on one's threshold for stimulation (either internal, such as emotional responses; or external tactile preferences, i.e. moisture, stickiness, other sensory qualities). In general , fixed media promote organization (internal structure, containment) because of their controlled nature (precise, unchanging). During a lively conversation, fellow Meliorist Antonia Rathbun-Lindsey explained: "Psychology focuses rather on what is happening in the mind, whereas neurology is concerned with what is happening in the brain. The mind is full of programs and sub-programs. The brain is full of connections and regions that coordinate functions so that those programs will run. In essence, our hardware needs to be in the best shape possible for us to run well. It is hard to run certain programs when some hardware regions aren't in the typical configuration, or when the networks between regions aren't connecting as expected. Programs may run inefficiently when regions or their connecting networks blink off and on or function sporadically instead of consistently. There may be crashes. We will have to create patches to manage the crashes or

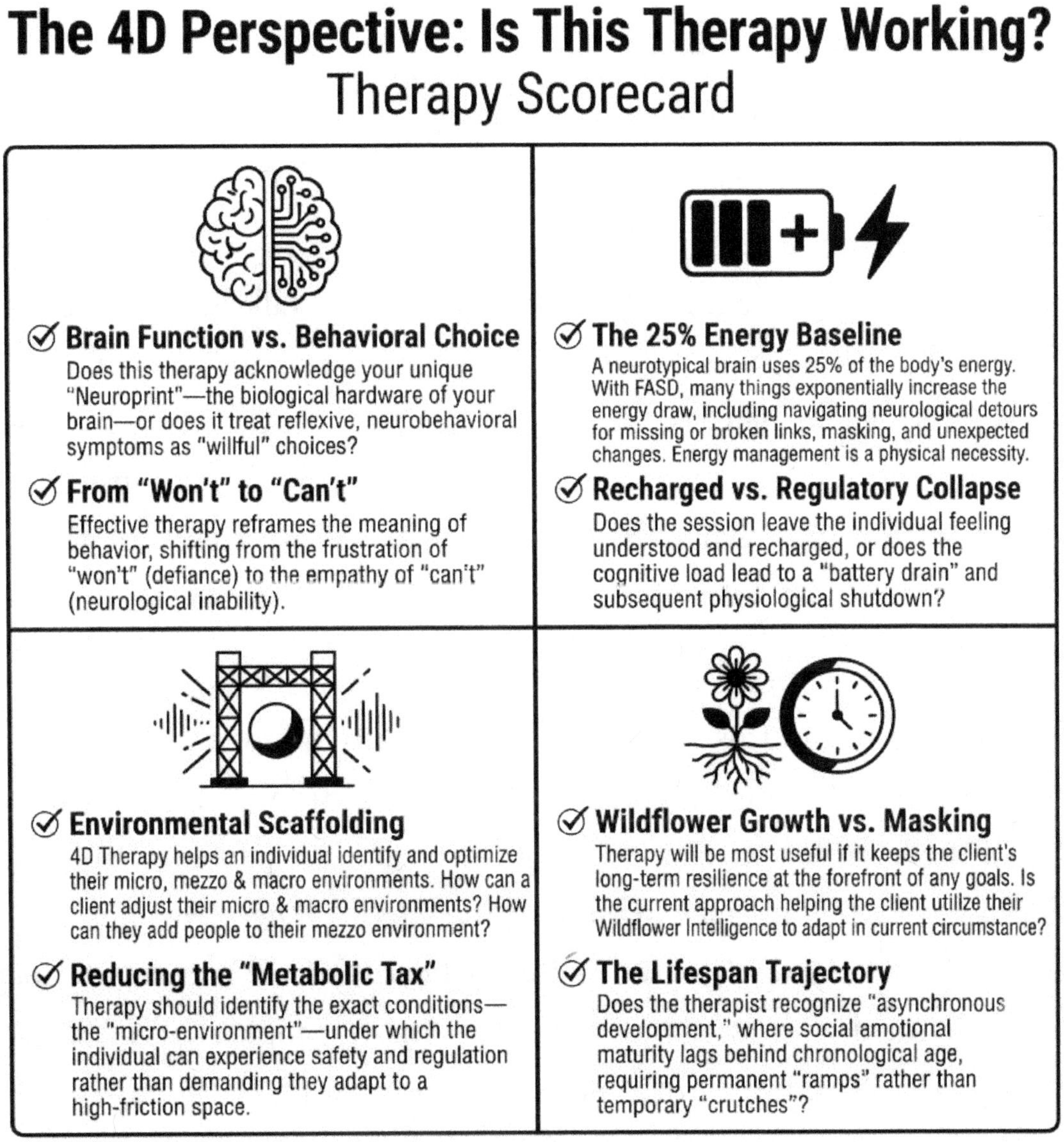

4D Living with FASD, Patricia Kasper, MA, ©2026

glitches. We can't just program things and assume the connections will work. We have to test what clicks and connects and what doesn't. We can't just replace the whole machine. What do we do? We can anticipate unevenness and find workarounds, since glitches may remain within certain networks or regions. We individualize each system so that we can run the best programs possible. That requires understanding the system configuration and how well each region works, not just picking from a catalog of existing programs to plug and play. We can't run Apple software on a Microsoft machine or vice versa."

The Danger of Talk Therapy

Traditional mental health treatments rely on a neurotypical standard that assumes intact executive functions and quick cognitive processing. When we assume a person with a scattered neuroprint will sit in a room, organize and appraise their thoughts and feelings, talk these out to gain insight that will change their behavior, we miss the obvious: all of that requires a person who can read their own mind, detect and decode body signals quickly, express emotions in language, and use insights to communicate and change their choices and actions; chains of activity depending on the very processing networks of the brain which are injured by prenatal alcohol exposure.

In clinical settings, this misalignment shows up in how therapists work with individuals who have FASD. Dr. Jerrod Brown states, "Insight-based therapeutic approaches often don't work for people with FASD because of the abstract reasoning deficits." When therapists use modalities like Cognitive Behavioral Therapy (CBT), they overload the individual with many questions that many people with FASD are biologically ill-equipped to handle. Dr. Brown warns, "If you're asking that person a ton of how and why questions, you may not get good, accurate responses."

This is not just a communication mismatch; it is a clinical threat. When a therapist demands an answer that a client's neurophysiology cannot produce, the brain defaults to a survival response to fill the gap. Dr. Brown explains this effect, noting that "if you ask a bunch of how and why questions to someone with FASD and their brain doesn't generate an answer, they may fill that blankness in their memory with something inaccurate and create a confabulated memory."

By insisting on answers where there is only neurobiological emptiness, overwhelm, or confusion, we are unintentionally encouraging them to fabricate reality just to survive the therapeutic encounter.

Because mainstream talk therapy is trained to focus solely on psychological processes rather than neurological realities, it often blames the environment or the individual's family history for their struggles. Adult self-advocate Neil Turley powerfully captures this harmful dynamic, stating, "I could make a cogent argument that all of my issues just come from a dysfunctional family, nothing else, because all of the evidence is there, all of the therapists could point to it." When a therapist concentrates only on family dysfunction or psychological trauma, they completely overlook the brain injury, leaving individuals to spend years analyzing their childhoods without ever receiving the tailored neurological support they need to help the body regroup and cope with better tools for their unique engine and immediate environments.

The Paradigm Shift in Practice

Traditional Talk Therapy	Neuro-Informed Habilitation
Focuses on psychological origins. It looks at family dysfunction or trauma as the sole root of struggles, missing the biological reality of brain injury.	**Focuses on structural neurophysiology.** It treats the whole body and recognizes changes in functional parameters.
Relies on abstract reasoning and verbal processing. It expects the individual to process spoken language, quickly analyze their internal state, and then verbalize descriptions in the moment.	**Utilizes sensory safety, expressive media, and animals.** It bypasses cognitive and language-processing barriers by using movement, gesture, nature, art, drama, music, and creativity in sensory-based interactions that show, not just tell, to communicate.
Asks "how and why" questions that can trigger confabulation. When the brain cannot find an answer, it involuntarily creates false memories to survive the pressure of the questioning. These function like emotional snapshots that portray emotion, but are not the facts of what happened, though the emotions they portray are very real.	**Looks at signals to assess systemic overload.** It views dysregulation as a physiological stress response to unmet needs or sensory distress. Provides ways to show what is stuck, when, how, where, and what can help. Concrete information keeps content clear.
Expects linear progress. It assumes that learning and emotional regulation follow a steady, predictable timeline.	**Honors asynchronous development.** It respects differing developmental timelines and adjusts expectations to match the stage (not age) and pace of expanding adaptive skills.
Expects steady function once a skill is learned. Learning Theory assumes that the steps of a skill will hold, like links in a chain, no matter how great the load. When one link (or step) fails, the rest of the chain can't pull the load, so the load must be changed. (All chains differ: a necklace is a chain, but you can't pull a truck with it).	**Honors fluctuating skill levels and uses strengths to flex and match capacity.** Habilitation respects that waxing and waning ability is part of the person's physiological profile. Coping means accepting and using workarounds on harder days, and maximizing strengths on better days, flexing support within routine and setting. (Think of a bike with both gears and electric assist for hills; both are used depending on terrain and capacity).

Self-advocate Jake Tjapkes challenges professionals directly, asking, "Have we looked behind the behavior? Yes, it might be a behavioral attitude, but have we looked behind the behavior?" Looking behind the behavior involves recognizing that traditional systems miss how a unique nervous system recalibrates when overloaded. Neurological differences require habilitative methods to manage vulnerabilities through strengths that preserve our resilience.

However, a treatment modality called Neurodevelopmental Intervention Treatment (NDIT) emerged in the 1950s and 1960s; it was controversial at the time, but has since been adapted with new somatic insights and is gaining acceptance for FASD and other neurodevelopmental differences. It emphasizes early and individualized intervention, caregiver coaching, environmental adaptation, and repetitive, concrete skill-building to strengthen self-regulation, adaptive functioning, learning readiness, and participation in daily life. Grounded in the principle that behavior and development are shaped by reciprocal interactions between the child's neurobiology and lived environment, NDIT seeks to improve function by providing guided experiences, structured supports, and developmentally appropriate expectations that align with the child's unique profile and needs.

My 4D Framework fits solidly within this NDIT framework. See the NDIT - 4D Framework Alignment Document in the Appendix.

The 4D Perspective: Is This Therapy Working?

- **Neuroprint/Physical (D1):** Does this therapist acknowledge your neurological reality, or are they treating your behaviors as choices? If they are not working with your specific neurophysiological profile, they will recommend psychological, compliance-based tools and behavioral expectations to force a 'cure' of acting typical. You have a Neuroprint Passport; they need to respect it.

- **Metabolism/Energy (D2):** Does this session leave you feeling recharged and understood, or does it leave you depleted? Therapy should be a net gain for your energy, not a drain.
- **Environment (D3):** Does the therapeutic space itself (the office, the tone, the structure) feel comfortable and supportive? Or does the environment impose a strain of noise, light, smell, or other sensory factors that distract or fatigue? How about communication: is it clear, or do you leave drowned in words, with no workarounds?
- **Time (D4):** Is this therapy aimed at long-term wildflower growth, or is it focused on compliance and masking? If the goal is just to make you hide or seem more acceptable to others, it may not serve your long-term stamina or health.

By shifting our clinical focus from the behavior itself to the metabolic costs imposed by the environment, we stop asking, "What is wrong with this person?" and instead ask the more productive question: "What would need to change for this person's system to work better?" This perspective shifts the therapist's role from behavioral correction to environmental stewardship, recognizing that transitions, sensory inputs, and new tasks are significant energetic demands. Whether a person is "collapsed," conserving energy, or "hypervigilant," conserving safety, our goal is to identify that specific energetic signature and help create a space where their system can afford to settle, rather than demanding a performance their physiology cannot currently support.

We all operate with a hidden budget for our physical energy. According to functional medicine specialist Elias Delphinus, every thought we think, emotion we feel, and action we take burns real fuel. When our body's battery is running low, our nervous system naturally chooses basic survival over daily tasks and repair. Over time, our body simply learns the most energy-efficient way to stay stable when faced with stress. These energy-saving habits are so deep that we often mistake them for a person's actual personality.

For example:

- The person who tries to control everything is not being bossy; they are conserving energy because dealing with surprises and uncertainty costs too much of their emotional safety.
- The person who avoids things or pulls away is not being lazy; they are conserving energy because simply getting activated and starting a task requires a massive surge of power.
- The person who is hypervigilant and always on guard is spending their energy to protect their basic safety.
- The person who collapses or shuts down is simply saving whatever tiny bit of fuel they have left because their battery is empty.

When we look at behavior this way, we see it is actually an energetic code. Therapy and support must stop viewing these states as psychological or moral failures, and instead honor them as our body's natural, physiological response to its physical energy limits.

The current literature on FASD has historically prioritized cognitive-behavioral training to change mindware, attempting to alter our output without addressing neurophysiological workarounds for mental or sensory fatigue that slow our pace and stamina. To achieve true habilitation, we must pivot toward maintaining biological health. The following interventions provide the evidence base for this systemic shift.

Nature as an Environment

Neurodivergent brains rarely possess the internal resources to self-regulate under stress and often require a supportive external environment. Nature is not simply an activity; rather, it is a non-negotiable regulator for the nervous system that bypasses the need for words and engages the brain's safety centers directly.

For many caregivers, actively engaging in nature becomes a vital form of environmental support for preserving stamina and resilience. Carl Young credits this method with his son's success, sharing how they abandoned traditional therapies and instead would "take off and we would go explore state parks... and go fishing." The impact of replacing clinical demands with the natural environment was significant: "And that has paid off. He's not in jail. He's not on drugs. He's at the house."

Dr. Jerrod Brown offers strong biological evidence, explaining that "there's some really good research that shows getting out in nature reduces stress more (than artificial environments) and may actually enhance neuroplasticity." By supplying the brain with this essential sensory input, nature provides the exact physical scaffolding needed to calm the body, allowing the brain to heal, regulate, and grow.

Primitive Reflex Habilitation

When the underlying neurophysiology is fragmented, higher-order cognitive performance is fundamentally compromised. Primitive reflex habilitation is foundational work that anchors the body's basic systems.

Dr. Janet Oliver explains that early neurological and developmental delays can cause uneven development of a person's abilities. She notes that in the neurodivergent brain, "Some things are running really well and they're working, and other things are just completely shut down and not working." When the lower regions of the brain are shut down or misfiring, the individual is constantly in a fight-or-flight or freeze state.

Occupational therapy and primitive reflex integration, which physically retrains the nervous system to improve feeling safe, reset, and ready, fill in the neurological gaps created by alcohol exposure and pave the way for compensation through adaptive skills. Until we stabilize the sensory basement through safe, repetitive, bottom-up stimulation, the higher motor and cognitive functions remain offline.

The Gut-Brain Axis

True biological maintenance requires considering the entire body. For decades, traditional therapy has been fixated on trying to change behavior from the top down, but focusing on the gastrointestinal tract and the vagal system is a real frontier in mental and holistic health treatment.

Developmental neuroscientist Dr. Kristina Uban confirms that this is precisely the direction the field needs to pursue. She emphasizes that if we want to improve behavioral and emotional outcomes, we need to look outside the skull, noting: "Perhaps mental health symptomology and severity of that symptomology is more related to our gut biome than it is our brain... we really need to kind of get out of the brain. We've already documented that the brain is altered."

We also know that interoception is all about reading the body's core signals and better understanding what it needs by decoding the patterns that emerge. By examining the internal ecosystem, we stop trying to fix the neurological injury in isolation and instead focus on how it filters the environment. When we focus on gastrointestinal health, we provide essential biological intervention. We actively reduce the body's inflammation, stabilize the nervous system, and provide the brain with the best possible physical foundation for functioning, adapting, and healing.

The Systemic Mandate: The Macro Shift

We urgently need to redesign institutional and professional training models. It is unacceptable that clinical interns, often the first point of contact for families, lack specialized neurodevelopment training. Systems treat the individual as an isolated client who needs to be fixed in a vacuum.

We are operating under a dangerous statistical illusion. As AJ Locashio highlights, the average standard represents a tiny 1% of the population. By using this 1% as the baseline, the current therapeutic system is built on a myth.

We need a paradigm shift in which institutional settings prioritize somatic and neuro-informed interventions over talk therapy, and in which the family unit is seen as an interconnected biological system that requires collective support for all within it. We must stop imposing standard social expectations on specialized neurophysiology. It helps to view families through a lens of struggles and strengths, with distinct adaptations to culture, region, and environment, rather than polarized "dysfunctional" vs "healthy" stereotypes.

Pivot Points:
Putting Chapter 9 into Practice

- **For Professionals** — Relying on business as usual is no longer an option when working with clients who are statistically unlikely to be neurotypical, as you are using a model designed for a one percent anomaly. We must remind ourselves to remain genuinely curious and never assume we already know what our clients are experiencing. I invite you to reflect on a recent challenging session and consider shifting your focus away from asking why the client will not cooperate. Instead, I invite you to ask the only question that truly matters: "What is this unique neuroprint communicating?" When you let go of the expectation of success in talk therapy and begin treating the underlying biological system, you transform the therapeutic relationship from confrontation to collaboration. You are invited to support the connection between the client's biology (D1) and their environment (D3) rather than forcing them to navigate that space alone. Ensure you utilize concrete, structured, and visual "what, where, when, and how" inquiries rather than abstract "why" questions to prevent cognitive overload and protect their metabolic battery and prevent confabulation.
- **For Caregivers** — How confident are you in your advocacy? Traditional talk therapy often fails because it treats the neurotype (FASD) as just a standard presentation that needs behavioral correction. You are not being difficult or demanding when you push back at those who do this; you are an essential

advocate. I invite you to step into this role confidently, without asking for permission, and to skip generic counseling entirely. Instead, I encourage you to look for practitioners who are specifically trained in habilitative approaches. You can invite counselors or other providers to use 'what, where, when, and how' questions when seeking input to inform changes in care and communication about your loved one's neuroprint. Check their background with people with disabilities or chronic medical conditions and ask them for one or two examples of workarounds they have used to improve their situation or skills. This helps protect your loved one's metabolic energy (D2) from being drained by ineffective sessions.

- **For Individuals Living with FASD** — Embrace Your Wildflower Nature! You are not defective; you have a unique, specific neurophysiology. If talking feels like being cornered, or you don't know what to say, it is fine to show it; you do not have to say it! Bring your own journal (for thoughts, if you like to write) or a pad of paper to make a map or picture that shows what you mean. I invite you to remember that your neuroprint might need movement, nature, art, or a service animal to feel safe, ahead of the pressure to use spoken words. For some people, words follow the intervention: art and movement can circumvent words. Embracing this truth allows you to honor your own growth over time **(D4)** and to seek the exact support your unique biology requires.

Up next

In the next chapter, we dismantle the cultural cataracts of myths, misinformation, and medical gaslighting that distort how the world views Fetal Alcohol Spectrum Disorders. We will uncover the hidden truths that release our loved ones from moral judgment and reveal what they truly need to thrive across the lifespan.

Resources:
The Passport and the Matrix Map

To put these neuro-informed insights into daily practice, the 4D Framework utilizes two visual, companion scaffolding tools:

- **The Neuroprint Passport (Your Static Specifications):** Designed as your permanent "owner's manual" (built in the Chapter 8 workbook exercises), this portable tool outlines your baseline processing speeds, sensory sensitivities, and somatic triggers to establish immediate, respectful boundaries with providers, schools, or employers.
- **The 4D Matrix Map (Your Dynamic Dashboard):** Featured in Appendix C, this real-time tool plots those static parameters against fluid, changing circumstances (your immediate battery level and the sensory load of the room). It visually illustrates the phenomenon of sporadic mastery, proving that while a skill is documented on your passport, your body may not be able to afford the metabolic cost of executing it under stress.

Chapter 9
Podcast Guests

- **AJ Locashio** - Episode 110 *(Understanding Emotional Regulation in Neurodivergent Individuals)*
- **Antonia Rathbun-Lindsey** - Episode 77 *(The Now What: Tools for Parenting & Understanding FASD with Antonia Rathbun Lindsey)* and Episode 131 *(Unlocking Emotions Through Art: A Therapist's Perspective with Antonia Rathbun Lindsey)*
- **Carl Young** - Episode 129 *(Aging with FASD: Insights, Challenges, and Hope with Carl Young)*
- **Dr. Janet Oliver** - Episode 93 *(Trigger Points: How Reflexes Shape FASD Journeys, with Dr. Janet Oliver)*
- **Dr. Jerrod Brown** - Episode 22 *(Confabulation: What is it & How to help, with Dr. Jerrod Brown)*, Episode 29 *(FASD and Sleep Challenges, Part 1, with Dr. Jerrod Brown)*, Episode 98 *(Rewiring the Brain: Exploring Neuroplasticity & FASD with Dr. Jerrod Brown)*
- **Jake Tjapkes** - Episode 119 *(Navigating Life with FASD: A Personal Journey with FASD podcaster & educator Jake Tjapkes)*
- **Dr. Kristina Uban** - Episode 137 *(FASD in Real Life: Marriage, Stigma & Changing the Narrative)*
- **Neil Turley** - Episode 46 *(Refracted Realities: Exploring FASD Across Generations with Neil Turley)*

— Chapter 10 —

Cultural Cataracts

"Whenever you use a search engine, you're hit with the message
that FASD is 100% preventable.
That's such a damaging message...
as if to say, 'Oh, I'm broken, and I need fixing.'
No, you are not broken. You do not need fixing.
You need understanding."
— Dr. Emily Hargrove

Dismantling FASD Myths & Misinformation

Moving through the world with a neuroprint that functions differently is challenging, but doing so without an accurate map can feel nearly impossible. Standard medical training is designed to provide a reliable guide, yet for millions of individuals living with Fetal Alcohol Spectrum Disorder (FASD), standard diagnostic tools simply do not fit their reality. The status of "no diagnosis" or misdiagnosis does not reflect a person's truth, but rather a flaw in our systemic maps.

Dear Reader,

Throughout this book, we have explored the many ways Fetal Alcohol Spectrum Disorder can be overlooked, misunderstood, or addressed too late. Lack of training, limited access to assessment, and gaps in support all matter. Yet beneath these practical barriers lies another problem: cultural beliefs that distort what people think they see.

A cataract clouds vision. It does not change what there is; it changes how clearly it can be perceived. In the same way, cultural myths about FASD can prevent professionals, families, and communities from recognizing the real needs of the person before them. Fluctuating capacity may be mistaken for laziness. Dysregulation may be called defiance. A person who speaks well may be assumed to function well in every setting. An adult may lose needed supports because others assume FASD belongs only to childhood.

What happens when massive, market-driven misinformation crashes down on us when we face FASD? Recently, I reached out to my online FASD community, including individuals, families, and professionals, and asked them to share the most frustrating myths they encounter. The responses revealed deep misunderstandings. We must now expose the truths behind these perceptions: how symptoms are misread as choices, the fallacy of "smart enough", and the heavy burden of blame.

The constant battle to correct these myths is more than an intellectual frustration; it is a significant D2 challenge for the FASD community. Every time you have to explain that your neurotype is not a "character flaw" or your family's "parenting failure", you exhaust your limited energy. This is why misinformation is so dangerous: it forces us to use our limited energy defending our basic humanity and our family's resilience and dignity despite challenges, rather than thriving.

The 4D Perspective: Clarifying Reality

To address these corrosive narratives, we use the 4D Perspective.

- **Neuroprint/Physical (D1):** Does the myth imply that the person has a choice in their struggle? If so, it ignores biological facts. FASD is a structural neurophysiological condition, not a behavioral choice.
- **Metabolism/Energy (D2):** Does the myth suggest that increased effort or incentives will solve the problem? This ignores the metabolic cost of a chronic health condition, which demands more energy from a body operating with limited resources.
- **Environment (D3):** Does the myth frame the problem as behavioral misconduct? If so, this ignores environmental conditions that impact our health. It blames the individual rather than assessing whether the environment meets sensory requirements and supports growth, adaptation, and resilience.
- **Time (D4):** Does the myth treat FASD as a temporary phase? This fails to consider the life-span implications of a health condition. It blinds society to the fact that we are managing a lifelong condition, which we manage but for which there is no cure.

By holding these four dimensions up as a diagnostic filter, we can systematically dismantle the most pervasive misconceptions in our culture.

To help you navigate these false narratives when you encounter them in daily life, Appendix A provides practical, real-time "pushback scripts."

While this chapter deepens your clinical and somatic understanding of *why* these myths fail, Appendix A acts as your active shield, giving you the exact, disarming language to use when confronting systemic ignorance, medical gaslighting, or relational misunderstandings in real time. Use the explanations here to rebuild your internal narrative, and turn to Appendix A for the words to educate others.

Myth One: "You Do Not Look Disabled"

One of the most profound challenges of living with an FASD is the invisibility of the brain injury. Because our physical appearance often aligns with societal expectations of normalcy, the world assumes our internal neurobiology must function typically as well. This visual bias sets us up for constant, demoralizing misunderstandings and impossible expectations.

This bias is reinforced by a medical community that often refuses to recognize FASD without distinct facial features. Professionals frequently tell families, "You don't need a screening; you'd see it on their face if you had Fetal Alcohol Syndrome," insisting that a person cannot have FASD without the facial identifiers. This practice has severe clinical consequences. One mother reported that a geneticist at a major hospital told her that her son would show physical anomalies if he had FASD. Years later, Dr. Jeff Wozniak at UCLA Medical Center, who had trained that geneticist, noted that the clinician knew better. There are even examples of those who have the facial features but are no longer in the early childhood window when these features are most apparent. In one such case, a provider told a mother her son lacked characteristic facial features, so she "didn't have to worry". Four years later, a diagnostic clinic identified that the boy displayed all three facial features, which the local provider had missed.

Further, there is a harmful assumption that Fetal Alcohol Syndrome, the diagnosis that includes facial features, is more severe than an FASD diagnosis without them. Society assumes that if the face is affected, the brain must be affected to the same degree. This is incorrect. Facial features indicate only that alcohol was consumed during a specific window of fetal development. While the tissues that form the mid-face develop between days 17 and 21 of gestation, alcohol exposure impacts all cells it contacts throughout pregnancy. A person can have no facial features because the exposure missed that small window, while the exposure continued throughout the rest of gestation. In that case, a person can still be significantly affected by prenatal brain injury.

I witnessed the consequences of this "severity myth" in a case study. A mother had two sons; the older was diagnosed early due to his facial features and received appropriate support. The younger son, who lacked those features, was held to standard behavioral expectations. His underlying brain injury was ignored. He only received an FASD diagnosis and necessary supports at age 16, following a suicide attempt. Facial features enable early detection, diagnosis, and better outcomes by supporting intervention implementation.

Evaluating the "facial features" myth through the 4D framework reveals why this specific misunderstanding is so destructive. This myth can fail the individual across every dimension of their life:

- **D1:** The myth relies on a false correlation between mid-face development (appearance of a disability) and brain injury (functional disability). A person's "Neuroprint" is a complex, structural, and whole-body reality. Facial features only indicate that alcohol exposure occurred during a narrow window in the first trimester (days 17–21 of gestation). By focusing on the face, society ignores the primary biological reality: that alcohol exposure can damage the developing brain at any point during gestation, with or without impact on the mid-face. The myth misleads by equating disability with appearance, instead of function. Alcohol kills or alters whatever cell it contacts, regardless of which body system or function it serves.

- **D2:** When a person lacks these facial features, their cognitive struggles are dismissed. The physical effort required to mask their struggles and try to "pass" as neurotypical drains their daily metabolic battery, leading to chronic exhaustion.
- **D3:** Because the person "looks normal," the environment is not adapted. They are denied the sensory scaffolding and environmental accommodations they need to function safely.
- **D4:** This myth fails to account for an individual's lifespan. Relying on facial features, which change significantly from childhood through puberty, is a static, short-term view of a lifelong condition. By treating the disability as something that must be "seen" to be believed, society ignores the dynamic, lifelong trajectory of the brain injury. It prevents the implementation of the permanent, long-term health and functional supports necessary for resilience, instead offering only temporary or nonexistent interventions.

Fetal Alcohol Syndrome (FAS) represents fewer than ten percent of overall cases on the spectrum. Relying on facial features to validate a brain injury systemically ghosts the ninety percent of individuals who have typical facial structures. We must stop checking faces and start checking brains.

Myth Two: "They Are Being Defiant"

If the Visual Trap prevents identification, the Defiance Delusion prevents support. Our society habitually judges human behavior by intent, assuming that rule-breaking or struggle is a conscious choice to disobey. When applied to FASD, this perspective is dangerously inaccurate, resulting in individuals being punished for the involuntary symptoms of a physical brain injury.

Exhausted families are routinely bombarded with harmful advice to increase discipline, being told that individuals "can behave if you teach them better." This mindset ignores the injury's biological reality. Assuming behavior is always intentional leads to damaging character labels like "lazy." Self-advocate Jessica Birch shared her painful experience with this: "Honestly, I had to do so much therapy around the word 'lazy'. I am quite triggered if someone suggests I am lazy because it is not my character. It is my disability."

The Masking Trap compounds this misunderstanding. Because individuals try desperately to hold it together during the school or work day, they arrive home completely neurologically depleted, resulting in massive meltdowns in their safe environment. When exhausted parents report these struggles, professionals see a child who seemingly performs fine in public and incorrectly assume the mother is making up, exaggerating, or causing the symptoms. This lack of FASD education directly leads to mothers being accused of Factitious Disorder (formerly known as Munchausen's Syndrome by Proxy). As social worker and adoptive parent Allison McCormick experienced: "No, no, they said I was causing it... because they were totally uneducated in her disability."

The Myths of Lying and Denial: We must also distinguish between intentional lying and confabulation.

As Dr. Jerrod Brown explains, confabulation occurs when the brain attempts to fill in memory gaps. It can seem like lying, but there is no intent to deceive. Someone who intentionally deceives tells one storyline over and over; people who confabulate may offer five different explanations within fifteen minutes, completely unaware that the stories conflict or are physically impossible (for example, having the object in their hand while saying that another person is holding it, placed it there, or the object doesn't even exist at all and they know nothing about it). Individuals are also often highly suggestible; if an authority figure insists that something happened a certain way, the individual may adopt that narrative to please the authority figure or as a fawning reflex towards the stress of prolonged confrontation.

This misunderstanding of confabulation is especially tragic in legal and therapeutic settings, where standard questioning techniques can actively provoke these false memories and lead to false confessions.

Relying on a choice-based framework can turn a neurological mismatch into blame. Self-advocate Patrick Bross contests this behavioral assumption, noting that when a person's reflex system signals that the demands of the moment exceed capacity, we cannot enforce conformity: "Because that is not how people work. Because you do not just make a choice just because you want something or because you are afraid of something." Demanding conformity from someone with executive functioning weaknesses adds load, when we could instead change the loading structure to fit their neurotype and battery capacity better.

The long-term cost of this myth is significant. Because the diagnostic rate for FASD is approximately 0.01 percent, most individuals grow up being blamed and punished for involuntary symptoms of their unique neuroprint. We internalize harmful messages from repeated punishment and misunderstanding, with devastating results that can include substance use, an inability to obtain or maintain stable housing and employment, and severe mental health challenges. This cycle leaves us vulnerable to the school-to-prison pipeline of the justice system.

Myth Three: "They Can Do It When They Want To"

One of the most frustrating aspects of living with FASD is "sporadic mastery," the biological reality that an individual can perform a task perfectly on Monday, but find that same task completely impossible on Thursday. To an uneducated observer, this fluctuation looks like willful manipulation or a lack of effort. "If they did it yesterday, they must be choosing not to do it today."

But as our 4D lens reveals, a person's accessible capacity is not a static possession. It fluctuates wildly based on energy reserves, stress levels, health, and context. If a child can tie their shoes or process a complex direction at 10:00 AM, it is because their D1 physical reflexes are calm, their D2 battery is at 80%, and their D3 sensory room is quiet. If they lose that same skill at 4:00 PM, it is not a failure of character or memory; it is a physical, biological reality of their neuroprint moving through Time.

Once the system has categorized the individual, it relies on the "Rulebook/Conformity" myth. This is the belief that rule-breaking is the direct, conscious choice to disobey an established order of things. This paradigm assumes that every individual can see all the details of cause and effect and act on them consistently. When we try to enforce conformity through negative consequences, we are attempting to "reward away" or "punish away" a brain injury, which is as futile as trying to punish away an asthma attack.

Myth Four: "They Will Grow Out Of It"

One of the most persistent and harmful misconceptions about Fetal Alcohol Spectrum Disorder (FASD) is that it is solely a childhood condition. Our culture expects that if a person does not reach developmental milestones by adulthood, they have failed. In the context of FASD, this is known as "The Graduation Myth". It assumes that the effects of prenatal alcohol exposure are temporary or that an individual will outgrow the neurological impacts of their injury by age 18 or 21.

This myth creates a tragic societal blind spot. As self-advocate CJ Lutke observed: "People tend to think that once someone has become an adult, all those struggles magically disappear. Where are all the adults with FASD in the minds of the public? Only these pitiful children. No one stops to think that those same children have grown up." Jake Tjapkes adds: "FASD doesn't disappear once you turn 18, once you become an adult."

FASD is a lifelong neurodevelopmental disorder. Although the brain can rewire itself over time, neuroplasticity is not a cure for the consequences of prenatal alcohol exposure. It does not repair the structural damage caused by alcohol during pregnancy.

FASD is a whole-body diagnosis. The effects of prenatal alcohol exposure impact skeletal, immune, cerebral, and metabolic development and persist into adulthood. If a skeletal anomaly, an endocrine difference, or a metabolic regulation issue exists in childhood, it continues. Saying someone "outgrows" FASD ignores the lifelong biological differences in their system. Expecting an individual with FASD to outgrow their condition is like expecting someone with a missing limb to grow a new limb or a diabetic to grow a new pancreas at 18, disregarding the pervasive biological reality of the injury.

The "Graduation Myth" creates a service cliff. Because society assumes the disability vanishes by adulthood, support services often end the moment an individual turns 18. Debbie Michaud noted the frustration of this transition: "There's this idea that somehow somebody can transition out of their support. You can outgrow the need for support." Sandra Flach emphasizes that graduation is not the end of the need for accommodation: "Just because our kiddos graduate from high school or homeschool or whatever amount of education they get doesn't mean that FASD disappears. It will carry over on the job or on whatever else they do into adulthood. They're always going to need some kind of accommodation." Dr. Christie Petrenko warns of the scarcity of resources: "We also recognize that FASD is a lifelong condition, and if you think there is little for families, there's even less for adults."

Applying the 4D Perspective to the Graduation Myth highlights the systemic failure that results from viewing FASD as a temporary condition:

- **D1:** FASD is a permanent, whole-body neurodevelopmental disability. The structural and physiological changes caused by prenatal alcohol exposure, including those affecting the skeleton, endocrine system, and metabolism, do not resolve upon reaching adulthood. Treating this as a condition one "outgrows" denies us access to how to manage a lifelong neurophysiological difference.

- **D2:** The "service cliff" forces adults with FASD to navigate systems not designed for their needs. Without accommodation, we must exert excessive energy to perform daily tasks and maintain employment. This creates a chronic metabolic deficit, as the energy required to survive in an unaccommodating world accelerates exhaustion and erodes stamina and resilience.
- **D3:** The Graduation Myth justifies the removal of needed supports at age 18, leaving a person with neurodevelopmental disability adrift to navigate high-friction settings without manageable solutions. We don't grow out of needing glasses to correct vision, inhalers for asthma, or crutches for mobility impairments. True support for neurocognitive differences remains a lifelong requirement as well.
- **D4:** Maturation in FASD progresses on a different developmental timeline. While our chronological bodies move forward, our social and emotional development progresses more slowly. Many individuals experience a beautiful "Cognitive Bloom" in their thirties and forties, stepping into their creative purpose once the pressure to conform is removed.

The "Smart Enough" Myth (IQ vs. Executive Function)

A major barrier to recognition and support of individuals with FASD is the "Smart Enough" myth. Society prioritizes IQ scores, treating them as definitive indicators of a person's capabilities. IQ testing was originally designed as a screening tool to identify those who need additional assistance, not as a criterion for denying them that help. However, these scores are often the institutional barrier that prevents access to necessary services. Professionals and families assume that verbal intelligence equates to the ability to manage the complexities of daily life, that talk is the same as walk. This creates a major barrier. Showing what is needed, rather than just giving verbal instructions, frequently breaks down because receptive and expressive language rely on different neural networks.

These stereotypes confound access and support. IQ ranges for individuals with FASD span from 29 to 142. Focusing solely on "book smarts" ignores the painful reality of the disability due to the functional differences at play across different settings. People with FASD can indeed have intellectual disabilities, but many do not meet those criteria. The disability is often located in the gap between verbal fluency and executive functioning, the ability to apply spoken information to daily life actions. When we can repeat a phrase but cannot apply its meaning to what has to be done, others get frustrated.

Dr. Stephen Greenspan challenges the focus on IQ numbers, stating, "The main problem if you have FASD or other developmental disability is altered executive functioning. That's much more important than IQ."

This fixation on intelligence creates a service gap for those whose cognitive abilities mask their neurological injuries. Jessica Birch, an Australian FASD self-advocate, describes this struggle: "I have a normal IQ, but my adaptive, affective, academic, and executive functioning have been deeply impacted." Because people viewed her as intelligent, they overlooked her injury. She notes, "I was told again and again and again, 'You're capable. You're like everybody else, just as smart, just as able as everybody else, and you were expected to achieve what everybody else is'." Carl Young observes this discrepancy in his son, who has an IQ over 110 but adaptive functioning scoring only in the lowest 1st percentile range. Facts are only as good as the context in which they apply and are used. Intelligence scores are not at all the same as adaptive skill levels.

What a painful paradox: an individual is intellectually aware of their struggles but lacks the neurological capacity to change them. Mary Byrnes recalls her husband's question: "How could you be so smart and stupid at the same time?" Her response remains a reality for many: "Easily, I have a brain-based disability. And there's no shame in that."

The gap between expressive language and executive capacity is often a minefield of misunderstanding. When persons with FASD have strong expressive vocabularies, others assume their sequential, spatial, or other reasoning processes are equally advanced. Dr. Kathryn Page identifies this issue: "The expectation that the world has of me and that I have of myself is that I can think just as well as I can sound. I can figure things out, but this is not true." Dr. Jerrod Brown calls this a "cloak of competence" or "superficial chattiness." Barb Clark notes that this allows individuals to pass as competent in brief interactions: "Our kids can appear like they comprehend something, because they know what to say in the moment, right? But they don't always comprehend it."

We must stop using IQ as the axis of capacity. Providing support must be based on actual daily functioning rather than select segments of performance for others. Failing to distinguish between intelligence and adaptive functioning leads to systemic abandonment. When society mistakes high intelligence for functional capability, this ignores our actual needs, setting us up for burnout, clinical depression, loss of self-worth, and further blame from others.

Applying the 4D Perspective to the "Smart Enough" myth clarifies why this misunderstanding is destructive:

- **D1:** FASD is a neurological, whole-body reality. Relying on IQ ignores the biological fact that an individual with high verbal intelligence can still have challenges in the prefrontal cortex networks that manage regulation, planning, and impulse control. The pattern of abilities and gaps is highly individual and varied. Our abilities are often quite uneven across daily tasks.
- **D2:** Masking, talking with verbal fluency to hide other executive functioning deficits, draws down enormous energy. When systems deny support because a person appears "smart enough" because they are articulate speakers, the pressure to hide gaps grows worse. Limited energy reserves are spent on overcompensating, dancing as fast as one can with words, worsening chronic fatigue and physiological collapse.
- **D3:** Forcing an FASD neuroprint into an Autism or ADHD rulebook prevents the creation of FASD-informed environmental scaffolding. If environmental supports don't match one's functional adaptive capacity, we are left to navigate a high-friction load beyond our stress threshold and physiological resources.
- **D4:** This myth creates a static, short-term view of a lifelong disability. Assuming that intelligence equates to uniform capacity across all cognitive activities ignores the lifespan trajectory of FASD and the role of fatigue over time in environments.

This is compounded by the "Close Enough" diagnostic myth. Many well-meaning professionals, wanting to avoid the maternal stigma of alcohol, will purposefully label a child with Autism or ADHD instead of FASD. Speech-language pathologist Elizabeth Kriston warns against this practice. Incorrect labels lead to interventions, like Applied Behavior Analysis (ABA) or rigid behavioral conformity plans, that focus on consequences and cause-and-effect thinking. These strategies are often entirely ineffective and even traumatizing for a brain impacted by FASD. Furthermore, these alternative diagnoses completely fail to monitor for the 428 physical co-morbidities associated with prenatal alcohol exposure.

Deconstructing the Blame/Shame Cycle

When our society insists on finding a single point of failure for FASD, we choose blame over real solutions. This constant focus on individual fault traps vulnerable families in a cycle of silence and shame. By treating a neurobiological reality as a moral failing, we fail to build the environmental scaffolds and physical supports that truly allow our wildflowers to thrive.

To heal, we must actively deconstruct these harmful narratives, release birth mothers from moral judgment, and celebrate the beautiful, resilient adaptations of our neuroprint. We must challenge the assumption that mothers purposefully harmed their children. Many women consume alcohol before they even know they are pregnant, following the standard cultural practices of our society. Carl Young offers a shift in perspective that redirects the narrative toward grace: "If I don't blame my mom for my having FASD, then nobody else gets to blame her either. That was in a time period where every doctor was telling mom it was okay to drink while she was pregnant. That was 1972."

Debbie Michaud adds: "Nobody is going out to hurt their children on purpose. Who wants to go around in the world having a terrible relationship with your parents because of something they didn't mean to do?"

Dr. Ken Jones, who has spent fifty years advocating for families and is fierce about ending the stigma that causes communities to blame birth mothers, provides a bulletproof clinical shield against maternal shame: "Addictions are very real struggles. Very. There really is no space for judgment and condemnation. Zero space for it."

Furthermore, the science of epigenetics and generational impact removes individual blame. Research demonstrates that a father's alcohol use before conception can alter the epigenetic programming of his sperm, carrying vulnerabilities down to the child. Additionally, because a female fetus develops all of her eggs while she is still inside her mother's womb, a grandmother's unintended exposure to alcohol can directly alter the genetic expression of her future grandchildren. When we recognize that FASD is a multi-generational biological reality, the impulse to point fingers dissolves.

To stop the cycle of silence, we must dismantle the specific myths of stigma:

- **The Slogan of "100% Preventable":** This phrase is factually misleading and deeply damaging. Dr. Emily Hargrove explains its impact: "Whenever you use a search engine, you're hit with the message that FASD is 100% preventable. That's such a damaging message. Because if you're a person on the spectrum and you read that, it's interpreted as, 'Oh, I was preventable,' or 'Oh, I'm broken, and I need fixing.' No, you are not broken.

You do not need fixing. You need understanding." We must focus on preventing prenatal alcohol exposure, not preventing the existence of people.

- **The Violent or Criminal Stereotype:** Because of skewed historical statistics, the public often fears individuals with FASD as inherently dangerous. RJ Formanek actively fights against this: "We're largely misunderstood. Many people think we're violent or we're this or that. And we need to change that." Dr. Ken Jones provides clinical validation: "Millions more people with this disorder don't kill people than those who do." Crime is not a symptom of FASD; it is a symptom of a system that fails to provide basic environmental scaffolding.
- **The Myth of the "Incompetent Parent":** We must reject the prejudice that suggests a different neurological hardware configuration precludes the ability to nurture a child. Individuals with FASD are highly creative and resourceful, utilizing brilliant organizational workarounds to raise their children successfully.

Pivot Points: Putting Chapter 10 into Practice

These pivots are the framework for a new system of care, moving from managing individuals to supporting the whole human.

- **For the Professional** — I invite you to review your diagnostic intake workflow. Reflect on the diagnostic labels you use most often, and consider whether shifting to this 4D lens would offer more effective, long-term support for your patient.

Moving from observing behavior to understanding the hidden neurodevelopmental reality transforms your practice from demanding compliance to fostering true functional support. Assess your clinical, educational, vocational, or social service environment for barriers to your clients and create workarounds for genuine access based on their unique D1 & D2 parameters. Share the workarounds with your staff and support services so your agency becomes a safe and therapeutic setting. As you do this, become aware that some of your coworkers and support staff may benefit as well, due to hidden PAE.

- **For the Caregiver** — I invite you to reflect on the period before you came to understand your loved one's health condition. How does the 4D Perspective help you come to terms with past struggles of thinking your loved one was lazy or defiant? Consider what you will do instead to support prevention and intervention efforts. Those who profit from sales and distribution must pay the freight of restitution and reduction of ongoing risk.
- **For the Individual** — Your lived experience is the most valid data we have. Trusting your experience and forgiving your history is an act of profound strength. You are not defective. You possess Wildflower Intelligence, a perspective that needs exploration, understanding, and inclusion. As Dr. Emily Hargrove reminds us: "We are not broken. We do not need to be fixed... We have a perspective that needs to be explored and understood and brought to the table."

Up Next

We have dismantled damaging myths and exposed the industry normalization and misdirection that shields one of the world's most powerful industries from accountability for its product's fallout. We have examined how it profits from our collective silence, negative stereotypes, or invisibility. We have scrutinized the systemic gaslighting that keeps our community isolated and blamed for our natures. We have moved through the wreckage of old systems to see the services and support landscape clearly for what it truly is. In the next chapter, we will explore the undeniable resilience and Wildflower Intelligence that bloom in our lives. We'll see how our diverse, neurodivergent neurophysiology, far from being broken, is the precise adaptation required for a constantly shifting world. Welcome to the new growth.

Chapter 10
Podcast Guest

- **Alice Foote** – Episode 124 *(FASD & Masking with Alice Foote)*
- **Debbie Michaud** – previously interviewed for my first book, *Sip by Sip: Candid Conversations with Adults Living with FASD.*
- **Elizabeth Kriston** – Episode 17 *(Diagnosing ND-PAE with Liz Kriston, LSLP)*
- **Kelly Rain Collin** – Episode 36 *(FASD & Education: Beyond the Diagnosis in IEP Meetings with Kelly Rain Collin)*

- **Dr. Ken Jones** – Episode 27 *(A 50-Year Look Back and Hope for the Future with Dr. Ken Jones)*
- **Patrick Bross** – Episode 33 *(Thriving with FASD: Candid Advice for Parents with Patrick Bross)*

— Chapter 11 —

Lacing Up Our Boots

"Resilience is not about performing neurotypically.

It is about finding the supports that allow a person's strengths to be expressed.

One day the world's going to realize that they need us."

— RJ Formanek

The Tenacity of the Wildflower

Moving through the world with a neuroprint that functions differently is challenging, but doing so without an accurate map can feel nearly impossible. Standard medical training is designed to temic maps.

The Foundational Shifts

What is resilience? Society often defines it as "bouncing back," or returning to a baseline of normalcy after a shock. For people living with FASD, that definition misses the point. A brain shaped by prenatal alcohol exposure will not "return" to a neurotypical baseline. Resilience is the daily 4D practice of honoring a unique Neuroprint/Physical reality (D1), protecting Metabolism and energy reserves (D2), creating supportive environments (D3), and sustaining life over Time (D4).

Resilience is not a personality trait, a moral victory, or proof that someone can endure unlimited demands. It is a systemic outcome of support, practical accommodation, connection, and realistic expectations. This remains true through childhood, adolescence, adulthood, and later life.

The wildflower is our metaphor. A wildflower does not fail because it cannot become a cultivated rose. Its nature shows in how it responds to the conditions around it—how it uses available light, finds room in altered soil, and persists through changing weather. Our Wildflower nature is not conformity; it is adaptive life.

When parents, caregivers, partners, friends, and professionals meet setbacks with curiosity, flexibility, humor, and connection, they help create conditions for resilience to grow. The question is not, "Why is this person not trying harder?" It is, "What is hard here, and what will help?"

Moving Beyond Doom Narratives

For decades, much of the public language around FASD has been dominated by pessimistic predictions. Early research often emphasized the most visible and severe presentations, while overlooking the breadth of the spectrum and the effect of support, relationships, accommodations, and opportunity.

Dr. Kristina Uban describes her early experience of the field this way: "And so, now, flash-forward, we realize the spectrum is much broader than many researchers think. And I still see that as a huge limitation in FASD research." She also names the difficulty of shifting long-held narratives: "I just see how limited and flawed research has been."

Dr. Uban adds, "If I'm going to be provocative, it's what I see in FASD research as well. The people who still hold a lot of the power and a lot of the funding and get to pick who newbies come up and all of these things still don't want to shift this narrative of FASD that it could be any of us and that negates their life's work... A lot of them are still very threatened about retiring. Their whole life's work is going to be irrelevant."

Dr. Emily Hargrove describes what many individuals and families encounter when they first seek information: "If you go on the internet or go to a conference because now you're curious, you're immediately hit in the face with pessimistic prognoses. And you're immediately hit in the face with all the things you're supposedly not going to be able to accomplish."

She remembers an early conversation with the man who later became her husband: "I told him that I was passionate about educating and self-advocating for fetal alcohol spectrum disorders, then explained what it is. After that conversation, he turned to Google and highlighted a study conducted in Canada. According to that study, the average age of the individual to pass away in a hospital with FASD, in this study, was thirty-four.

RJ Formanek directly challenges the thirty-four-year lifespan myth: "We need a researcher to stand up and say that was bad science; do not follow it." Dr. Hargrove likewise explains, "However, that was based on one study that did not have proper context... Fetal alcohol spectrum disorders are real, and the struggle is, too. I have plenty of friends who live past the age of thirty-four."

That number has frightened many families, particularly when it is repeated without its study context. It cannot be used as a personal forecast for everyone with FASD. I know what it is to be given a limiting prediction: doctors told my parents that I would not live past eight years old. Yet here I am, more than five decades beyond that prediction.

Emily continues, "Part of what I do is acknowledge that there will be a struggle, but every single person struggles. But there is hope, there is help, and there is healing. All of these things can be for everyone." Jenn Wisdahl of FASD United reports that stories of hope and resilience have helped influence legislators to support the FASD Respect Act.

Gina Schumaker learned at age fifty that FASD helped explain why money, math, and time management had been so difficult throughout her life. Her diagnosis gave her room to use straightforward supports without shame. A purse with designated places for keys, identification, and credit cards reduced the mental work of tracking essential items. Today, Gina creates content to counter the assumptions that people with an FASD often encounter soon after diagnosis: "just because you have an FASD doesn't mean you're going to be homeless or on drugs."

The 4D Resilience Framework: Sustaining the Bloom

- **D1: Honor your neuroprint.** A brain-based tool, routine, visual support, or reminder system can reduce cognitive load and make participation more possible.
- **D2: Protect your battery.** Energy is a physical currency. When metabolic reserves are depleted, tasks, decisions, emotion regulation, and transitions may require far more effort. Reducing, sharing, delaying, or adapting demands can preserve capacity.

- **D3: Shift the burden to the environment.** As we age, we take on the vital responsibility of modifying our environments to fit our changing neurobiology. This self-advocacy is not a solo pursuit of isolated independence, but a collaborative act: we learn to map our unique neuroprint and explicitly direct our support teams on exactly how to help carry the load.
- **D4: Protect the next decade.** Resilience includes building a life that remains workable over time, rather than sacrificing health and stability to the immediate demands of the moment.

The Mechanics of Connection and Growth

The Neuroscience of Hope and Healing

A realistic understanding of resilience makes room for hope without denying challenges. Brains are dynamic. Prenatal alcohol exposure can involve lasting structural and functional differences, while people can also develop new skills, build supportive routines, and find workarounds that fit their lives.

Dr. Jennifer Fraser says, "The neuroscience is clear that our brains are wired to repair and recover. It doesn't matter what's happened to them. They can rebuild most stunningly." The original effects of prenatal alcohol exposure do not disappear, but new pathways, accommodations, relationships, and repeated experiences of success can expand what is possible.

Strengths and Wildflower Intelligence

Strengths-based language does not deny disability. It recognizes that a full picture includes capacity, creativity, loyalty, justice, persistence, and insight, as well as areas of genuine difficulty.

Jodee Kulp describes an early homeschooling experience with her daughter, Liz: "The first day of school for Liz, we took a learning disabled book, and I gave her a red pen, and I said, find all the disses in this book and let's cross them out because they're not going to be in our school." Their focus became what Liz could do and the supports that made learning accessible.

Dr. David Gilbert similarly emphasizes that "it's very important to identify the positives and the strengths of individuals... and leverage those positives to be able to help them live."

Mary Byrnes offers a useful reframe: "Yes, we perseverate, but over time, it actually becomes a strength." Focused interest can become deep expertise, advocacy, research, creativity, or loyalty when it is understood and supported. Mary also observes, "There's something I think about being neurodivergent that we are so attuned to fairness. So attuned to equity." A strong sense of justice can contribute meaningfully to families, workplaces, and communities.

Lived Experience and Adaptation

A deficit-only model can leave individuals with FASD and those who love them feeling frightened or fundamentally broken. Lived experience offers a fuller, more authentic view: people adapt, implement custom tools, build supportive communities, contribute, and develop lives of deep meaning.

Advocate Mary Byrnes spent decades navigating this exact developmental divide. While she excelled academically, she struggled intensely with peer relationships, social awkwardness, and the physical toll of multiple co-occurring chronic health conditions. Lacking an explanation for these invisible challenges, she spent her life internalizing the friction as a personal character flaw, keeping a painful emotional loop of self-blame active since early childhood.

Similarly, as I shared with Mary in that conversation, discovering I had FASD later in life—self-identifying at fifty-six and receiving my formal diagnosis at sixty—completely transformed my perspective. The diagnosis silenced that lifelong loop of self-reproach, allowing me to make sense of my history finally.

Mary found that it also gave her a definitive answer to a question her husband had once asked in frustration: "How could you be so smart and stupid at the same time?" Mary's response now is clear, steady, and entirely free of shame: "Easily, I have a brain-based disability, and there is no shame in that."

Today, Mary has channeled her lived experience into tireless systemic action, founding the charity Harrison's Hope to dismantle the public stigma surrounding the spectrum and educate families.

RJ Formanek also received an FASD diagnosis in his late forties after years of mental-health diagnoses that did not adequately explain his experience. He reflects, "I was charming. I could talk my way out of things and into things... But that always allowed me to lead the situation and not deal with it."

Understanding his neurology helped RJ seek accommodations that suited him. He became an international speaker, founded the Flying with Broken Wings support group, and co-founded the global Red Shoes Rock awareness movement. His view of wildflower intelligence is clear: resilience is not about performing neurotypicality. It is about finding the supports that allow a person's strengths to be expressed. As RJ says, "One day the world's going to realize that they need us."

Resilience Is a Team Sport

Resilience rarely develops in isolation. It grows through relationships in which people can be known, believed, and supported without shame.

Retired art therapist Antonia Rathbun-Lindsey notes that humans are remarkably resilient when they feel a sense of connection again, because it is all about relationships. RJ Formanek likewise describes the value of trusted people who can offer feedback and help interpret situations that may be difficult to read alone.

The role of a neurodiversity interpreter, similar to the Collaborative Support Triad that Carl Young and Joel Sheagren speak of in their books, can be especially valuable in clinical and everyday settings. Tami Eller describes her work as helping neurotypical people understand the neurodivergent experience. Carolyn Kiel and I discussed a mother who attended medical appointments with her adult daughter to support working-memory needs and add context when communication was misunderstood. AJ Locashio expands this idea, describing the value of a medical interpreter who can help translate medical information and help a provider understand a person's silences, responses, and behavior.

AJ Locashio also explains that connection and shared stories engage systems involved in exploring new experiences and regulating the nervous system. As AJ says, "connection is definitely a way that people can regulate." Jennifer Henczel frames connection as "the window and the door to every resource and thing that you need to bring into your life."

Shannon Butt shares that she has experienced suicidal thoughts for much of her life. She credits family, rural FASD programs, and sober and neurodivergent communities with giving her essential support: she would not be here without her dad, stepmom, and the communities she built. Connection made the dark thoughts take up less space. Connection can save lives.

Tenacity and "Half a Loaf"

Living with invisible brain-based differences in systems that often misunderstand them requires real endurance. Yet tenacity does not mean constant pushing. It includes rest, repair, practical support, and beginning again.

Carl Young calls his life motto "NEGU," an acronym for "never give up." He describes success as returning after a fall: "no matter how many times he falls, he gets back up and tries again." He adds, "I've fallen a lot of times."

Jodee Kulp describes that shared endurance simply: "Our boots go back on and in we go." She also offers the balancing wisdom to "let off the gas but not park the car." Rest is part of resilience; then, when capacity returns, the boots go back on.

Josh Bechtel names a more humane measure of success: "I got half a loaf. And half a loaf is better than none... even if the half of the loaf they got has a few stones in it." A partial accomplishment still matters. It can protect the battery, preserve hope, and make tomorrow more possible.

Kyle Perkins (Episode 114) uses small, manageable steps to approach overwhelming projects: "If I can just work on one paragraph for two minutes, that's all that needs to happen." He describes the value of "just being able to get that smaller task done and have that sense of accomplishment." Smaller steps can reduce overload while building momentum.

Environmental Anchors and Joy

The Gift of Grace is not simply letting someone off the hook. It is equipping a person with environmental support, sensory safety, and structure that make a task or goal more accessible.

Jodee Kulp has long advocated for practical, sensory-aware accommodation: modifying the physical environment, adjusting lighting, using a service dog, and creating a place where someone can safely de-stress. Her work with Expanding Minds of Canines for Persons with Neurodiversity shows how environmental support can reduce daily friction. When a brain doesn't have to spend all its energy surviving and masking, it has more energy for learning, relationships, and participation.

A positive emotional environment also matters. Families and individuals can become exhausted by behavior management, appointments, financial strain, and systems that do not understand FASD. Dr. Jerrod Brown (Episode 48) points to the value of positive relationships and meaningful activities. He says, "If you are a family focused on laughter and joy and gratitude and optimism and empathy and compassion and kindness and warmth, that shows profound benefits for the child's brain, their physical development, their social development."

Joy is not a denial of hardship. Laughter, warmth, pleasure, and connection can help settle an overworked nervous system and help people remain available to one another.

The Gift of Diagnosis and Celebration

An accurate FASD diagnosis can replace years of moral judgment with brain-based understanding. Diagnosis does not define the whole person, and it can explain why certain expectations have carried such a high cost. Shannon Butt observes that people often feel relief when they understand that their reactions are rooted in physiology rather than personal failure. Dr. Emily Hargrove describes diagnosis as the beginning of understanding.

This understanding creates room for everyday celebration. A milestone may be remembering medication, using a workaround, completing a difficult call, repairing a relationship, taking a needed rest, or returning after a setback. Jodee Kulp reminds us that we can celebrate milestones again and again. What matters is not what we lack; it is how we use what we do have.

Purpose in Pain

Living with FASD—or loving, raising, partnering with, or supporting someone with FASD—can be hard work. Some days bring exhaustion, misunderstanding, and collisions with societal expectations. Those challenges do not determine a person's trajectory.

Patrick Bross expresses this determination when he confronts the statistics often assigned to the FASD community: "Even if it were a statistic, it wouldn't be the first statistic I broke. So, it won't be the last."

I understand the weight of a prognostic statement. When I was diagnosed with Type 1 diabetes on my second birthday in 1965, during what I call the medical dark ages, my parents were told that I would not live past eight years old. I have now lived more than five decades beyond that prediction.

I have also lived with peripheral neuropathy, arthritis, and degenerative disc disease. In 2012, I received a Diabetic Alert Dog, a black Lab named Tzaylie (Hebrew for "My Shadow"), after realizing my body was no longer providing warning signs of low blood sugar. Even with the best technology available to me at the time, I once woke with a blood sugar of 30 and no symptoms. Diabetes had become a disability. From her placement in October 2012 until I retired her during COVID-19 to protect her from exposure, Tzaylie alerted me to impending critically low blood sugar 54 times, always sooner than my technology, and often 45 minutes sooner.

Long before Tzaylie, there were occasions when I knew I was still here by the grace of God. One happened while my husband, my mother, and I were glamping (RV camping) five miles outside Yosemite National Park's west gate. We drove into the park for the Sentinel Dome and Taft Point trailheads.

Because exercise with a blood sugar above 250 can create further physiological stress, I checked my blood sugar before beginning the downhill hike. It was around 270. I gave myself a small dose of insulin through my pump, expecting the exercise to lower it as we began the one-mile hike.

At the Taft Point Overlook, however, my blood sugar had climbed another 100 points. My pump calculated and delivered more insulin. Twenty minutes later, it was higher again. After this happened twice more, I pulled the pump from my pocket and saw the problem: the cartridge tip where the tubing attached had broken. The tubing had disconnected from the pump. I had started the day with a new set and hadn't brought extras, trusting the three-day insulin supply inside the pump.

I sat at the base of a tree and prayed. I told God that I was ready to take a dirt nap until Resurrection Day if my purpose had been fulfilled. But, for the sake of my husband and mother, whose vacations would be ruined, I asked for help.

Then came a sudden reminder: the disconnected tubing held exactly 15 units of insulin.

We made our way slowly back up the trail to avoid stressing my body further. My husband and I took turns blowing into the tubing to force those 15 units into my body, earning headaches far worse than those from blowing up too many balloons. The campground was only about 30 miles away as the crow flies, but the mountain roads made it a 90-minute drive. When we arrived, my blood sugar was 110. Perfect.

The intervention felt so undeniably miraculous that my agnostic mother shared the story at church a few days later, just before I was ordained as an elder.

People often ask how I keep going through the compounding weight of invisible disabilities and chronic health conditions. For me, faith is central. I have long believed that, when I have fulfilled the purpose for which God created me, He will allow me to sleep and rest in Him. The fact that I am still here, despite medical odds, close calls, and exhaustion, tells me that He is not done with me yet.

Dr. Emily Hargrove echoes this in her own journey, saying that when we lean on the One who created us, our purpose is fully understood. Carl Young reflects on that sense of preservation as well: "There are a lot of times when I look back, and there's another set of footprints there... I'm still here, so there's got to be a reason."

When we lead with insatiable curiosity, use environmental supports instead of blame-based strategies, and make room for an individual's strengths alongside real disabilities, we change the story. The Gift of Grace, connection, and joy do not erase FASD. They create conditions for people to live more fully.

4D resilience is also communal. When we share workarounds, accommodations, stories, and practical wisdom, we lighten one another's metabolic load. Wildflower Nature is not merely personal; it is a shared way of adapting in complex, shifting landscapes. Our resilience is strengthened through the community we build together. As Jennifer Henczel says, "connection is the window and the door to every resource that you need to bring into your life."

Pivot Points: Putting Chapter 11 into Practice

- **For Professionals** — Consider your own resilience through the 4D Perspective. When burnout or frustration rises, notice whether neurotypical compliance is being required at the expense of D1 needs. Consider how shifting from correction to connection might protect your D2 battery as well as your client's. Sensory-aware accommodations and partnership in D3 can support growth over D4 and build a more sustainable practice. As Antonia Rathbun-Lindsey reminds us, humans are remarkably resilient when they experience connection.

- **For Caregivers** — Caregiving requires tenacity, and it is not meant to be done in isolation. Notice your own 4D reality. Are your D2 reserves being depleted by the effort to enforce neurotypical expectations? The Gift of Grace can include grace for you. When D3 supports carry more of the burden, you can protect your energy and make room for genuine joy. Community can help share the load over time. As Jodee Kulp says, we can rest, and then "our boots go back on and in we go."
- **For Individuals Living with FASD** — Resilience may be part of your daily work in a world not consistently designed for your brain. Honor **D1** needs, protect **D2** reserves, and seek **D3** workarounds that allow your wildflower intelligence to be expressed safely across **D4** time. Celebrate everyday victories. Remember Josh Bechtel's wisdom: half a loaf is better than none. Connection with people who understand can make it easier to set down the mask and live from a more truthful place.

Up Next

We have moved beyond the myth that resilience means bouncing back to a standard that never fit. A brain with FASD may require different tools, different energy management, and a wider field of grace. Resilience also does not grow in a vacuum. In the final chapters, we will step beyond our immediate circle and explore how FASD belongs within the broader neurodiversity conversation.

Chapter 11
Podcast Guests

- **Angela (AJ) Locashio** - Episode 110 *(Understanding Emotional Regulation in Neurodivergent Individuals)*, and Episode 120, *(Finding Calm in Chaos: Practical Strategies for Emotional Regulation with AJ Locashio)*
- **Antonia Rathbun Lindsey** - Episode 43 *(Unlocking Emotions Through Art: A Therapist's Perspective with Antonia Rathbun Lindsey)*, Episode 77 *(The Now What: Tools for Parenting & Understanding FASD with Antonia Rathbun Lindsey)*, and Episode 131, *(Unlocking Emotions Through Art: A Therapist's Perspective with Antonia Rathbun Lindsey)*
- **Carl Young** - Episode 129 *(Aging with FASD: Insights, Challenges, and Hope with Carl Young)*
- **Carolyn Kiel** - Episode 108 *(Exploring Neurodivergence: Communication Challenges)*
- **Dr. David Gilbert** - Episode 56 *(Bridging the Gap: FASD, Law Enforcement & Research with Dr. David Gilbert)*
- **Dr. Emily Hargrove** - Episode 41 *(The Superpower Within: FASD and Embracing Inner Strengths)*
- **Gina Schumaker** - Episode 2 *(Our Candid Conversation with Gina Schumaker)*
- **Dr. Jen Fraser** - Episode 116 *(Bullying and Gaslighting with Dr. Jen Fraser)*

- **Jennifer Henczel** - Episode 117 *(From Tragedy to Triumph: A Journey of Resilience & the Power of Community)*
- **Jenn Wisdahl** - Episode 109 *(Takeaways from FASD National Impact Week with Jenn Wisdahl)*
- **Jodee Kulp** - Episode 53 (*Kickstarting Season Two of Living with FASD)*, Episode 86 (*Habilitation & FASD, Part 2: Reading the Body to Build the Brain)*, and Episode 100 *(Celebrating 100 Episodes: Reflections & Revelations on the Meliorists' FASD Journeys)*
- **Josh Bechtel** - Episode 39 *(The Mosaic of Mind: Josh Bechtel on the Art of Navigating FASD)*
- **Mary Byrnes** - Episode 127 *(Harrison's Hope: Building a Lifespan Support System with Mary Byrnes)*
- **Patrick Bross** - Episode 133 *(Thriving with FASD: Candid Advice for Parents with Patrick Bross)*
- **RJ Formanek** - Episode 4 *(From Misunderstood to Mentor with RJ Formanek)*
- **Shannon Butt** - Episode 113 *(Empowering Change: Shannon's Insights on FASD and Mental Health)*
- **Tami Eller** - Episode 106 *(Understanding Perseveration in FASD with Tami Eller)*

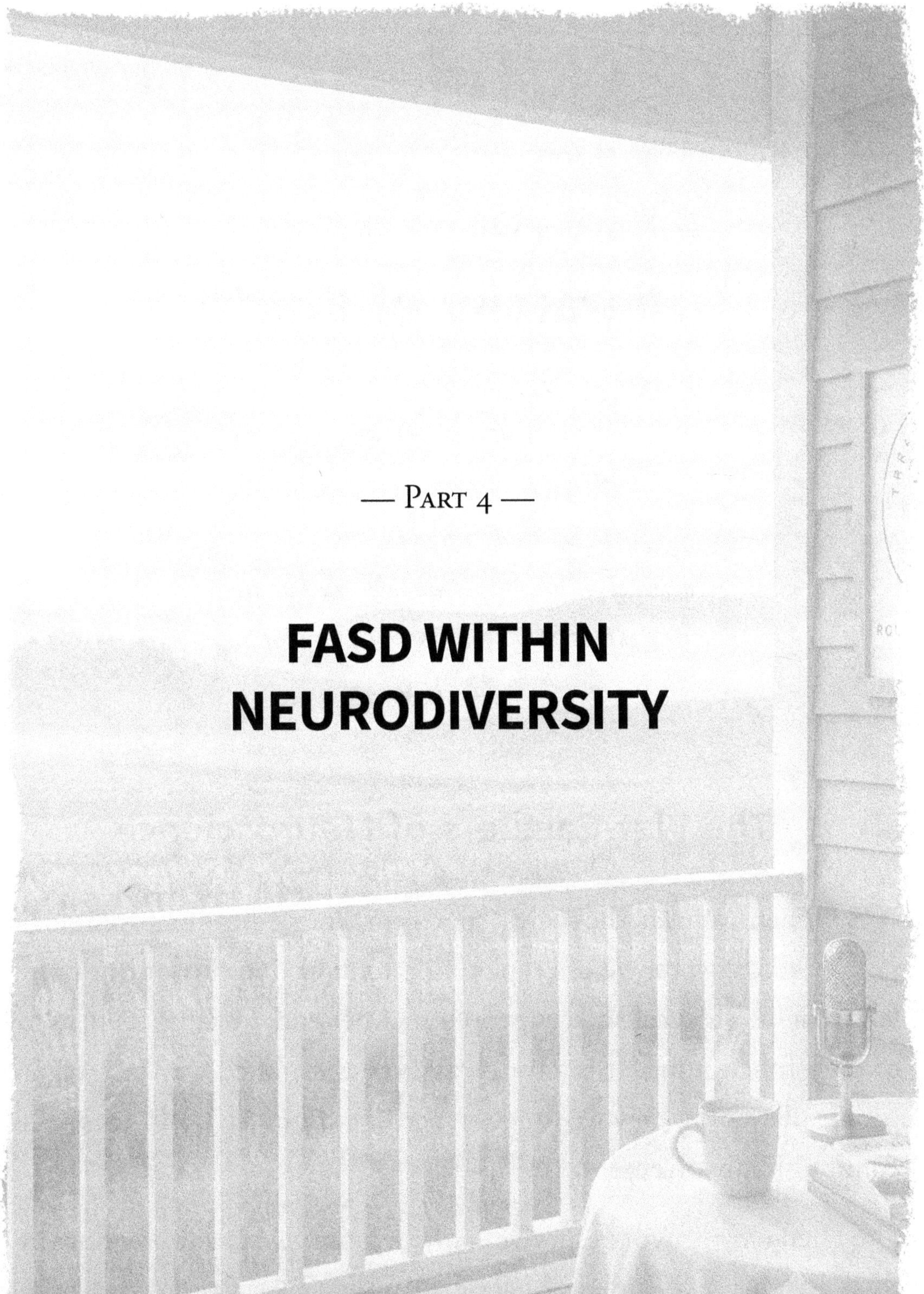

— Part 4 —

FASD WITHIN NEURODIVERSITY

— CHAPTER 12 —

Hierarchy of Worth

"There is significant bias and hierarchy
within the neurodiversity space itself,
especially around FASD...
where some neurotypes are celebrated as diverse,
while FASD is viewed as damaged."
— Aeris Wren

The Flat-Earthers of Neuroscience

When we hear the word "spectrum" in medical or psychological diagnostics, we often picture a straight line, a continuum from left to right. This scale places people at either end, labeling them as low- or high-functioning. It is a rough and oversimplified way to categorize people, flattening how we function across education, health, work, and community involvement.

The Hierarchy of Worth survives only because we are viewing humanity through this two-dimensional lens. When we flatten the human experience, we naturally create a rigid, moralized ranking between the "capable" and the "disabled." In this model, the Intellectual Quotient

(IQ) becomes the supreme gatekeeper of human value. Anyone with an IQ over seventy-five is considered "capable enough" to navigate the world independently, meaning their needs are systematically ignored, while those below are institutionalized or written off.

But human biology is not a flat line, and as we have established, the only flat line is on a dead person. The multi-dimensional 4D Framework destroys this linear sorting. When you view every individual through the coordinates of their unique Neuroprint (Dimension 1), their Metabolism and daily energy capacity (Dimension 2), their Environment (Dimension 3), and Time (Dimension 4), we no longer look at arbitrary scores on standardized tests. Instead, we have a map to read. You cannot compare a wildflower to an oak tree; you can only understand the specific environment required for each to bloom.

By treating the professions as separate, isolated clinical categories, the medical and educational networks operate in fragmented silos. As Dr. Elizabeth Cleveland notes, the helping professions are highly siloed: mental health is its own silo, behavioral health is its own silo, and communication between them is limited. We are treated as a collection of isolated diagnoses, rather than a whole, interconnected human being.

Dismantling the "Normal" Setting

When we are forced to navigate systems never designed for us, we constantly crash against a statistical phantom: the myth of the "average" human.

The so-called "neurotypical average" is not a massive, dominant majority. It represents a razor-thin, one percent sliver of the population at the absolute center of the curve. The rest of humanity, ninety-nine percent of us, actually lives along the sloping sides, experiencing our own unique, natural variations.

Yet, our schools, our hospitals, and our workplaces are built entirely around the demands of that fictional one percent. We are told that "normal" is the baseline, the default, the expectation.

But as I like to remind people, "Normal" is just a town in Illinois. It is a physical coordinate on a map, not a baseline for human biology. Yet, our institutions behave as if we are all meant to live there, forcing us to squeeze our beautiful, complex, and uneven biological configurations into a single, rigid, default setting.

Forcing ninety-nine percent of diverse humanity to conform to a default setting designed for a fictional one percent extracts a heavy physical toll. This is not some abstract social theory; it is a literal somatic drain. When you are neurodivergent, you have to spend an enormous amount of your body's limited physical energy just trying to survive in environments that constantly trigger your nervous system's survival responses.

Think of the cumulative wear-and-tear of having to continually explain, justify, and fight for your very right to exist and be supported. Whether you are advocating for yourself or desperately trying to protect a loved one, that constant friction is an exhausting, unpaid second job. Every school meeting, every doctor's appointment where your reality is dismissed, and every system crossover drains your battery. It leaves families and individuals running on empty, trapped in a relentless state of vigilance just trying to get through the day. Diversity is the norm, not the exception.

The Stigma of Origin (Acquired vs. Inherited)

There is an unspoken bias in society that a neurotype is only valid if it is entirely genetic. People assume that true neurodivergence must be inherited rather than shaped by external factors. This fosters a harmful hierarchy of worth that marginalizes the FASD community, separating us from those with genetic conditions.

We see this most clearly in the genetic double standard applied to ADHD. Dr. William Curran points out the hypocrisy of this belief, noting that ADHD does not have a confirmed genetic code and is completely invisible on an MRI. Yet, it is widely welcomed in the neurodiversity space, while FASD is systemically ghosted.

Dr. Steve Greenspan points out that professionals often equate brain-based differences solely with genetics. He corrects this by reminding us that organicity goes far beyond genetics, with FASD as a prime example. Whether a brain-based difference was written into the DNA at conception or shaped by an environmental teratogen in utero, the physiological result is the same: an organic, physical change in how the brain functions.

This is where the science of epigenetics offers a beautiful, leveling reframe. Epigenetic tags act like the “Do Not Disturb” signs on hotel doors. The body’s cellular machinery, much like the housekeeping staff, passes by, leaving those specific genetic instructions unread. Whether a genetic pathway is bypassed because of a hereditary mutation or because of prenatal alcohol exposure, the resulting neurology demands our absolute respect.

To clarify this tangled landscape, consider how we understand environmental "causes" themselves. For years, the scientific community pointed to Dr. Ira Chasnoff's landmark research, which suggested that prenatal exposure to tobacco is the primary environmental cause of ADHD. In popular circles, people took this as a direct, biological teratogenic fact. Yet, modern genetic epidemiology has since revealed a more complex truth. When we compare siblings raised by the same mother, the direct biological link of nicotine on the brain is heavily challenged. Instead, the association is largely driven by genetic and environmental confounding: parents who carry ADHD genes are statistically much more likely to smoke cigarettes to self-medicate, passing those same genes to their children.

The irony is breathtaking. ADHD, which is heavily associated with maternal smoking and genetic confounding, is celebrated as a blameless, natural variation. But FASD, which is also an environmental exposure, is pathologized and excluded because society wants to hold onto a moral stick to beat the birth mother. No child chooses their own neurodevelopmental challenges, and no parent harms their child on purpose. It is time to stop drawing arbitrary lines between "blameless" genetics and "preventable" acquisitions.

"Othered" Within the Margins

As we try to build bridges across different neurotypes, we must face a very painful truth within the neurodiversity movement itself. The movement often relies heavily on "superpower" metaphors or on the suggestion that being neurodivergent is a hidden gift. While empowerment is important, this story is deeply isolating for those of us living with FASD, whose challenges are often seen by society only through the lens of brain damage and deficit checklists.

As youth advocate Aeris Wren notes, there is significant bias and hierarchy within the neurodiversity space itself, especially around FASD. This creates a divide where some neurotypes are celebrated as diverse, while FASD is viewed as damaged. Aeris warns that this bias creates a highly unhelpful hierarchy, because everyone in this space has individual strengths and needs that mainstream society does not prioritize.

We know how awful it feels to be othered. We expect the neurodiversity space to offer absolute inclusion. Yet, we feel othered by the very people who refuse to put this neurotype on their lists. If we only support the neurotypes that we find socially acceptable, convenient, or blameless, we are not practicing true neuro-inclusion. We are simply implementing a new, painful form of exclusion.

Sovereign Grace: Building Our Own Table

How do we break free from this hierarchy? We do not do it by begging for a seat at a table that was never designed to hold our weight. We do it by building our own table.

This is the ultimate, forward-looking power of Sovereign Grace.

In Chapter 6, we undertook the intimate, retrospective journey of self-forgiveness. We looked back at our histories, realized our past "failures" were biological mismatches rather than moral flaws, and found emotional peace. But while self-forgiveness unties the heavy knots of our past, Sovereign Grace equips us for the path ahead.

If grace means *equipping*, then Sovereign Grace is the active, aggressive engineering of our physical and relational environments. It is the fierce declaration that we have an absolute, non-negotiable right to exist, participate, and thrive exactly as we are.

Sovereign Grace means you no longer wait for a clinical signature, a school board's permission, or a doctor's rubber stamp to protect your nervous system. You do not apologize for needing a quiet space to recharge. You do not feel guilty for using visual schedules, timers, noise-canceling headphones, or needing to rest when your daily battery is depleted. You stop trying to force your unique wildflower brain to bend to a standardized, flat ruler.

When we reclaim our right to be uncomfortable with the world as it is currently designed, we take back our power. Our body's reactions, the exhaustion, the sensory overload, are not failures of character; they are accurate biological data.

As Dr. Emily Hargrove beautifully reminds us, we are not broken, and we do not need to be fixed. We have a unique, profound perspective that needs exploration, understanding, and bold presentation. By practicing Sovereign Grace, we actively build that table. We stop trying to survive a system that gaslights us, and we begin to engineer a world where our wildflower intelligence can finally, beautifully take root and bloom.

Pivot Points:
Putting Chapter 12 into Practice

- **For the Professional** — I invite you to review your diagnostic intake workflow. Reflect on the diagnostic labels you use most often, and consider whether shifting to this 4D lens would offer more effective, long-term support for your patients. When you stop dividing your care into rigid, clinical silos and begin recognizing the universal human need for nervous system safety and support, you shift from being a gatekeeper of diagnoses to becoming a partner in human flourishing. Assess your clinical, educational, or vocational environment for barriers to your clients, and create workarounds for genuine access given their unique parameters.

- **For the Caregiver** — I invite you to reject the "independent-only" narrative that society forces on your family. Success does not mean standing alone in isolation; it means thriving in absolute, supportive interdependence. Focus your limited energy on building a customized, "nested" environment at home where your loved one's nervous system can co-regulate and find safety. This is not a passive surrender; it is the active, loving provision of the scaffolding they need to bloom.
- **For the Self-Advocate** — I invite you to claim the absolute validity of your unique neuroprint. You are not a damaged version of a neurotypical standard; you are a resilient, beautifully configured wildflower. Stop apologizing for your battery limits, your sensory needs, or the workarounds your body requires to function. Practice Sovereign Grace by aggressively protecting your energy, designing your own supportive spaces, and standing tall in the truth of your Wildflower Intelligence.

Up Next

We have found our place within the broad neurodivergent community, but realizing we aren't alone is only the first step. When multiple diagnoses overlap, medical and educational systems often default to confusion or, worse, dismissal. How do we navigate the 'complicated cases' in which one symptom masks another and the 'standard' protocol fails? In the next chapter, we move from shared neurodivergent identity to the complex, often overwhelming reality of comorbidity, learning how to untangle the chaos and advocate for care that sees the whole person.

Podcast Guests Quoted in this Chapter

- **AJ Locashio** - Episode 110 *(Understanding Emotional Regulation in Neurodivergent Individuals)* and Episode 120 *(Finding Calm in Chaos: Practical Strategies for Emotional Regulation with AJ Locashio)*
- **Aeris Wren** - Episode 128 *(Dismantling the Myth of "Neurotypical": A Conversation with Youth Advocate Aeris Wren)*
- **Dr. Elizabeth Cleveland** - Episode 80 *(Adult Neurodiversity Diagnostic Services: Dr Elizabeth Cleveland's Fusion Center)*
- **Dr. Emily Hargrove** - Episode 76 *(Embrace the Whole Self: Faith & FASD with Emily Hargrove)*
- **Dr. Steve Greenspan** - Episode 57 *(Gullibility & FASD: the Untold Story of Social Challenges with Dr. Stephen Greenspan)*
- **Dr. William Curran** -Episode 101 *(The Invisible Struggle: Addressing FASD in Child Welfare, with Dr. William Curran)*

— Chapter 13 —

The Habilitative Shift

"If something in our authenticity feels threatening to that connection with the caregiver, then authenticity is set aside to maintain that attachment... there will come a point when we lose our authenticity completely."

— *Morgane Borzée*

Beyond the Illusion of Choice

Dear reader, our society operates under a single, deeply flawed assumption known as the behavior paradigm: the belief that every action is a deliberate, conscious choice. This model shapes our schools, psychiatric clinics, child welfare programs, courts, and households. We operate as if the right reward or consequence will inevitably force individuals to conform. Because this approach succeeded in B.F. Skinner's labs with pigeons and rats, our public institutions blindly assume it applies to the entire range of human behavior. Dr. Lyelle Palmer, professor emeritus of educational psychology, explains that this focus became a profound distraction for the helping professions for decades. While behaviorism can serve as a simple motivational tool for typically developing brains, it is not a workable solution for neurodivergent human development.

When we rely on behavior modification to address Fetal Alcohol Spectrum Disorder (FASD), we operate in a two-dimensional vacuum, treating complex somatic reactions as simple choices. This flat view completely ignores our Dimension 1 reality. The brain is not a static machine that can be programmed through simple carrots and sticks; it is a prenatally altered, living neural network. We try to patch behavioral "software" while the brain's physical "hardware" struggles with basic regulatory energy. Retired art therapist and family clinician Antonia Rathbun Lindsey insightfully observes that while we can tinker with the software, the biological hardware has certain non-negotiable configurations. To support this unique neurobiology, we must stop expecting a sensitive wildflower to survive in an environment that drains its very capacity to live. We must move beyond two-dimensional behavioral checklists and embrace a four-dimensional, organic reality.

In my decades of practice in child welfare, every system I encountered operated under this same choice-based assumption. When a student or client struggles with regulation, and professionals cannot identify an obvious trigger, they default to the clinical trap of "secondary gain": assuming the individual is faking or choosing a struggle to avoid work or manipulate others. When rewards and consequences inevitably fail, the system blames the caregivers for undermining the therapy, or labels the individual as defiant and incorrigible. This leads to a tragic, self-perpetuating loop of two outcomes. First, families are forced into "provider shopping": moving from one uneducated clinician to another in a desperate search for answers. Second, the system resorts to "family shopping": shuffling vulnerable children from one foster home or group placement to another, driven by the false belief that a stricter enforcer of compliance will finally break the child.

The 4D Habilitative Lens: From Punishment to Support

To dismantle this compliance cycle, we must run every moment of distress through the multi-dimensional filter of our 4D lens:

- **Neuroprint/Physical Baseline (Dimension 1):** Does this response stem from a somatic safety alarm, a sensory overload, or a prenatally acquired, bio-structural difference? If the underlying biological neuroprint is configured differently (much like a wildflower that requires distinct soil and shade), punishing the plant for not performing like a cultivated garden rose is not only ineffective; it is a systemic violation that adds trauma to injury.
- **Metabolism/Energy Balance (Dimension 2):** Is the individual in a state of regulatory collapse? When their biological battery is depleted, no reward can buy regulation, and no consequence can motivate performance. The only solution is active energy restoration and somatic refueling, not sticker charts or isolation.
- **Active Environmental Inputs (Dimension 3):** When we throw out the carrot and the stick, what real-time demands in this room are overtaxing the nervous system? This is the core of habilitation: we stop demanding that the individual adapt to a hostile space, and instead redesign the environment to match their unique biology.
- **Temporal Context & Rhythm (Dimension 4):** Are we chasing a quick, superficial fix to close a clinical file, or are we building a sustainable, long-term life trajectory? Habilitation is not about suppressing a behavior for an hour; it is about honoring a unique developmental timeline and preserving regulation across a lifetime.

Antonia Rathbun Lindsey often cites advocate Robert Taylor's profound analogy from the late 1980s to expose this systemic blind spot. Imagine a child playing baseball who is accidentally struck in the head by a bat and knocked unconscious. After ten minutes, he regains his senses and stands back up. But an hour later on the field, he begins stumbling, dropping routine catches, and misjudging the ball's trajectory. If the coach misinterprets this clumsy coordination as deliberate clowning or laziness, they might bench the child to teach him a lesson. Yet we would be horrified by such a response. We would recognize that the child has suffered a physical head injury. We would expect the adults in the room to stop the game, protect the child, and get him immediate medical care rather than punishing him for involuntary physical symptoms. Yet, when a child or adult prenatally exposed to alcohol stumbles over the cognitive and executive hurdles of daily life, our institutions relentlessly punish them for their biological struggles.

This mismatch demands a professional reckoning. Master educator and behavior specialist Deb Evensen faced a profound crisis of confidence early in her career when her traditional behavioral training failed her. She recalls sitting at her desk, watching her students struggle, and realizing she was looking at them through the wrong lens: she saw bad choices rather than a lack of understanding. Deb notes that this shift is exactly the revolution our systems need, moving us away from moralizing behavior as "good or bad choices" and toward the realization that we are all configured differently, we are all doing our best, and we must learn how to support one another.

This invisible physicality (the unseen, metabolic toll of managing an unaccommodated disability) is the primary reason traditional rehabilitation fails. Standard rehab assumes that an individual possesses the physiological stamina to practice a skill repeatedly until it runs on autopilot. However, for a brain prenatally altered by a teratogen, the biological pathways for automaticity were never established. Every single action (from maintaining posture to filtering out background noise) requires a continuous, active, and exhausting manual override.

To help us visualize this, imagine a metal chain where a few critical links are made of thin, fragile copper wire, while the rest are forged from heavy iron. If you attempt to lift an ordinary daily load, the iron links will hold, but the fragile wire links will quickly stretch and snap. Traditional behavioral plans demand that our loved ones pull heavier loads, promising a reward at the end, without ever realizing that no amount of motivation can make a thin copper link support the weight of an iron one.

Habilitation, by contrast, respects the bodily battery. It honors the unique biological configuration and finite energy capacity of the individual's physical system, rather than demanding that a car keep running on an empty tank.

The Fundamental Distinction: Rehabilitation vs. Habilitation

In clinical practice, *rehabilitation* aims to restore a lost function, assuming a healthy baseline once existed and merely needs a restart. But for a brain prenatally altered by alcohol, that baseline was never established. As Dr. Lyelle Palmer explains, when prenatal alcohol exposure disrupts the early formation of the central nervous system, certain foundational pathways in the brainstem and midbrain are never fully developed.

This is why our work must be strictly habilitative: we are not restoring an old baseline or repairing a broken mechanism; we are building physical scaffolding and adaptive workarounds for skills that were never built in the first place. Shifting our focus from recovery to construction is not a semantic game; it is a clinical and ethical necessity. When we stop searching for a baseline that does not exist, we can finally begin supporting the living, breathing organism that does. We must start where the individual's nervous system is, rather than where society expects them to function based on chronological age.

Dr. Palmer explains that living with an unintegrated startle response is physically exhausting, noting that these reflexes, when active, keep the body in constant discomfort. Traditional therapists attempt to teach our loved ones to calm themselves using psychological or verbal tools, but habilitation recognizes that the alarm is physically stuck in the nervous system. This approach identifies the Moro reflex as the gateway to the other infant motor loops and focuses on physically integrating it at the core somatic level.

The Spinal Galant and STNR Reflexes: The 'Wiggle' Baseline

Because public schools view a student's restlessness through a psychological lens, they assume a child is choosing to wiggle, slouch, or kick their desk. But Dr. Palmer clarifies that a neurologically organized child can sit still without effort. If prenatal alcohol exposure disrupted their early development, reflexes like the Symmetrical Tonic Neck Reflex (STNR) or the Spinal Galant Reflex remain active.

Whenever their back touches a chair or their head tilts forward to read, their nervous system fires involuntary, automatic motor signals. The child is essentially trapped in a physical loop. We cannot build a sturdy conduit of executive functioning or teach abstract cognitive skills to a brain that is still expending all its energy managing basic infant motor reflexes. Habilitation requires us to return to these physical roots, helping the body organize and complete the developmental steps it missed.

To support a sensitive nervous system, pediatric occupational therapist Kokeb McDonald cautions that we must stop chasing the "smoke" of surface behavior and instead target the "fire" of neurological distress. Behavior is simply the visible smoke; trying to correct it through rewards or consequences is futile because the signal can look like defiance, panic, or laziness. The true work is to find where the fire lives (whether in unintegrated reflexes, metabolic depletion, or environmental mismatch) and address it directly through core, physical organization.

Kokeb notes that we must return to the somatic foundation where natural movement is coded in our bodies, using purposeful, movement-based habilitation to bypass the cognitive bottlenecks and directly access the brain's safety centers. Through this bottom-up coordination, we help the brain integrate its foundational pathways, stabilizing the links in our physical chain so the body can finally manage the daily weight of school, work, and community life.

To shift our perspective from judgment to curiosity, we must completely redefine how we engage with neurodivergence. As leaders, caregivers, and practitioners, we must stop focusing on repeated execution errors and asking, "What is wrong with you?" Instead, we must ask with limitless, compassionate curiosity, "What is happening in your body right now, and what support do you need to succeed?"

By replacing compliance-based behavioral charts with genuine environmental scaffolds, we stop treating a physical battery depletion as a failure of character, and instead honor the natural growth and distinct environmental needs of our Wildflower Nature. This is the habilitative shift. Neurodevelopmental Intervention Treatment (NDIT) provides the broader, historical philosophical boundary for this somatic work. At the same time, our 4D FASD Framework supplies the step-by-step, real-world habilitative mechanics to put it into action.

The Safe Soil Audit

Adapted from the collective wisdom of Dr. Lyelle Palmer, Dr. Janet Oliver, Kokeb McDonald, Dr. Maude Champagne, Eileen Devine, AJ Locashio, Jodee Kulp, Antonia Rathbun Lindsey, and Mary Byrnes.

Before you attempt to address any challenging behavior, consider these foundational elements of safe soil:

- **Audit for Safety (The Neuroprint Check):** Are active primitive reflexes or sensory overloads locking the nervous system in a chronic state of alarm? Before expecting cognitive focus or emotional control, have you given the individual the somatic tools they need to feel safe? This might look like a strategic movement break, a complete pause in verbal communication, using white noise headphones, walking outside, or retreating to a pre-assembled, quiet sensory nest.
- **Audit the Micro-Environment (The Input Check):** Is the immediate setting configured to minimize the sensory load on a sensitive neurotype? If the immediate room is loud, the individual's biology cannot be quiet. Have you actively tuned down the flickering lights, background noise, and visual clutter that consume their regulatory reserves?

We are finished with the exhausting, futile pursuit of compliance. We choose a calming, slow connection. We are done trying to normalize the human spirit; we are finally ready to honor the neuroprint's physical reality.

Pivot Points:
Putting Chapter 13 into Practice

Before you turn the page, I invite you to linger and choose just one perspective to carry with you. Imagine how your practice, your relationships, or your self-concept would transform if you allowed this single shift to take root.

- **For Professionals** — I invite you to consider a shift in focus: moving from a search for 'secondary gain' to an exploration of the individual's real-time metabolic battery and environmental triggers. What might change in your clinical practice or educational approach if we stopped asking what a person is trying to get, and instead wondered how much energy the immediate environment is actively draining from their system? When we recognize that uneven performance often reflects a fluctuating battery rather than a lack of willpower, our entire relationship can shift from enforcement to collaborative accommodation. I invite you to explore how they best cool down when overwhelmed, how their body resets, and what simple, physical modifications their system needs to function reliably.

- **For Caregivers** — I invite you to pause when a behavior becomes challenging, and instead of trying to prune or paint the visible behavioral leaves of the system, look first at metabolic battery depletions and environmental sensory overloads. In Jodee Kulp's beautiful words, we can stop trying to paint the leaves gold to force compliance when the physical root system of the tree is actively starving. By offering a safe, quiet space to recharge, we support the roots first and let our loved ones bloom in their own time.
- **For Individuals Living with FASD** — I invite you to lay down the heavy burden of the 'try harder' narrative. Your uneven performance is a biological hallmark of your prenatally altered neuroprint, not a failure of character, effort, or willpower. I invite you to claim your right to the environmental workarounds and permanent scaffolding that allow your unique wildflower intelligence to bloom beautifully, exactly as you are.

Next Up

We have dismantled the behavioral paradigm and introduced the Habilitative Lens, shifting our perspective from compliance-driven behavior to the organic reality of the biological battery. We have replaced the ineffective "choice" model with the precise, multi-dimensional 4D Framework necessary to create real, sustainable stability. However, even with the right lens, we cannot fully understand this hardware (or the courageous effort required to live with it) without facing the reality of its environment.

In the next chapter, we explore what happens when a unique, survival-wired neuroprint is forced to navigate a world that does not honor its biology. We will encounter the **"Bear in the Neuroprint"**: the physiological and environmental clash that occurs when a sensitive, structural adaptation meets a rigid, unyielding world.

Chapter 13
Podcast Guests

- **Antonia Rathbun Lindsey** - Episode 43 *(The Now What: Tools for Parenting & Understanding FASD with Antonia Rathbun Lindsey),* Episode 51 *(Crafting Calm: Exploring Art Therapy in FASD)* and Episode 131 *(Unlocking Emotions Through Art: A Therapist's Perspective with Antonia Rathbun Lindsey)*
- **Deb Evensen** - Episode 14 *(Deb Evensen: Creator of 8 Keys for Adults with FASD)*
- **Kokeb McDonald** - Episode 99 *(The Hidden Power of Reflexes: with Occupational Therapist Kokeb McDonald)*
- **Dr. Lyelle Palmer** - Episode 103 *(Reflexology with Dr. Lyelle Palmer)*

— Chapter 14 —

The Bear in the Neuroprint

"It's not like the person wants to be mean or has bad intentions.
When the brainstem detects a threat,
it completely bypasses the logical prefrontal cortex.
The resulting aggression is simply the
neurological hardware trying to keep the body safe."
— Dr. Maude Champagne

The Blueprint of Connection

Dear Reader, human connection underpins our existence. However, for individuals living with Fetal Alcohol Spectrum Disorder (FASD) and other neurodivergent conditions, navigating relationships and establishing a true sense of safety can be a deeply complex process. To genuinely foster supportive relationships throughout life, we must examine how our earliest environments and neurological makeup influence how we connect, trust, and feel secure.

During a presentation I gave on Intergenerational Trauma in February 2026, I examined the biological basis of how these relationship patterns develop. Let's start by understanding how our biological ledger is maintained, or as Dr. Bessel van der Kolk would say, how our bodies keep score. We often discuss trauma as a single, terrifying event, such as a car accident, a natural disaster, or a major illness. We usually label the aftermath of these shocks as PTSD. With this type of "Big T trauma", the event generally occurs after our attachment systems have already formed and isn't caused by our caregivers. Typically, caring individuals buffered us from stress, teaching our nervous systems that even if the world feels unsafe at a moment, it remains a safe place to live.

In contrast, when a person lives in a climate of Complex Developmental Trauma (CDT), the trauma is less like a sudden storm or season and more like a permanent climate. This trauma begins during those vital years when our brains are still learning how to be safe. It is caused by the confusion our systems face when the same people we depended on for food, shelter, and nurturance become the source of physical or psychological danger. Our brains do not know whether to attach or flee. It is like trying to build a new road in the middle of a perpetual earthquake. This explains why our nervous system gets stuck on High Alert: it had to be, just to survive the climate in which it developed.

The Cortisol Bath and the Bear

When a person lives in a climate of Complex Developmental Trauma, their brain is constantly immersed in what we call a Cortisol Bath, which is the ongoing flood of stress hormones. Cortisol is perfectly designed for a temporary surge of energy to fight or flee. Still, when your brain is exposed to it for decades, it alters the physical structure and configuration of your neural pathways and metabolic system.

On one of my visits to Glacier National Park in Northern Montana, we hiked to a beautiful, remote mountain lake. It was a peaceful, quiet trek going up, but on our way back down, we spotted fresh grizzly bear scat right in the middle of our path. It had not been there when we walked up.

In that split second, what happens to your biology? Your heart rate jumps, your breathing halts, and your skin prickles as your body is instantly immersed in what we call a Cortisol Bath: a sudden flood of stress hormones. Cortisol is perfectly designed for a temporary surge of energy to fight or flee, a life-saving evolutionary gift when a real grizzly might be lurking around the next bend in the trail. It mobilizes every ounce of your physical energy to keep the organism alive.

But we must ask: what happens when your daily life is permanently situated on that high-alert trail? What if your nervous system is forced to treat the classroom, the clinic, or the kitchen table (the very places where you are supposed to feel safest) as a dense thicket where a predator is actively tracking you? When the threat of a sudden encounter is ongoing and inescapable, your biological survival switch never flips back to Off. You remain on high alert for ten, twenty, or thirty years. Your brain isn't broken; it's simply become an expert at navigating a high-risk wilderness.

This is how our neuroception becomes conditioned. Similarly, if you have previously been frightened by a snake while walking on a park's sidewalk, your cortisol bath starts running every time you notice a crack in the sidewalk. Your brainstem does not wait to perform a high-resolution analysis of whether that dark line is a harmless gap or a venomous threat; it fires the alarm first and asks questions later. To keep you alive, your amygdala operates on a low-resolution survival scan, choosing speed over accuracy. It would rather jump at a hundred harmless sidewalk cracks than miss a single venomous snake. After such a frightening encounter, it can take weeks or even months of walking that same path before your nervous system stops doing an involuntary double take every single time you see a dark line on the ground.

Now, let us bring this biological reality into the womb, where we find the ultimate, foundational bear in the neuroprint. If a biological mother experiences chronic, unmitigated stress during pregnancy, a developing baby spends a significant portion of their gestation swimming in a prenatal Cortisol Bath. Just as my family and I remained hyperfocused on every snapping twig and shifting shadow for the remainder of our hike down that Montana mountain, and just as it takes weeks or months to stop doing double takes at harmless cracks in the pavement, a gestation period spent under the shadow of high cortisol exposure (compounded directly by the neurotoxic insult of prenatal alcohol exposure) permanently damages the developing threat thermostat. Before birth, this delicate regulatory system is thrown completely out of kilter, leaving the body struggling to balance the sympathetic 'heater' of fight-or-flight with the parasympathetic 'air conditioner' of felt safety. Consider the monumental physical toll on an individual's system from all the subconscious stress audits they must perform every day just to verify true safety, maintain regulation, and preserve their relationships. They are not choosing to be hypervigilant or difficult; their biological battery is simply being rapidly depleted by an internal defense system that has been running on high alert since the womb. For an individual living with a prenatally altered nervous system, the modern world is filled with these innocent cracks in the sidewalk. Their brainstem constantly misinterprets ordinary, low-level sensory inputs as immediate, deadly snakes, forcing them to spend precious metabolic energy validating safety in spaces the rest of us take for granted.

This systemic blindness creates a disastrous cycle. Dr. William Curran highlights that our institutions fail to intervene effectively, stating that we are graduating those children into the juvenile justice system, into the homeless system, and into the mental health system. An intergenerational blind spot in our reunification plans worsens this tragedy. As a social worker, I often overheard colleagues complain about birth parents failing to complete simple reunification case plans, assuming they didn't care enough to regain custody of their children. However, if the system recognizes the intergenerational pattern of substance use and understands that these children are often in care due to prenatal exposures to various substances, why does it fail to see that the birth parents likely struggle with similar, unaddressed, intergenerational brain injuries where there are patterns of intergenerational substance use? When the child welfare system punishes birth parents for their own invisible, unsupported disabilities, it perpetuates the cycle of trauma. It keeps the front door of our intake process wide open.

The Biology of Attachment

When we examine Mary Ainsworth's attachment model, we can see how childhood environments directly influence our relationship habits. Our childhood attachment strategies were not flaws in our personality; they were smart biological responses to the challenges we faced when our environments couldn't properly support us.

- **Type A (Connection Avoidant):** This often develops in an environment where caregivers are physically present but emotionally distant. The nervous system learns that trying to connect deeply is often met with no response. To stay safe, the person concludes that depending on others is risky, so they must be their own safe space. In adulthood, this often shows up as the Reliable Provider who cares for everyone else but doesn't let anyone care for them, or the Quiet Perfectionist who asks for nothing to avoid rejection.

- **Type C (Connection-Seeking or Fawn):** This develops when caregiving is inconsistent. The nervous system learns that safety is a moving target and can be achieved only by being hypervigilant about others' needs. The biological logic becomes a belief that *I am only safe if you are okay*. In adulthood, these individuals become the household's Mood Monitor, sacrificing their own needs to prevent a storm, or the Chameleon, changing their personality to match what others need to keep the peace.
- **Type B (Securely Attached):** This reflects an internal belief that says, "It is safe for me to be me, and it is safe for you to be you. We are safe together." Someone with a secure attachment style is comfortable with an open-door approach to discussing differences, shared roles, decision-making, and collaboration. They see conflict as an important opportunity to clarify boundaries. Although only about 25 percent of people grow up with naturally secure attachments, it is important to recognize that this is a flexible state we all can move toward, especially within a supportive community.

The Conflict Between Attachment and Authenticity

The systemic failure to create a safe environment is more than just an administrative mistake; it signifies a profound rupture within the sense of self. When a child is moved repeatedly from home to home, and their neurological differences are punished instead of understood, they learn a devastating lesson: their true self is a threat to their survival. To secure the attachment they desperately need, they begin the slow, painful process of eroding their own identity to meet the expectations of the adults around them.

Emotional intelligence expert Morgane Borzee explains this paradox with clear insight. Drawing on the work of Dr. Gabor Maté, Morgane points out that every child is born with two essential needs: attachment and authenticity. As mammals wired for connection, we rely on attachment to a caregiver to survive. Morgane describes the tragic biological trade-off that happens for neurodivergent children, noting that if something in our authenticity feels threatening to that connection with the caregiver, then authenticity is set aside to maintain that attachment. She warns that if we continue this pattern, we will eventually lose our authenticity completely.

This conflict between who they are (their individual neuroprint) and the persona they must create to be compliant is the main struggle for many. It is a form of survival masking that eventually spills into adulthood, leading to a life in which the person constantly feels like an impostor in their own skin.

For Morgane, the pressure to conform to neurotypical expectations was a fundamental assault on her ability to form deep, authentic connections. She openly shares her lived experience with this fawning response, describing it as a submissive response rooted in her inability to express herself and her strong concern about maintaining relationships. She sacrificed her authenticity to prevent anything that could jeopardize the relationship. While this performance of normalcy may bring temporary acceptance, it comes at a terrible cost. Every moment spent pretending to be someone she is not is a moment in which the true attachment she longs for remains just out of reach. You cannot be truly loved if you are never truly seen, and when the system demands a performance of compliance, it makes authentic intimacy nearly impossible.

Biological Protectors in Childhood

To cope with chronic stress and a lack of safety, the autonomic nervous system activates biological protective responses. These are not behavioral choices, personality flaws, or deliberate acts of defiance. They are reflexive, primitive survival responses wired into the nervous system specifically for safety.

Professor Emeritus Dr. Lyelle Palmer explains that many of these responses arise from unintegrated primitive reflexes, such as the Moro reflex, which functions as a fundamental alarm system. He reminds us that "a newborn comes with more than 40 reflexes." These patterns are designed to integrate as higher-level brain development progresses. Before a young person can think through danger, the nervous system may react automatically. Noise, unexpected movement, touch, crowded spaces, or sudden changes in routine can register as threats rather than inconveniences, leading to fight, flight, freeze, shutdown, or urgent attempts to escape. In fear-paralysis reflex (FPR/FTR) integration models, this early protective freeze response emerges about 5–8 weeks after conception and becomes inhibited as the Moro reflex develops. The Moro—an established infant startle reflex—can be observed by about 25 weeks after conception and is generally established by 30 weeks. When a startle response is unusually strong or easily triggered, sudden sounds, visual surprises, touch, or balance changes may produce a jolt, muscle tension, rapid breathing, and a heightened urge to fight, flee, freeze, or shut down. A young person may then appear oppositional, impulsive, avoidant, or emotionally reactive when they are actually overwhelmed.

Pediatric occupational therapist Kokeb McDonald explains how this survival instinct also manifests as the fear-paralysis reflex. When a child's sensory system becomes overwhelmed, their body enters a deep freeze response. As Kokeb describes, their visual field narrows, and because their brain focuses entirely on safety, they abandon everything else. She notes that a child might talk very articulately and appear totally fine in a calm home environment, but when they enter a challenging, noisy classroom, the fear paralysis kicks in, and they shut down. She observes that their behavior becomes almost like selective mutism. The child becomes speechless and tries to become invisible to the threat.

When these biological protectors turn outward, systems of care often mistakenly label the child as defiant. Dr. Maude Champagne notes that aggressive or withdrawn behaviors often reflect hostile attribution bias, in which individuals misinterpret situations as threatening. For example, a child might hit a classmate after an innocent bump in a crowded hallway because their brain genuinely perceives the accidental bump as a deliberate physical attack. Dr. Champagne emphasizes that this is a neurological reality, stating that "it's not like the person wants to be mean" or has bad intentions. These behaviors are responses to unmet needs or survival instincts. When the brainstem detects a threat, it completely bypasses the logical prefrontal cortex. The resulting aggression is simply the neurological hardware trying to keep the body safe.

What Felt Safety Actually Looks Like

True safety occurs when we stop demanding forced compliance and instead offer co-regulation and compassion. Speech-language pathologist Elizabeth Kriston reflects on the heartbreak of using traditional discipline on a child whose brain is stuck in a biological survival response. Looking back, she vulnerably shares how she parented her daughter using standard consequences, noting, "Brain injuries do not respond to bribes or punishment." She recognizes the damage this caused, explaining that her daughter "doesn't understand why she was being corrected or being chastised or being punished for things that she had no control over and she didn't want to do them."

Sometimes, safety requires highly creative, sensory-based accommodation that directly targets the autonomic nervous system. Social worker Allison McCormick shared how she trained her service dog, Star, to provide deep pressure by straddling her daughter during a meltdown. Allison explains that applying pressure to the shoulders "releases oxytocin, which is a feel-good hormone." She notes that when Star would lie across her daughter and apply that pressure, it would trigger oxytocin release, and the meltdown would simply vanish.

This isn't pampering; it's neurobiological scaffolding. By offering external regulation that the child cannot yet produce independently, these interventions help the child relax their biological defenses and breathe freely. When we shift from trying to fix behavior to regulating biology, we stop battling the brain and start working with it.

The Adult Cost of Masking

As we transition into adulthood, navigating romantic partnerships, workplace dynamics, and deep friendships with a neurodivergent brain brings an entirely new set of complexities. In adulthood, chronic masking frequently evolves into profound codependency.

Emotional intelligence expert Morgane Borzee shares her own lived experience with this dynamic. She explains, "In my case, I grew up in an environment where there was a lot of anger, and I relate anger to unsafe, to being in danger. So it meant that I would do anything to avoid any anger." To protect herself and her relationships, she adopted what she calls a submit response, sacrificing her own needs to ensure she did not do "anything that could make the relationship go bad".

When the Five-Year-Old Takes the Wheel

When this internal stress bubbles over into adult conflicts, our autonomic nervous system activates the same biological protectors. The program Morgane founded uses very accessible characters to describe these responses: the Tiger for the fight response, the Seagull for the flight response, the Deer for the shutdown response, the Bunny for the fawn response, and the Koala for the clingy attachment response.

Morgane beautifully shows how these protective parts form when we are very young. She explains it like this: "You can think of it like you are the adult and you're driving your life. You know, you are driving the car; you are in the driver's seat; everything is fine. And then you see something. You see something, and then you have your five-year-old on as the copilot." She describes how the nervous system reacts, noting that the five-year-old part of the brain "says, I've seen this. I remember this. I know how to act. And the five-year-old takes the wheel of the car and starts driving with either fight, flight, or freeze."

When adult relationships break down, it's essential to step back and ask whether you're talking to your adult partner or to the five-year-old reacting to an old wound. As Morgane reminds us, we need to pause and ask ourselves, "Am I talking to the adult here, or am I talking to the five-year-old who is just vividly remembering something that has nothing to do with the present moment but with their own wounds and troubles?"

Sensory Overload and Adult Shutdowns

Adult relationships are heavily affected by the intense exhaustion that comes with navigating a neurotypical world. Adult advocate Kyle Perkins, who lives with AuDHD, describes a physiological point where sensory and cognitive demands become overwhelming. He points out that when a manager pressures him or a customer loses control, he reaches a breaking point and can't keep going. As he explains, "If I push through it, I'm going to damage myself. And to me, I thought it was just burnout, but instead it happened to be shutdown."We see this same biological limit even in childhood. In our conversations, Jodee Kulp often recounts how her daughter would hold it together in a neurotypical environment all day, only to come home and release that immense tension by melting down on the floor to decompress safely. It was not misbehavior. It was a necessary physiological release.

Whether it manifests as melting down on the floor, pressing into a car seat, or going nonverbal for days, we observe the same phenomenon. When the brain is overwhelmed with too many inputs, it reaches a hard physiological limit. The shutdown is the body's ultimate protective response. When we view this as a brain-based survival strategy rather than a behavioral issue, we stop telling people to "just get over it."

Instead, we focus on what we can do to create a safe environment that keeps their nervous system functioning.

Rewiring Adult Relationships

Because our attachment styles form in childhood, changing our patterns in adulthood takes significant effort. Healing occurs when we shift toward Type B, the Securely Attached style. This internal state reassures us that it is safe to be ourselves, safe for others to be themselves, and safe for us to be together. By replacing a constant need to perform with authentic presence, we move away from the isolating myth of complete independence and embrace the supportive reality of interdependence. Self-advocate Kenny LaJoy offers a helpful perspective, noting that our society would not function without an unspoken reliance on interdependence.

The 4D Safety & Connection Framework

Before attempting to repair a relational rupture or force a connection, pause and run the situation through this 4D scan:

- **D1:** Is the person's nervous system currently focused solely on survival? When someone is highly aroused, their nervous system may be prioritizing threat detection over reflection, problem-solving, and self-control. In that moment, avoid lengthy explanations, demands for insight, or attempts to reason them out of distress. Instead, use a calm voice, few words, physical space, predictable choices, and supports that help restore a sense of safety. As arousal decreases, the person can better access the prefrontal cortex skills needed for conversation, learning, reflection, and logical problem-solving.

- **D2:** Is there enough metabolic reserve left to support social connection? If the bear has been active for hours, the system is probably deeply depleted. Connection demands significant cognitive energy, and right now, they have none to spare. We must remember that operating in a neurotypical environment depletes energy reserves much faster, and a meltdown is often just a physiological shutdown caused by an empty cognitive battery.
- **D3:** What is the environmental cueing? Is the tone of voice, the physical space, or the rhythm of the interaction inadvertently triggering the bear? As Antonia Rathbun-Lindsey points out, when someone feels uncomfortable or triggered, we must reduce the situation to neutral and slow down to ensure everyone feels safe first. Safety isn't just an emotion; it's a physical state the nervous system senses.
- **D4:** Are we judging this moment as a permanent failure, or are we recognizing it as a transient bear state? True connection is rooted in long-term safety, not in the success or failure of a single interaction. We must view this through Dimension 4, understanding that inconsistent performance is a biological hallmark of brain-based differences, not a willful behavioral choice.

Pivot Points:
Putting Chapter 14 into Practice

In this chapter, we have mapped the systemic and biological barriers to connection. The following pivots invite you to shift your internal lens gently. Once you change your perspective, your actions will naturally follow.

- **For Professionals** — I invite you to shift your focus from identifying misbehavior to evaluating the autonomic nervous system. Instead of asking what a child is doing wrong, consider asking which biological response (fight, flight, or freeze) is currently controlling this individual's brainstem.
- **For Caregivers** — I invite you to step away from the role of a disciplinarian trying to enforce compliance, and instead embrace your role as a safety partner who protects the space so the bear is not triggered. When your loved one struggles, I invite you to let go of rigid expectations based on chronological age and instead offer developmental support that matches their actual, asynchronous maturity.
- **For Adults Living with FASD** — I invite you to look at your emotional meltdowns, sensory shutdowns, or intense reactions with profound self-compassion. They are not proof of a failure of willpower or character; they are smart, ancient biological protective responses that kept your system safe when you had to survive a world that did not understand your wiring.

Next Up

We have explored why the behavioral lens fails in relational spaces, replacing the demand for compliance with a neurobiological map for felt safety and connection. However, mapping these relational dynamics is only the beginning. How do these survival-driven states interact with our larger public systems (our classrooms, our clinics, and our courtrooms)? In the next chapter, we step into the machinery of public care to examine why traditional behavior modification fails so spectacularly at scale, and how we can begin building permanent, institutional ramps.

Chapter 14
Podcast Guests

- **Allison McCormick** - Episode 89 *(FASD & Trauma: How Social Services Fail & Dogs Help, with Alison McCormick)*
- **Antonia Rathbun-Lindsey** - Episode 43 *(The Now What: Tools for Parenting & Understanding FASD with Antonia Rathbun Lindsey)*, Episode 61 *(From Rupture to Repair: Healing FASD Family Dynamics with Antonia Lindsey)*, and Episode 131 *(Unlocking Emotions Through Art: A Therapist's Perspective with Antonia Rathbun Lindsey)*
- **Barb Clark** - Episode 97 *(The Truth They Ignore: System Denial and FASD)* and Episode 118 *(Denial, Anosognosia & Delayed Remorse with Barb Clark)*
- **Carolyn Kiel** - Episode 108 *(Exploring Neurodivergence: Communication Challenges)*
- **Elizabeth Kriston** - Episode 17 *(From Diagnosis to Dialogue: An SLP's Dual Lens on Prenatal Alcohol Exposure)*
- **Jodee Kulp** - Episode 34 *(Embracing Neurodiversity & FASD: a Candid Conversation with Jodee Kulp)*, Episode 53 *(Kickstarting*

Season Two of Living with FASD, with author Jodee Kulp), and Episode 81 *(Unveiling Stories: The Impact of Jodee Kulp's Writing on FASD Awareness)*

- **Kenny LaJoy** - Episode 11 *(It's Okay to be You: A Candid Interview with author Kenny LaJoy)*
- **Kokeb McDonald** - Episode 99 *(The Hidden Power of Reflexes: with Occupational Therapist Kokeb McDonald)*
- **Kyle Perkins** - Episode 114 *(Navigating Neurodivergent Life with Kyle Perkins),* and Episode 126 *(Top Strategies to Manage RSD and Overthinking with Kyle Perkins)*
- **Dr. Lyelle Palmer** - Episode 103 *(Reflexology with Dr. Lyell Palmer)*
- **Dr. Maude Champagne** - Episode 94 *(Understanding Aggression in FASD: a Conversation with Dr. Maude Champagne)*
- **Morgane Borzée** - Episode 124 (*Unlocking Emotional Intelligence for Neurodivergent Minds: A Conversation with Morgane Borzée)*
- **Dr. William Curran** - Episode 101 *(The Invisible Struggle Addressing FASD in Child Welfare, with Dr. William Curran)*

— Part 5 —

RETHINKING THE FRAMEWORK

— CHAPTER 15 —

Bribing the Blind: Behaviorism's Illusion of Choice

"Our story follows our state.
When a nervous system registers threat or overwhelm,
its behavior will reflect self-protection."
— Eileen Devine

Much of modern society revolves around the behavior paradigm: the pervasive assumption that all human action arises from a conscious, voluntary choice. This model shapes educational classrooms, psychiatric care, child welfare systems, judicial structures, and family dynamics. Built on traditional learning theory, it assumes that offering rewards or applying consequences will reliably motivate an individual to comply with authority. Behavior is the downstream expression of an organism attempting to preserve stability with the energy and neural pathways available to it.

When these motivational tools fail, conventional systems rarely question their underlying premise. Instead, professionals are trained to uncover "secondary gain," assuming the person is intentionally choosing noncompliance to escape a task or gain attention.

Advances in neuroscience reveal why this approach falls short. Human beings are biological organisms with physical survival reflexes that activate automatically under stress. We cannot navigate a multidimensional neurobiological landscape using a flat, one-dimensional model. Involuntary reflexes—such as startle responses, fight-or-flight activations, or protective sensory shutdowns—are not volitional acts. They trigger instinctively when a biological threshold is crossed.

Prenatal alcohol exposure causes diffuse, whole-body impacts that alter physical neural networks and central nervous system communication. As clinician Antonia Rathbun-Lindsey notes, drawing on the clinical writings of Robert Taylor, severe harm occurs when physical and neurological conditions are mistaken for psychological or moral failures. The brain and body operate as an integrated ecosystem; when neurological pathways are injured, expecting typical responses through sheer willpower is biologically impossible.

Consider a simple athletic analogy. If a young baseball player suffers a concussion from an errant bat, adults immediately recognize the injury. If he stumbles or drops a routine catch an hour later, a coach does not bench him for "clowning around" or demand that he try harder to focus. We understand that swelling and altered pathways create an involuntary coordination deficit that requires medical care, rest, and environmental protection.

With FASD, the developmental brain injury is diffuse, whole-body, and invisible. Expecting behavioral incentives to override a physical neurological difference is like demanding that an athlete run on a broken ankle or telling a visually impaired student to try harder to read a distant blackboard.

The 4D Perspective: Evaluating the Behavioral Paradigm

Evaluating standard behavioral modification through the 4D Framework clarifies why compliance-driven methods break down:

- **D1:** Behaviorism assumes a uniform nervous system. It overlooks the fact that prenatal alcohol exposure alters structural pathways, leaving an individual with physical regulatory limits that rewards cannot alter.
- **D2:** Coerced compliance, point sheets, and loss of privileges place heavy processing demands on a nervous system that is already metabolically vulnerable. External rewards cannot recharge a drained biological battery.
- **D3:** Traditional systems blame the person when their nervous system buckles under environmental friction. The 4D lens shifts focus to environmental accommodations and workarounds that match the individual's authentic processing pace.
- **D4:** Behaviorism prioritizes immediate, short-term compliance. The 4D Framework protects long-term health, dignity, and lifespan stamina.

Siloed Systems and the Prescription Mismatch

When institutions fail to recognize whole-body neurobiology, support becomes siloed. Medical, mental health, and educational providers assess individuals through separate diagnostic lenses, often assigning familiar labels like ADHD, Autism, or Oppositional Defiant Disorder for administrative expediency. As Goethe observed, *"We see what we look for; we look for what we know."*

This siloed approach produces an environmental mismatch. In both school and workplace settings, people assume an individual with high verbal intelligence has equally strong executive functioning across all tasks. When performance fluctuates, employers and teachers frequently misinterpret this scattered profile as disrespect or poor motivation.

Navigating everyday expectations with FASD often feels like managing multiple complex tasks on a five-percent battery. We would never expect a phone on low-power reserve to stream high-definition video. Yet, neurodivergent individuals are routinely expected to operate at the razor's edge of their stamina without a recharge.

When we hear from neurodivergent self-advocates and clinicians, a strong chorus of validation arises about this systemic depletion. Self-advocate Shannon Butt notes how quickly an empty battery triggers systemic overwhelm, describing a snowball effect of stress on a fragile physical system when unmanaged demands accumulate. Clinician Tami Eller highlights the persistent risk of evaluating individuals based solely on their best days, mistaking a temporary high-water mark for a sustainable baseline and failing to realize the massive biological toll and recovery required afterward. Neurodivergent voice AJ Locashio summarizes this metabolic reality simply: "It's all about energy... And we only have so much of it." Straining to perform on that depleted red reserve bar burns an enormous amount of biological fuel simply to maintain basic coherence. Without a 4D lens to provide perspective, individuals internalize this friction as personal inadequacy rather than an environmental mismatch, accelerating chronic burnout, anxiety, and relational rupture.

The Futility of "Try Harder"

As Morgane Borzée notes, when an institution demands compliance for a missing neurological pathway, *"'try harder' becomes the wound rather than the work."*

When an individual experiences working-memory drops, multi-step directions simply vanish from retrieval. Demanding that they try harder to remember inflicts profound emotional distress.

Similarly, when sensory overwhelm triggers alexithymia (the temporary inability to identify and vocalize internal emotions) traditional talk therapies that demand verbal expression push reasoning further offline. Antonia Rathbun-Lindsey addressed this by using visual art and concrete workarounds, allowing clients to map internal stress states nonverbally and exit high-friction environments safely before reaching survival thresholds.

Visible physical differences receive standard accommodations (such as curb cuts, ramps, and braille signage)without social debate. However, when a disability is invisible, individuals are often forced to justify their needs repeatedly, draining finite energy reserves just to secure basic access.

Cognitive Rigidity vs. Relational Flexibility

Cognitive rigidity is frequently misinterpreted as willful stubbornness or defiance. Clinical social worker Eileen Devine explains that individuals with executive processing differences experience an intense internal panic when plans shift unexpectedly.

Devine reframes cognitive flexibility not as a moral attitude, but as an advanced relational cognitive skill. When an individual lacks the immediate neural bandwidth to navigate rapid changes, demanding sudden compliance destabilizes their nervous system.

Drawing on the polyvagal insights of Dr. Stephen Porges and Deb Dana, Devine reminds us that *"our story follows our state."* When a nervous system registers threat or overwhelm, its behavior will reflect self-protection. Cultivating safety must precede cognitive flexibility.

The Harm of Public Behavior Charts

Classroom token economies, public sticker charts, and color-coded behavior trackers assume that a child possesses the real-time executive capacity to pause, evaluate, and alter their responses on command.

Educational advocate Kelly Rain Collin points out that when a student is operating in sensory overload, physical survival mechanisms override cognitive reasoning. Public behavior charts do not teach regulation; they publicly display involuntary neurological distress, exposing the child to peer rejection, shame, and compounding trauma. A sticker chart cannot soothe an overstimulated nervous system.

Aggression as a Survival Mechanism

Aggressive outbursts are rarely planned malice; they are physical survival responses. Dr. Maude Champagne explains that neurodivergence and chronic stress can create a **hostile attribution bias**, causing the brain to misinterpret neutral environmental stimuli (such as an accidental bump in a crowded hallway) as immediate threats.

Antonia Rathbun-Lindsey's work with Dr. David Potter clarifies this through neuroscience:

- **Anxious Aggression:** A protective, reactive reflex driven by alarm circuits in the lower brainstem.
- **Drive Aggression:** A calculated, goal-directed behavior.

Most FASD-related outbursts are anxious, reactive responses to an overwhelmed sensory system.

Additionally, many individuals actively seek proprioceptive feedback—craving deep physical pressure, heavy lifting, or intense movement to ground their bodies in space. When we mislabel an unaccommodated sensory need as deliberate aggression and punish it, we miss the underlying biological signal. We must adopt a "swap, not stop" strategy, utilizing occupational therapy supports, physical tasks, and sensory breaks rather than punitive isolation.

Traditional Paradigm

Fix the Person (Rewards / Punishment) > Masking & Burnout

Neuro-Informed 4D Lens

Modify the Space (Workarounds / Pacing) > Regulation & Safety

The Developmental Horizon: Chronological Age vs. Biological Reality

Society often assumes that turning eighteen automatically grants adult executive function and impulse control. For individuals with FASD, reaching the age of majority rarely matches a sudden leap in neurological maturity. As counselor Tami Eller notes, the sudden withdrawal of youth supports leaves young adults navigating complex adult expectations with developmental tools that are still taking root and maturing at their own natural pace.

During my years in foster care and adoption social work, evening on-call rotations often meant responding to late-night crises involving Transitional-Aged Youth (TAY). Without training in prenatal alcohol exposure, staff frequently mislabeled calls about lockouts or roommate conflicts as "attention-seeking" or "manipulation."

We were measuring young people by chronological age rather than developmental reality. Expecting adult independence from a maturing nervous system without transitional scaffolding sets up severe systemic vulnerabilities.

Moving Beyond the Legal and Educational Pipeline

When childhood accommodations disappear, systems often transition from support to policing. While many individuals with FASD develop strong self-advocacy and live stable, fulfilling adult lives, those who encounter the legal system face significant danger.

Retired attorney David Boulding points out that legal environments rely on abstract concepts and linear logic models that do not account for neurodevelopmental differences. A suggestible individual who confabulates under interrogation, or experiences an involuntary startle reflex, is easily mislabeled as guilty or defiant.

Author Melissa Jacobus (*The Accomplice*) documented this when her daughter was manipulated into taking the blame for a financial crime, with the legal system interpreting developmental vulnerability as calculating intent. Replacing choice-based assumptions with capacity-based understanding prevents the criminalization of neurodivergence.

Comparing Frameworks

Core Dimension	**The Behavior Paradigm**	**The Neuro-Informed 4D Lens**
View of Behavior	A deliberate, voluntary choice.	A communication of internal biological state.
Primary Goal	Outward compliance and conformity.	Autonomic regulation and genuine connection.
Core Intervention	Modify the person through incentives.	Modify the environment and provide workarounds.
Guiding Question	*"Why won't you comply?"*	*"What does your nervous system need right now?"*
Long-Term Outcome	Masking, depletion, and chronic burnout.	Sustainable capacity, resilience, and dignity.

Supporting Caregivers: Moving Past Systemic Blame

When traditional behavioral interventions fail, providers sometimes shift blame onto parents, misinterpreting the child's brain-based symptoms as inconsistent parenting. Dr. Maude Champagne notes that assessing parental competence based on a neurodivergent child's behavioral presentation is a flawed clinical metric.

This dynamic creates a safe parent paradox. As podcaster Carolyn Kiel explains, children often mask all day at school, burning every ounce of energy to conform, only to collapse in the emotional safety of their home.

Blaming parents for this biological depletion damages the parent-child attachment bond, turning advocates into disciplinarians. When we look beneath visible behaviors to assess root neurobiology, we restore trust and collaboration within families.

Pivot Points: Putting Chapter 15 into Practice

- **For the Professional** — I invite you to explore shifting your clinical intake from assessing surface compliance to evaluating the client's sensory load and metabolic battery. Consider replacing punitive rubrics with collaborative workarounds that gently accommodate their scattered profile.
- **For the Caregiver** — I invite you to consider introducing a five-percent battery check into your daily routines. When a task stalls, you might pause and look for gentle signs of biological depletion rather than asking your loved one to "try harder," giving regulation space to take root before re-engaging the task together.
- **For Individuals Living with FASD** — I invite you to gently reframe the "try harder" wounds of your past. Consider that inconsistent performance is never a moral failure, but the natural response of a living nervous system navigating load. You might allow yourself the grace to honor your biological needs and design spaces where your authentic wildflower resilience and natural strengths can truly bloom.

Up Next

Having examined why reductive behavioral methods fail, we turn next to the physical foundations of regulation. In Chapter 16, we explore how unintegrated primitive reflexes shape daily body responses, and how bottom-up somatic support lets us nourish the biological roots rather than merely prune the leaves.

Chapter 15
Podcast Guests

- **AJ Locashio** - Episode 110 *(Understanding Emotional Regulation in Neurodivergent Individuals)*
- **Allison McCormick** - Episode 89 *(FASD & Trauma: How Social Services Fail & Dogs Help, with Alison McCormick)*
- **Antonia Rathbun-Lindsey** - Episode 43 *(Parenting Your Porcupine, Part 1, with Antonia Rathbun Lindsey)*, Episode 51 *(Crafting Calm: Exploring Art Therapy in FASD with Antonia Lindsey)*, Episode 61 *(From Rupture to Repair: Healing FASD Family Dynamics with Antonia Lindsey)*, and Episode 131 *(Unlocking Emotions Through Art: A Therapist's Perspective with Antonia Rathbun Lindsey)*
- **Carolyn Kiel** - Episode 108 *(Exploring Neurodivergence: Communication Challenges)*
- **David Boulding** - Episode 31 *(David Boulding: the Intersection of FASD and both the Law & Sex)*
- **Dr. Maude Champagne** - Episode 94 *(Understanding Aggression in FASD: a Conversation with Dr. Maude Champagne)*

- **Eileen Devine** - Episode 112 *(Understanding Cognitive Rigidity with Eileen Devine)*
- **Kelly Rain Collin** - Episode 36 *(FASD and Education: Beyond Diagnosis in IEP Meetings with Kelly Rain Collin)*
- **Mary Byrnes** - Episode 127 *(Harrison's Hope: Building a Lifespan Support System with Mary Byrnes)*
- **Melissa Jacobus** - Episode 28 *(Supporting our Young Adults with FASD: a Candid Conversation with author Melissa Jacobus)*
- **Morgane Borzée** - Episode 124 *(Unlocking Emotional Intelligence for Neurodivergent Minds: A Conversation with Morgane Borzée)*
- **Neil Turley** - Episode 46 *(Refracted Realities: Exploring FASD Across Generations with Neil Turley)*
- **Tami Eller** - Episode 106 *(Understanding Perseveration in FASD with Tami Eller)* and Episode 115 *(The Spectrum of Experience: Moving Past Labels in FASD with Tami Eller)*

— Chapter 16 —

Restoring the Unestablished

"The way I look at symptoms is like smoke...
Smoke is a sign that there's a fire somewhere.
I can't chase the smoke because it can go anywhere
and look like it came from anything.
So the trick will be to find the fire."
— Kokeb McDonald

As helping professionals, our efforts to help clients identify obstacles and achieve success are undermined by the belief that behavior is chosen and intentional.

The Limits of the Behavioral Lens

To support people with FASD well, professional training and practice need to move beyond the assumption that behavior generally arises from choice. When a person's reflex system signals that the demands of the moment exceed capacity, a choice-based framework can turn a neurological mismatch into blame.

Carrots, sticks, rewards, and consequences can be useful tools for some kinds of motivation. They do not explain or resolve biological brain fatigue, sensory overload, unintegrated reflexes, communication differences, or a depleted metabolic battery. When the reason for a struggle is unclear, behavioral training may look for "secondary gain"—the belief that a person is unconsciously choosing a difficulty to gain attention or avoid a task. Yet the behavior may be the body's fire alarm, warning that the system is overloaded.

Dr. Lyelle Palmer, professor emeritus of educational psychology, describes the impact of this shift in the field: "Along came behavioral psychology, and that was supposed to be the answer to everything. And so that was a huge distraction for about 20 years." He adds that "behavioral psychology is important for motivation... It's not the end-all, be-all."

A behavioral lens can measure one visible dimension of experience. It cannot, on its own, account for the brain and body, the environment, energy demands, relationships, or the effects that accumulate over time. That is why the 4D Framework matters. It provides a whole-of-life view of FASD rather than reducing a person to a behavioral output.

I warn professionals in my own training, "If we presuppose a client is motivated by secondary gain, then we no longer have to be compassionate or address inequities. Instead, we judge them." When we blame people for what does not fit, we miss the supports that may help.

Protective Stress Responses

Traditional compliance strategies fail because they overlook the physiological states driving an individual's stress response. These somatic reactions are biological data, signaling how the nervous system manages threat, uncertainty, pain, sensory overload, relationship strain, or capacity-stretching demands.

Morgane Borzée introduces the Equanima emotional intelligence system to describe how these survival responses intensify or settle in relation to our surroundings. Her system uses cards depicting five animals to represent the most common nervous system defenses: Tiger (Fight), Seagull (Flight), Deer (Freeze), Bunny (Fawn), and Koala (Attach). These representations create a healthy, protective distance between the individual and their overwhelming reactions, facilitating productive discussions without re-triggering the brain stem's alarm system.

Reframing these defenses as protective measures opens a pathway for collaborative curiosity once regulation returns. Instead of escalating shame or isolation, a support partner (whether a parent, teacher, clinician, or spouse) can ask: "Oh, I see your Tiger came out today. I wonder what your Tiger saw?" This question invites mutual discovery without denying the real-world impact of behavior.

Hardware and Software

The distinction between hardware and software helps explain why people can work extremely hard and still struggle with tasks that seem simple to others.

In 4D terms, D1 is the Neuroprint/Physical body. Prenatal alcohol exposure can alter the development of the brain, organs, and systems that connect them. These differences are not undone through effort, discipline, rewards, or insight alone. People can adapt, build skills, and find workarounds, but they are building with the hardware, the brain and body they were born with.

Traditional therapies often concentrate on software, the learned strategies, skills, and ways of interacting with people and environments. Art therapist and clinician Antonia Rathbun-Lindsey observes that people with FASD and their families are frequently given psychological advice for neurological problems. She offers this illustration: "If motivational strategies worked on neurodevelopmental issues, then telling a person missing a thumb to grip a coffee cup harder would work."

Rathbun-Lindsey explains the necessary shift: "You can fiddle with the software all you want, but the hardware has certain configurations. Unless we respect and understand that, we can't even begin to know what additional components might help and which software to try gently."

Rewards, consequences, and talk therapies may have a place, but they cannot repair a brain-based difference on their own. Effective support begins by matching strategies to the person's hardware, capacities, sensory needs, communication style, and available energy. The behavior paradigm ignores the physical injury and its impact on how the brain is organized and how it runs its software. As Antonia notes, "We cannot run Apple software on a Microsoft machine."

Primitive Reflexes and the Battery

As discussed in Chapter 13, primitive reflexes—such as the Moro, STNR, and Spinal Galant—are automatic neural circuits that support early movement and sensory development. When prenatal alcohol exposure disrupts development, some reflexes may remain unintegrated. The result can be greater difficulty with posture, stillness, sensory filtering, coordination, or maintaining regulation under demand.

The central 4D implication is D2: Metabolism and energy. When automatic processes require conscious effort, the brain may need to continually override them to complete ordinary school, work, social, or daily-living tasks. Occupational therapist Kokeb McDonald emphasizes that this ongoing compensation can drain limited battery reserves and result in significant physical and cognitive fatigue.

This fatigue is physiological. It is not a lack of discipline, an intentional choice, or proof of behavioral opposition. Jodee Kulp describes unintegrated reflexes as developmental roots that need attention. When systems try to prune outward behaviors such as fidgeting, leg extension, or sensory shutdown without addressing the underlying nervous-system needs, they punish a body already running on an empty battery.

Kokeb McDonald makes the distinction clear: "The way I look at symptoms is like smoke... Smoke is a sign that there's a fire somewhere... I can't chase the smoke because it can go anywhere and look like it came from anything. So the trick will be to find the fire." The work is to understand what the signal is telling us and to address the neurological, sensory, relational, environmental, or energy-related need beneath it. To truly help an individual, we must stop chasing the smoke of behavior and address the neurological fire. The solution is not more cognitive software, but core physical work.

From Rehabilitation to Habilitation

Rehabilitation often aims to restore a lost function or return an individual to a prior baseline. That model can be appropriate after an injury or illness when a person had a previous skill level. In contrast, FASD calls for a habilitative approach: building capacity and supports from the body and brain a person has, rather than trying to restore a neurotypical baseline that was never present.

Question	Rehabilitative model	Habilitative model
Goal	Return to a prior baseline	Build capacity where foundations are incomplete or still developing
Assumption	A skill was lost	A skill may be delayed, uneven, or need a different pathway
Focus	Correct the software	Understand the hardware and match supports to it
Outcome	Independence from support	A meaningful life supported by accommodations, workarounds, and strengths

Habilitation recognizes that development continues across the lifespan. A child, adolescent, adult, or older adult with FASD may build new skills and still need environmental accommodations. Growth and support are not opposites.

Nourishing What Supports Growth

This is where we must pivot to Habilitation: building capacity where none existed before, tailored to the individual's unique neuroprint. Think of this shift as the difference between "Pruning the Leaves" and "Nourishing the Roots." Jodee Kulp frequently uses a plant metaphor to describe where our focus must be as partners, whether caregivers or professionals. Plants are composed of three main parts: the roots (the Autonomic Nervous System, which functions as our foundation), the trunk (Executive Functioning, which functions as the conduit for all information and regulation, but which is fragile), and the leaves (behavioral output).

Dimension 3 (D3) encompasses this pivot. With the 4D Framework, we move beyond efforts to suppress behavior and toward environments that fit a person's hardware, sensory needs, strengths, and available battery. Jodee's observation remains vital: "We treat behavioral output like the leaves on a tree, pruning, shaping them, and expecting them to flourish, without ever checking the health of the soil or the stability of the root system." Her reminder is equally direct: "You simply cannot motivate a tree to grow by painting its leaves gold."

Likewise, a person does not need to be reshaped into a neurotypical ideal. They need practical scaffolding: accessible communication, sensory safety, predictable routines, enough time, opportunities for movement or recovery, and relationships that make it safe to ask for help. Wildflower intelligence grows in conditions where it can use what is available and where its distinct nature is understood.

Interdependence Across Time

D4 invites us to look beyond a fixed chronological milestone of adulthood. Society assumes that an individual can eventually transition out of their support, outgrowing the need for accommodations. We see the tragedy of this assumption when school districts look at accommodated students who are thriving and erroneously assume they are "cured," mainstreaming them back into traditional classrooms only for them to flounder and drop out. Support needs fluctuate across a lifespan, and changing needs do not mean an individual has failed or regressed. No one outgrows their neurological profile, and no one outgrows the fundamental human need for relationship and community.

We do not ask a wheelchair user when they will outgrow the need for a ramp, or a person who wears glasses when they will no longer need vision correction. Environmental accommodations are not a failure of independence. They are practical tools that allow participation.

Mental-health clinician and FASD self-advocate Tami Eller names the inequity in many systems: “Even neurotypical 18, 19, 20-year-olds need support to be independent. I am sorry, but we are holding individuals to an expectation that is completely unfair, inequitable, and unrealistic. And then we blame them for their failures.”

We do not outgrow our neurobiology. We must redefine our ultimate goals. Success is not the absence of support. Success is access to the effective support that allows a person to have safety, contribution, connection, choice, and quality of life. The sustainable goal is not total independence; it is interdependence.

The Habilitative Checklist

Use this checklist to identify when an intervention drifts toward a behavioral paradigm that treats struggle as a choice, or a rehabilitative mindset that seeks to restore a baseline that does not exist.

D1: Neuroprint / Physical Body

- **Somatic Primacy:** Are we demanding an outward behavior, such as impulse control or sustained stillness, before considering reflex integration, sensory safety, communication access, and basic physical needs?
- **Individual Baselines:** Are we working from the individual's actual physiological baseline and unique neuroprint rather than comparing them to a neurotypical peer?
- **Biological Signaling:** When we see difficulty, are we asking what unintegrated reflex, unmet physical need, or systemic mismatch the body is signaling?

D2: Metabolism/Energy

- **Battery Capacity:** Is the current load too heavy for the individual's available metabolic battery?
- **Conservation Strategies:** Would rest, nutrition, hydration, pacing, reduced demands, or a change in timing preserve their capacity?
- **The Cost of Masking:** Is masking draining vital energy by requiring the individual to hide hardware differences of difficulty sustaining attention, physical posture, or processing speed?
- **Proactive Recovery:** What adjustments can reduce metabolic fatigue before the battery reaches empty?

Dimension 3 (D3): Environment

- **Sensory Fit:** Does the physical and social environment accommodate the individual's needs for sound, visual input, physical proximity, movement, pace, and social demand?
- **Tailored Scaffolding:** Is the environmental support specific to this individual's unique neurotype rather than a generic, standardized solution?
- **Structural Adjustments:** Can the task be broken into smaller steps, communicated visually, offered with more processing time, or moved into a setting that requires less energy?

D4: Time

- **Developmental Timelines:** Does the plan respect a unique developmental timeline and allow supports to adjust flexibly as needs fluctuate across the lifespan?

- **Ongoing Scaffolding:** Are necessary supports treated as permanent, flexible tools rather than temporary interventions removed based on chronological age?
- **Lifelong Well-being:** Does the plan prioritize long-term well-being, relationships, authentic participation, and the individual's opportunity to use their wildflower intelligence?

Toward a Neuro-Informed Framework

For decades, systems have attempted to manage human variety through behavioral charts, compliance training, and the pursuit of an abstract idea of "normal". There is only one place in the United States officially named Normal—a town in Illinois. As a label, it belongs on a map, not on a human being.

The neurotypical average is a statistical construct, not a requirement for a worthy life. A neuro-informed framework asks systems to become more flexible, accessible, and humane, rather than asking people with FASD to erase differences to belong.

Habilitation is an expression of respect. It begins with the person as they are, recognizes the reality of their hardware, and protects their right to a supported and meaningful life. When we stop trying to reward away a brain-based disability, we make more room for people to breathe, participate, and flourish.

Pivot Points:
Putting Chapter 16 into Practice

- **For Professionals** — Think of a recent challenge through a habilitative lens. What might change if you considered D1 neuroprint needs and D2 battery demands before asking for compliance? Notice how the physical setting, appointment length, pace of dialogue, communication tools, sensory load, materials, and opportunities for movement influence a client's capacity to participate. Create settings in which clients can show you what fits.

- **For Caregivers** — It is understandable to be drawn toward correcting visible difficulties. Pause and ask what the body may need beneath the outward behavior. Consider your own habilitative needs as well: your brain and body also have a battery, sensory needs, and limits. When environments are adjusted, and tasks are broken into smaller steps, families can build traction through strengths. What blooms follows what we nourish.
- **For Those Living with FASD** — Notice what your body feels like when your battery is full,l and name three physical signals that tell you stress is rising. Consider what helps you use less energy at home, at work, at school, or around other people. A photo reminder, step-by-step plan, phone timer, quiet nest, noise-canceling headphones, white-noise machine, water, movement, or a planned break may help your nervous system stay available.

  Respect your physical body. It is working hard. Recharging is part of living well, not a failure. Trust your hands, your heart, your strengths, and your wildflower ways.

Up Next

We have established the habilitative lens: a shift from visible behavior to the unique brain and body, from blame to curiosity, and from forced self-sufficiency to practical support. Next, we move from family and immediate environments to broader systems of care—including child welfare, education, and the justice system—and examine the consequences of punitive bureaucracies.

Chapter 16
Podcast Guest

- **Antonia Rathbun-Lindsey** - Episode 77 *(The Now What: Tools for Parenting & Understanding FASD with Antonia Rathbun-Lindsey)*
- **Jodee Kulp** - Episodes 85 and 86 *(Habilitation & FASD: Reading the Body to Build the Brain, parts 1 and 2)*
- **Kokeb McDonald** - Episode 99 *(The Hidden Power of Reflexes: with Occupational Therapist Kokeb McDonald)*
- **Dr. Lyelle Palmer** - Episode 103 *(Reflexology with Dr. Lyelle Palmer)*
- **Morgane Borzée** - Episode 124 *(Unlocking Emotional Intelligence for Neurodivergent Minds: A Conversation with Morgane Borzée)*
- **Tami Eller** - Episode 115 *(The Spectrum of Experience: Moving Past Labels in FASD with Tami Eller)*

— Chapter 17 —

The Great Narrowing

"Children with, or suspected of having,
FASD do not enter foster care by chance;
they are funneled through standard intake processes
that lack neurodevelopmental screening tools."
— Dr. William Curran

• Profit, Policy, and Institutional Blindness

The Child Welfare Front Door: An Unrecognized Population

Child welfare is the primary entry point for unsupported neurodivergence. Dr. William Curran notes that children with, or suspected of having, FASD do not enter foster care by chance; they are funneled through standard intake processes that lack neurodevelopmental screening tools.

In the United States, foster care systems serve between 330,000 and 345,000 children at any given time. Dr. Curran's research indicates that 20 to 25 percent of these youths meet the formal diagnostic criteria for FASD. Experienced frontline practitioners suggest the actual rate exceeds 70 percent when probable and suspected cases are included.

Because alcohol is a legal and socially normalized substance, biological mothers rarely disclose its use due to societal stigma and fear of punitive legal consequences. Consequently, official case records reflect artificially low confirmation rates, leaving the vast majority of affected youths classified as "exposure unconfirmed," despite presenting clear neurodevelopmental needs. Dr. Susan Rich cites Child Welfare League of America data showing that up to 95 percent of child welfare removals involve substance exposure, making high estimates very realistic. Across decades in child welfare and addiction recovery, the pattern remains consistent: alcohol use frequently co-occurs alongside other substances, yet stigma suppresses accurate disclosure.

Comprehensive neurodevelopmental assessments can cost several thousand dollars per child. Lacking specialized diagnostic budgets and neurobehavioral training, systems default to outdated behavioral methods that misinterpret involuntary symptoms as deliberate misconduct, missing the opportunity to build family coping workarounds.

When a multi-dimensional human life is managed through a flat, one-dimensional administrative checklist, complexity is stripped away in favor of standardized compliance.

The Institutional Dilemma: Policy Constraints and Systemic Inertia

Child welfare organizations are composed of dedicated professionals—caseworkers, supervisors, and administrators—who strive to support families within outdated structural guidelines. Frontline staff frequently recognize the complex neurodevelopmental struggles children face, yet programmatic protocols often reduce support to general reassurance, assuming that a stable home alone will resolve biological injury.

Deviating from established guidelines to advocate for specialized environmental accommodations can create professional friction. Furthermore, agency leadership answers to oversight boards and community leaders whose expertise is rooted in finance or public administration rather than neurodevelopment. In industrial production, standardized uniformity ensures efficiency; in human biology, standardized expectations overlook the reality of individual profiles.

Professional reflection also carries profound weight. Looking back after decades of service and realizing that well-intentioned advice lacked a neurodevelopmental foundation can bring deep grief. Acknowledging that standard practices require systemic modernization asks professionals to rethink long-standing practices. Systems remain stationary not out of malice, but because confronting institutional momentum is deeply challenging.

The Schrödinger's Paradox: Why Systems See Behavior Instead of Biology

To understand why our macro-systems resist neurobiological variation, we can look to a core principle of physics: wave-particle duality. In quantum physics, matter can exist in dual states, behaving simultaneously as both a discrete, physical entity (a particle) and a fluid, shifting manifestation of energy (a wave). Think of a raindrop, which can be viewed as an isolated drop of water or as the ripple that expands across the surface of a pond, depending on context and environment.

The paradox Erwin Schrödinger famously illustrated is that an observer cannot measure both states simultaneously; the act of observing forces the system to collapse into one state or the other.

When viewing a human being, this exact dynamic is at play:

- **The Particle:** The underlying, physical neurobiology (D1)—the permanent developmental neuroprint of FASD.
- **The Wave:** The visible behavior—the fluid, shifting, and unpredictable way that unique biology interacts with stress, fatigue, and environmental load.

The conventional behavioral paradigm focuses exclusively on the wave. By observing only the outward behavior, the system collapses human complexity into a simple question of compliance, naturally missing the underlying biological particle. Caseworkers, educators, and administrators are often just as trapped by this observational blind spot as the families they serve. They are trained to track and manage the wave, while the biological particle remains completely unaddressed beneath the surface.

Selective Systemic Vision: The Library of Support

Institutions see what their established frameworks prepare them to look for. In the history of developmental advocacy, medical pioneers searching major research libraries noted that the vast majority of accessible literature focused on visible, physical disabilities, leaving cognitive and neurobehavioral conditions largely unaddressed.

Macrosystems can and do adapt when public awareness and policy align. In the early 1990s, administrative and clinical frameworks for Autism and ADHD were sparse. As clinical identification grew, systems evolved: specialized funding was allocated, educational support codes were established, and sensory accommodations became standard practice.

The slower institutional evolution for FASD reflects policy priorities and persistent social stigma. Conditions framed primarily through a genetic lens are more readily accepted as differences requiring accommodation. In contrast, FASD carries the weight of maternal scapegoating and commercial influence. When regulatory oversight of alcohol shifted to the Treasury Department's Alcohol and Tobacco Tax and Trade Bureau (TTB), public attention was steered toward revenue collection rather than public health transparency. Acknowledging the true prevalence of FASD requires confronting the widespread impact of alcohol as a teratogen, a reality institutions have historically avoided.

Evaluating Policy Through the 4D Lens

Applying the 4D Framework to institutional policies clarifies where traditional practices fall short:

- **D1**: Acknowledges unique biological baselines and somatic strengths rather than expecting developmental uniformity.
- **D2**: Replaces the assumption of infinite stamina with an understanding of real-time battery reserves and metabolic drain.
- **D3**: Adjusts environmental load, intensity, and sensory inputs to prevent autonomic collapse.
- **D4**: Honors natural developmental horizons and lifelong interdependence rather than forcing arbitrary timelines for case closure.

When systems screen out complex profiles, individuals are absorbed into juvenile justice, emergency care, or adult assistance—leaving administrative data clean while real human need remains unaddressed.

Intergenerational Patterns and Cultural Scripts

Standard compliance-driven models closely mirror authoritarian caregiving styles, prioritizing immediate obedience over mutual regulation. At the same time, structured routines provide safety; rigid compliance without relational warmth strains a neurodivergent nervous system. When a child cannot meet arbitrary expectations, their physical symptoms are easily misinterpreted as willful defiance.

Dr. Jennifer Fraser explains that broader institutions often reinforce this authoritarian dynamic, training children to submit to authority without validating their internal state.

Because alcohol use and its neurodevelopmental impacts can span generations, parents navigating their own unrecognized injuries often fall back on the rigid patterns they experienced growing up. Advocate Patrick Bross notes that true growth requires breaking cycles of forced obedience: "There's a big difference between telling someone what to think and teaching them how to find the answers to what to think."

Sustainable growth occurs when we cultivate a secure base, pairing consistent structure with deep relational nurture.

The Historical Shift: How the Medical Model Narrowed

To understand modern institutional resistance to neurodevelopmental variation, we must look to the evolution of American medicine.

- **Pre-1910 (The Holistic Era):** Health care functioned primarily as a relational, community-based practice that recognized human variation as part of the social fabric.
- **1910 (The Flexner Report):** The Flexner Report established biomedical laboratory science as the sole standard of modern

medicine. While it brought scientific rigor, it sidelined holistic, relational, and community-centered models of care.

The Shell Game: Shifting focus to evade systemic responsibility.

- **The 1960s (Managed Pharmaceuticals):** As psychiatric care decentralized, long-term human-centered habilitation—such as Professor Hugo Maynard's communal living models on the Oregon coast—was replaced by mass-marketed psychotropic medications focused on outward symptom management.

The Great Narrowing: A History of the Medical Lens

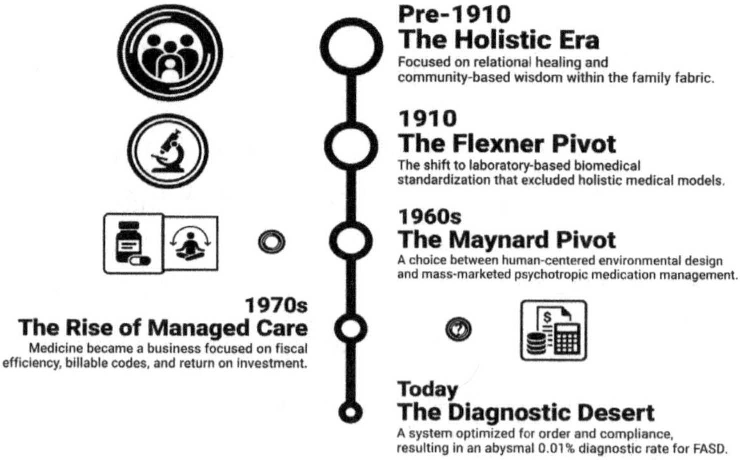

- **The 1970s to Present (Managed Care and the Diagnostic Desert):** Healthcare administration adopted third-party billing codes, prioritizing standardized, short-term pharmaceutical interventions over long-term, relationally intensive developmental support.

As I explained in a training I gave in spring 2026, Dr. Alison Escalante points out that normal human suffering and developmental differences are often categorized as billable psychiatric disorders to fit insurance reimbursement schedules. While medication can provide essential stabilization when used thoughtfully, it cannot serve as a complete substitute for sensory accommodations, supportive environments, and relational community.

Pivot Points: Putting Chapter 17 into Practice

- **For Professionals** — I invite you to explore your role within institutional systems. When evaluating a client with a scattered profile, consider documenting their distress not as willful defiance, but as an involuntary biological response to an environment that has not yet adapted to their needs.
- **For Caregivers** — I invite you to trust your daily observations of your loved one's strengths and fatigue. Consider releasing the pressure to force immediate compliance, recognizing that your need for respite and flexible routines is a natural part of supporting a unique developmental journey.
- **For Individuals Living with FASD** — I invite you to recognize that past labels of being "treatment-resistant" reflect systemic

limitations, not your personal worth. Consider identifying three accommodations or environmental adjustments that help your nervous system feel settled and supported.

Up Next

Having examined how historical policies narrowed modern care, we turn next to specific public institutions. In Chapter 18, we examine the intersections of child welfare, education, medicine, and the judicial system, exploring how the 4D Framework can transform these spaces into responsive, neuro-informed environments.

Sources and Resources

- Alison Escalante, Medical Contributor, *Forbes Magazine*, "Researchers Doubt That Certain Mental Disorders Are Disorders et al," August 11, 2020

Chapter 17 Podcast Guests

- **Dr. Jennifer Fraser** – Episode 122 *(Bullying & Medical Gaslighting with Dr. Jennifer Fraser)*
- **Dr. Susan Rich** – Episode 7 *(A Candid Conversation with Dr. Susan Rich)*, Episode 23 *(Our Ongoing Love Affair with a Toxin: a Candid Conversation with Susan Rich, MD)*, Episode 32 (FASD, Foster Care & Future Generations, with Dr. Susan Rich), and Episode 38 *(The Better Safe than Sorry Project with Dr. Susan Rich & Fatima Iqbal)*

- **Dr. William Curran** – Episode 101 *(The Invisible Struggle: Addressing FASD in Child Welfare, with Dr. William Curran)*
- **Patrick Bross** – Episode 33 *(Thriving with FASD: Candid Advice for Parents with Patrick Bross)*

— CHAPTER 18 —

The Medical and Mental Health Systems

"Silos in the medical community cause one person who has FASD to need a GI doctor... a rheumatologist... a psychiatrist... and an orthopedic surgeon without anyone seeing the bigger picture."

– Dr. Susan Rich.

Recombining the Silos

Beyond Medical Isolation

The medical and mental health systems arguably need a macro-level paradigm shift most urgently. Despite extensive scientific evidence demonstrating the interconnected nature of the human body, where neural networks in the gut, heart, and fascia communicate continuously with the central nervous system, an artificial separation between mind and body persists. Modern medicine remains highly siloed and often overlooks the comprehensive, whole-body reality of FASD.

Currently, individuals navigate a diagnostic desert of fragmented specialties, none of which has fully integrated comprehensive FASD training into standard medical or doctoral curricula. As neuropsychologist Dr. Paul Connor reflects on his doctoral training: "What I learned about

FASD? Zilch. Nothing. Not a peep... and it was kind of eye-opening that there was so little where neuropsychology kind of has a big play in FASD." Dr. Christie Petrenko points to this same educational gap among mental health providers: "They don't get trained in it. It's not their fault. It's just not part of their training programs."

Because practitioners cannot utilize tools they were never given, they rely on familiar, narrow frameworks. Dr. Susan Rich emphasizes that this fragmentation bounces patients among specialists who address isolated symptoms without connecting the overarching clinical burden of associated health conditions.

The Neuro-Informed Primary Coordinator

One essential solution is to establish a dedicated neuro-informed primary coordinator, or to provide standardized neurobehavioral training for existing clinical case managers, primary therapists, and medical social workers. This professional serves as a central anchor, viewing the patient through the lens of their unique neuroprint and metabolic battery rather than a collection of unrelated diagnostic codes.

When complex symptoms confuse a fragmented medical system, individuals often face medical gaslighting. Self-advocate Jessica Birch noted that repeated dismissals and the minimizing of physical symptoms during her journey to diagnosis caused prolonged, unnecessary suffering. Without a neuro-informed coordinator to identify how sensory sensitivities and biological baselines interact over time, unsupported families frequently encounter systems that become increasingly punitive.

The Child Welfare System: The Front Door of Crisis

The child welfare system is tasked with protecting children facing severe family disruption. A high proportion of removals involve parental substance use, domestic trauma, or catastrophic life events. Yet the child welfare system continues to apply a traditional behavior paradigm, demanding that families conform to standardized expectations regardless of intergenerational medical or neurodevelopmental histories.

Social workers are historically trained in Bowen Family Systems theory, which often views a child's functional presentation as a direct reflection of parental boundaries and expectations. When birth parents struggle to complete a standard reunification plan, caseworkers may assume the parents are unmotivated or indifferent. This assumption overlooks the reality that parents may carry their own unrecognized, intergenerational neurodevelopmental profiles.

The longer a child remains in care without brain-based support, the greater the risk of compounded trauma. Involuntary reflex reactions are easily misread as willful defiance. Foster parents who can't correct these struggles with standard behavioral advice often face blame from workers, leading to placement disruptions that further damage attachment security. Social worker Angela Geddes explains that viewing neurodevelopmental distress as a character flaw causes systems to intervene incorrectly, unintentionally creating trauma within the very institutions meant to heal.

Educator Barb Clark highlights systemic hesitation in child welfare, recalling instances where agencies resisted offering FASD education to prospective caregivers for fear that parents would refuse placements. When institutions avoid identifying neurodevelopmental injury, the burden is displaced onto children and families.

The Education System: From Behavioral Modification to Environmental Scaffolding

Classrooms frequently operate within compliance-driven frameworks influenced by industrial-era models of uniformity. When a student's neurobiology makes it difficult to sit quietly under fluorescent lighting or process rapid verbal instruction, conventional systems often penalize the student rather than adapting the sensory space.

Educational advocate Kelly Rain Collin points out that standard behavior intervention plans focus almost exclusively on suppressing surface behaviors, ignoring the underlying stress alarms driving the distress. When schools ignore quiet requests for help but respond urgently to severe dysregulation, they unintentionally condition neurodivergent brains to view explosive outbursts as the only reliable way to access support. Self-advocate Jake Tjapkes describes learning this pattern directly in school, noting that he would intentionally lash out at physical surroundings simply to bring a staff member to his side.

To make genuine progress, we can redefine the IEP as an **Individualized Environmental Plan**. Pioneered by educators Deb Evensen and Antonia Rathbun-Lindsey, this model focuses on adapting the physical space and relational pacing to support the student's biological baseline. As Deb Evensen explains, understanding FASD equips educators to handle diverse classroom needs effectively without increasing teacher burnout.

The Judicial System: Preventing Miscarriages of Justice

The most severe consequences of the behavior paradigm occur when individuals encounter the legal system. Research by Dr. David Gilbert indicates that individuals with FASD are nineteen times more likely to encounter the justice system than the general population. Dr. Gilbert emphasizes that this reflects systemic vulnerability and environmental mismatch, not an inherent genetic predisposition to criminal behavior.

Dr. Stephen Greenspan notes that legal contexts must move away from moral assumptions of character and actively assess for underlying developmental brain injury.

When an individual with an unrecognized neuroprint enters a high-stress interrogation room, rapid questioning overwhelms processing capacity. Dr. Jerrod Brown explains that the power dynamics and cognitive demands of interrogations often trigger survival reflexes to please authority or escape confrontation, leading to confabulation and false confessions. Abstract legal procedures (such as entering pleas or understanding Miranda warnings) are often incomprehensible to someone with significant executive and receptive language delays, even while they appear to nod in agreement.

Dr. Ken Jones highlights this vulnerability at the most extreme level, observing that individuals with unrecognized prenatal alcohol exposure are tragically overrepresented on death row. Attorney David Boulding summarizes the lasting gravity of criminalizing an invisible disability: "When that cell door is shut, that's a noise nobody forgets."

Toward a Biology-First Paradigm

True success will not come from forcing individuals to navigate punitive systems in isolation. It requires creating accessible environments across clinics, welfare agencies, classrooms, and courts, replacing the myth of complete independence with the strength of **systemic interdependence**:

- **From Management to Habilitation:** Shifting the focus from controlling outward behavioral output to evaluating the somatic state: "Where is the body registering distress, and what physical baseline needs support?"

- **From Compliance to Environmental Fit:** Recognizing that biological battery capacity varies across settings, adjusting environmental friction to prevent autonomic collapse.
- **From Uniformity to Ecosystemic Support:** Redirecting institutional resources away from punitive enforcement and toward relational communities that support lifespan growth.

Pivot Points: Putting Chapter 18 into Practice

- **For Professionals** — I invite you to consider your role within institutional systems. When a client's distress is labeled as noncompliance, you might pause and document that reaction as an involuntary biological response to an environmental mismatch, identifying practical workarounds that support access.
- **For Caregivers** — I invite you to release the pressure to act as a compliance enforcer for rigid systems. You might stand confidently as your loved one's secure base, sharing observations about their unique neuroprint and advocating for the environmental scaffolds that allow them to flourish.
- **For Individuals Living with FASD** — I invite you to recognize that your lived experience is profound expertise. You are not broken or "treatment-resistant"; you are navigating institutions that were not originally built with your neurobiology in mind. Your self-advocacy helps dismantle outdated assumptions and illuminates the resilient wildflower strengths you bring to your community.

Final Thought: The Glass Box

The classic experiment of Schrödinger's Cat illustrates how easily systems fall into binary thinking. Because institutions historically could not see inside the opaque box, they felt forced to choose between the wave of behavior and the particle of biology, defaulting to managing only what was visible on the surface.

What happens when the box is made of glass?

When the container is transparent, the false choice dissolves. Looking through the glass, we no longer guess at internal intent; we clearly see the living neuroprint, the fluctuating battery, the sensory environment, and the passage of time interacting as a whole. Transparency lets institutions stop demanding impossible compliance and start providing genuine, biological care.

Up Next

Dismantling these institutional silos requires more than critique; it calls for a unified, actionable architecture that bridges the clinic, the classroom, the courtroom, and the home. Having examined the fractures across our public systems, we now turn from diagnosing the problem to constructing the remedy. In Chapter 19: The 4D Foundation: A Framework for Lifespan Care, we integrate the whole person into four clear, interlocking dimensions: honoring the physical neuroprint (D1), pacing the metabolic battery (D2), scaffolding the sensory and relational environment (D3), and navigating the asynchronous horizon of time (D4). Step inside to discover how this blueprint translates into compassionate, practical habilitation across the entire lifespan.

Chapter 18
Podcast Guests

- **Angela Geddes** – Episode 121 *(A Complicated and Beautiful Brain: Reframing FASD with Angela Geddes)*
- **Antonia Rathbun-Lindsey** – Episode 43 *(Parenting Your Porcupine, Part 1, with Antonia Rathbun Lindsey)*, Episode 51 *(Crafting Calm: Exploring Art Therapy for FASD with Antonia Lindsey)*, Episode 61 *(From Rupture to Repair: Healing FASD Family Dynamics with Antonia Lindsey)*, and Episode 131 *(Unlocking Emotions Through Art: A Therapist's Perspective with Antonia Rathbun Lindsey)*
- **Barb Clark** – Episode 118 *(Denial, Anosognosia & Delayed Remorse with Barb Clark)*
- **Dr. Christie Petrenko** – Episode 24 *(Current FASD Research with Dr. Christie Petrenko)*
- **Dr. David Gilbert** – Episode 56 *(From Biochemistry to FASD: Dr. David Gilbert's Story)*
- **David Boulding** – Episode 31 *(David Boulding: the Intersection of FASD and both the Law and Sex)*
- **Deb Evensen** – Episode 14 *(Deb Evensen: Creator of 8 Keys for Adults with FASD)*
- **Dr. Jerrod Brown** – Episode 69 *(Unmasking False Confessions in FASD Cases)*
- **Jessica Birch** – previously interviewed for my first book, *Sip by Sip: Candid Conversations with Adults Living with FASD*

- **Kelly Rain Collin** – Episode 36 *(FASD and Education: Beyond Diagnosis in IEP Meetings, with Kelly Rain Collin)*
- **Dr. Ken Jones** – Episode 55 *(Unmasking FASD: Insights from Dr. Kenneth Lyons Jones)*
- **Dr. Paul Connor** – Episode 13 *(FASD Diagnoses for Adults: Overcoming Inaccessibility)*
- **Dr. Stephen Greenspan** – Episode 57 *(Gullibility & FASD: the Untold Story of Social Challenges with Dr. Stephen Greenspan)*
- **Dr. Susan Rich** – Episode 23 *(A Candid Conversation with Dr. Susan Rich)*
- **Dr. William Curran** – Episode 101 *(The Invisible Struggle: Addressing FASD in Child Welfare, with Dr. William Curran)*
- **Jake Tjapkes** – Episode 119 *(Navigating Life with FASD: A Personal Journey with FASD podcaster & educator Jake Tjapkes)*

— CHAPTER 19 —

The 4D Foundation: A Framework for Lifespan Care

"We are not asking for a seat at the table
of the behavior paradigm.
We are building a new table
—one that sees the whole person."
— Me

The medical and mental health systems arguably need a macro-level paradigm shift most urgently. Despite extensive scientific evidence demonstrating the interconnected nature of the human body, where neural networks in the gut, heart, and fascia communicate continuously with the central nervous system, an artificial separation between mind and body persists. Modern medicine remains highly siloed and often overlooks the comprehensive, whole-body reality of FASD.

We are not asking for a seat at the behavior paradigm's table. We are building a new table – one that sees the whole person.

We began this journey by looking into the diagnostic desert, seeking to understand why Fetal Alcohol Spectrum Disorder remains so persistently hidden, misunderstood, and pathologized.

We have explored the limitations of the behavior paradigm—a model that mistakes involuntary biological reflexes for intentional choices and treats neurological injury as a moral failing. We examined the historical shifts that prioritized short-term, standardized interventions over human-centered, relational habilitation. And through the clarity of the glass box, we illuminated why systems must stop guessing at outward behavior and start observing whole-body neurobiology directly.

Moving beyond incremental adjustments requires establishing a completely new foundation—one centered on dignity, collaboration, and living neurobiology.

Foundational Elements of 4D Habilitation

Replacing compliance-driven models requires a clear, practical approach:

- **Moving Beyond the Behavioral Model:** Acknowledging that prenatal alcohol exposure alters structural and metabolic baselines, rendering rewards-and-punishment approaches ineffective and exhausting for the nervous system. Relying on compliance management rather than biological accommodation has historically stalled the creation of disability-informed support.
- **The 4D Framework:** Moving past flat, linear scales to evaluate the recursive interaction among the physical neuroprint (D1), real-time metabolic energy (D2), sensory and relational environment (D3), and lifespan rhythms across time (D4).
- **Environmental Scaffolding:** Shifting the responsibility of adaptation from the individual to the environment by constructing reliable physical, sensory, and relational supports that match processing pace.

- **Wildflower Intelligence:** Celebrating the sporadic brilliance, adaptive tenacity, and unique problem-solving capacities that emerge when an individual is provided with a safe, nourishing ecosystem. Variable cognitive processing is not a total loss of capacity; it is the natural expression of resilient wildflowers blooming on their own timeline.

The Four Dimensions in Daily Practice

To truly support our community, institutions and families must cultivate capacity across all four dimensions:

- **D1:** Acknowledge physical neurodevelopmental realities, treating differences as structural baselines requiring specialized scaffolding rather than volitional defiance.
- **D2:** Protect the biological battery by eliminating compliance-driven exhaustion and integrating restorative pauses that replenish capacity.
- **D3:** Shift the onus of adaptation to the space, modifying sensory friction, auditory volume, and visual demands so the individual is not forced to survive in a chronic state of alarm.
- **D4:** Replace rushed, short-term metrics with a sustainable, lifespan perspective that honors natural developmental rhythms and lifelong interdependence.

Honoring the Undiagnosed

Our attention turns especially to the millions of individuals living without a formal diagnosis—navigating a society that demands neurotypical execution while their nervous systems require understanding and accommodation.

These individuals carry the somatic and metabolic weight of systems that look only at outward compliance. To those navigating this space: your daily struggles are not signs of personal inadequacy, but evidence of an adaptive nervous system striving to maintain coherence in environments never designed for your biology.

We establish this framework so that supportive spaces and reliable workarounds are ready and waiting as community understanding grows.

Pivot Points: Putting Chapter 19 into Practice

- **For Professionals** — I invite you to consider how your assessment practices define progress. When evaluating client goals, consider shifting from measuring outward behavioral compliance to assessing biological regulation, energetic reserves, and environmental fit across all four dimensions.
- **For Caregivers** — I invite you to step away from the pressure of standardized developmental timelines. Consider viewing your home through the 4D lens, identifying which sensory adjustments (D3) can immediately help conserve your loved one's metabolic battery (D2).
- **For Individuals Living with FASD** — I invite you to recognize that your capacity is naturally fluid and non-linear. Consider honoring your body's energy signals without judgment, trusting that honoring your biological baselines creates space for your wildflower strengths to flourish.

Up Next

Now that we've laid out the four dimensions of our framework, we examine how this model comes alive through foundational somatic practice. In Chapter 20, we gather the threads of clinical history and the voices of neurodevelopmental pioneers to weave the tapestry of the 4D Framework.

— Chapter 20 —

Gathering the Threads

"The curriculum's not the issue, the kid's brain is.
It needs a tune-up, it's not disabled.
It's just disorganized."
— Toni Hager.

Honoring Our Somatic Pioneers and the Humble Tapestry of Living Experience

We began this journey by looking at the scattered threads of a magnificent, overlooked puzzle: the rich voices of those living with FASD, woven together with the quiet, brushed-aside wisdom of historical pioneers. In the second half of this book, we explored the history of "the great shrinking" (the era when managed care, accountant-driven billing systems, and narrow behavioral metrics shrunk our professional view and interactions with the human brain to a narrowed menu of top-down, conformity-driven goals. In that shrinking, the body's physical, sensory, and motor realities were pushed to the extreme sidelines. To build a framework that delivers genuine, daily relief, we do not need to fight our neighbors or blame professionals for what their training withheld.

Instead, we are invited to return to the very biological foundations of the central nervous system. This chapter recovers the profound, somatic history of the **Vortex Model**, a collaborative effort co-created by Jodee Kulp and pioneering neurodevelopmentalist Toni Hager. The Vortex Model proves that when we honor the brain's biological timeline and stabilize its sensory and sensorimotor baselines, we no longer need to force cognitive conformity; we simply watch the body, read the physical signals of safety, and co-create a supportive environment where our loved ones can thrive.

The Greyhound to Minneapolis: Habilitation vs. Rehabilitation

The Vortex Model's origin story begins on a cheap Greyhound bus traveling through the freezing cold of Minneapolis in January. Toni Hager, a young neurodevelopmental specialist fresh out of college, was traveling across the country to share a simple, revolutionary message: the brain is not a static, broken organ; it is dynamic, plastic, and, when disorganized, can be systematically developed and organized. Jodee Kulp, a desperate mother searching for answers for her daughter, Liz, caught wind of Toni's work on a homeschooling listserv and invited her to make a stop. Their first meeting took place at the Greyhound station in downtown Minneapolis in the middle of a freezing night, where Jodee met Toni with a thermos of hot cocoa and sandwiches during a brief layover. On Toni's return trip from the East Coast, Jodee brought Liz to meet her. When Toni first met Liz, the young teen was thirteen years old and in a state of profound sensory shutdown. Sitting silently in the corner of a room, a heavy winter parka pulled tight and a baseball cap shading her eyes, Liz did not speak or make eye contact. Traditional providers had already written Liz off as having severe, permanent, and unimprovable developmental deficits. But Toni held a core neurodevelopmental conviction that bypassed all clinical gatekeeping: "Brain's a brain, you always start at the bottom. Let's try it and see."

Toni evaluated Liz's sensory baseline and wrote out a highly tailored developmental program right there in the room. Three months later, Liz was a completely different person. She had begun the slow, miraculous climb out of neurological organization. This story highlights the foundational difference between rehabilitation and habilitation. In standard medicine, rehabilitation means returning an individual to a pre-existing, healthy baseline of functioning after an injury. But because prenatal alcohol exposure alters cells as they are replicating, those functional baselines were never fully established or developed in the first place. Trying to "rehabilitate" these functions is a biological impossibility that only causes a crushing "try harder" wound. Instead, our focus must be strictly on habilitation, building, establishing, and myelinating neural pathways for the very first time. Yet, habilitation is not a one-time project, it is a lifelong sanctuary of care. Over the decades, Jodee returned to the Vortex Model on four separate occasions when Liz suffered major physiological, sensory, or neurological setbacks and needed to re-establish her functional baselines: following a severe car accident, following a period where she went blind for several months, following a brain injury caused by neurosurgery, and following a bout of heavy alcohol use. In each instance, rather than trying to force cognitive or behavioral conformity through sheer willpower, Jodee bypassed the top-down demands and went straight back to the bottom of the Vortex, stabilizing Liz's physical sensory pathways and cooling her primitive reflex roots. And every single time, Liz's nervous system organized itself once more, allowing her to recover, adapt, and reclaim her life.

Bending the Line: Weaving the Spectrum into a Vortex

To understand why Toni's approach worked where years of traditional interventions had failed, we must look at how she and Jodee radically transformed the developmental maps of their era. Toni had been trained in the original Doman-Delacato model of the 1960s. That model was a flat, two-dimensional piece of paper outlining seven levels of brain development. But a flat piece of paper cannot capture the three-dimensional, dynamic reality of a human being. Just as we can step past the linear, two-dimensional spectrum ruler that ranks people from high to low functioning, we can look beyond rigid grids. As first responder Jake Tjapkes (Episode 119) observed:"Flat lines only fit dead people."

Toni expanded those seven linear levels into twelve precise developmental, neurological pathways. Together, Jodee and Toni literally bent the flat paper, twisting those twelve stages into a spiral Vortex. This Vortex represents a fundamental somatic truth: neurodevelopment is a spiral that starts at the absolute bottom. If an individual has disorganized functioning in the brainstem or midbrain (whether due to prenatal alcohol exposure, birth trauma, forceps injuries, or anoxia), organization needs a chance to establish in these basic networks before we can successfully chain on more advanced, higher-level functions. Instead of attempting to teach executive functioning, emotional regulation, or social reasoning to a brain whose lower pathways are in a constant, survival-driven state of alarm, we can choose to begin at the sensory and sensory-motor foundations and spiral our way up. While the Vortex Model maintained a beautifully holistic view of development, a splintered piece of this concept eventually migrated into standard clinical practice as "the ten brain domains" (such as executive function, motor skills, and memory). But when these domains are isolated and turned into a purely cognitive checklist, they can lose the essential physical, sensory-somatic, and environmental connections that the Vortex so beautifully emphasized. Instead of serving as a map for supportive environmental adjustments, the domains are often used simply to document static deficits rather than to identify adaptive solutions in daily life. As we explored in Chapter 16, Jodee's tree metaphor reminds us that standard behavioral methods only paint or prune the visible leaves of behavior. In contrast, neurodevelopmental habilitation nourishes the physical roots of the nervous system. When those physical roots are left with active, unintegrated primitive reflexes, they act like the smoldering embers of a forest fire buried deep underground that people mistakenly think is completely out. It takes very little (a tiny sensory spark like a slamming door or a sudden touch) for those hidden coals to flare back up, heating the surrounding soil and forcing our California poppy into instant, reflexive closure to survive. By using Toni's and Lyelle's somatic exercises as targeted cooling protocols, we systematically calm those active reflexes and quiet the heat beneath the surface, stabilizing the soil so the poppy can safely open its petals and thrive in its own season.

The Evolution of Care: The Hager-Kulp Vortex, the Ten Brain Domains, and the 4D Matrix Map

To understand how we navigate support today, we must look at how our diagnostic and developmental frameworks have evolved across time. The story of these models is not a collection of competing approaches, but a direct chronological lineage. It began with the foundational, bottom-up sensory-motor work of the **Hager-Kulp Vortex Model,** as described above. Later, this dynamic ecosystem was simplified into the mainstream ten brain domains. Today, we operationalize and expand these systems into an active, lifelong reality through the 4D

Framework and the 4D Matrix Mapping System. We can understand this evolutionary lineage through three critical distinctions:

1. **The Chronology of "The Great Splintering"** The somatic and developmental Hager-Kulp Vortex Model came first, establishing the essential sensory-motor, autonomic, and somatic foundations of neurodevelopment. The standardized ten brain domains are a splintered-off, two-dimensional subset of this original work. When mainstream medicine and education adopted these categories, they extracted the cognitive functions, effectively deflating the multi-dimensional, spiraling Vortex into a flat checklist. This oversimplification stripped away the underlying sensory-motor layers that allow higher-level cognition to develop. Reconnecting these deflated domains requires looking beyond a flat checklist to see the physical, somatic individual.
2. **Deficit Checklist vs. The 4D Matrix Mapping System** Because the ten brain domains were extracted and deflated, they became tools of documentation rather than active development. Standard domain assessments measure static deficits, cataloging what an individual cannot do. In contrast, the original Hager-Kulp Vortex Model serves as an active blueprint for habilitation. Today, we operationalize this blueprint through the 4D Matrix Mapping System. Instead of stopping at a static list of damaged brain functions, this mapping system plots how an individual's somatic neuroprint (D1) interacts with real-time metabolic energy (D2) and physical environments (D3) over chronological time (D4), providing a practical, dynamic guide for design rather than a catalog of failure.

3. **Bottom-Up Sequence and Lifespan Integration** The traditional model lost the critical understanding of developmental sequence by flattening the Vortex into separate categories. Standard clinical approaches often treat cognitive domains as isolated, top-down skills. The original Hager-Kulp Vortex Model exposed the biological fallacy of this top-down approach, proving that we must calm the somatic roots first. However, the 4D Framework is what systematically extends this bottom-up sequence across the entire lifespan. While early neurodevelopmental models focused heavily on the pediatric baseline of early developmental milestones, the 4D Framework recognizes that our neurobiology, metabolic battery, and environmental needs fluctuate across a lifetime. Under the 4D Framework, the ultimate goal is not a fixed, independent destination, but a state of supportive, lifelong interdependence.

The 4D Framework as an Assessment Compass

The 4D Framework gives this work a practical, whole-life structure:

- **D1: Neuroprint / Physical:** *Who is this person physically?* This is the holistic somatic baseline, the unique nervous system and physical organs as they were formed and programmed in utero in response to the specific timing, dosing, and co-exposures of prenatal alcohol. It includes the brain, brainstem, active primitive reflexes, and all physical body systems.
- **D2: Metabolism / Energy:** What is their metabolic battery level? This is the body's real-time energy economy, circadian rhythms, and somatic cost-benefit ledger. It tracks the standard metabolic cost of daily activities, the acute energy

tax (the physical depletions experienced when energy expenditure exceeds our reserves), and the energy deposits (somatic rest, hydration, and safety) that recharge the system.

- **D3: Environment:** How does this specific room speak to their senses? This is the sensory, spatial, physical, and relational profile of a space (zen vs. overwhelming). It recognizes whether an individual's unique nervous system is sensory seeking or sensory avoidant in that space. (With these factors identified, we then design the scaffolding, what we do to adjust the environment to fit their biology).
- **D4: Time:** How are fluid, temporal factors shifting the picture? This is the fluid temporal element of life, developmental pacing, age-role transitions, day-to-day shifts, and long-term fatigue (allostatic load). Most importantly, Time interweaves with all other dimensions, providing the biological explanation for why capacity is naturally fluid, non-linear, and changing.
  By assessing all four dimensions, we can accurately pinpoint the environmental and biological mismatches in play, allowing us to craft highly tailored, respectful workarounds.

The Pioneers: Dismantling the Silos and Aligning the Approaches

This bottom-up habilitative philosophy has been developed and championed by clinical pioneers like Dr. Lyelle Palmer, Dr. Carol Brown, and Dr. Janet Oliver, alongside modern, forward-thinking practitioners like clinical art therapist and family clinician Antonia Rathbun-Lindsey who recognize that the helping professions have historically operated in isolated, biased silos. When we evaluate the landscape of professional help, we see deep systemic splits:

- **Physical and Occupational Therapy (PT & OT):** These disciplines have historically been ahead of the curve in addressing sensory-somatic and reflex-based aspects of development. However, they often lack a deep appreciation of the cognitive, executive, and linguistic processing layers of the brain.
- **Mental Health Professions:** While pioneering counselors and psychologists utilize brilliant body-centered models like Polyvagal Theory, somatic experiencing, and mindfulness to help people notice their internal states, a critical gap remains. Standard mental health practices often lack training in foundational neurodevelopment, specifically how unintegrated primitive reflexes and embryonic motor loops lock the somatic baseline in a state of high alarm. Without this physical, bottom-up reflex integration lens, traditional talk therapies can easily miss the raw biological drivers of distress, attempting to analyze a nervous system that simply needs physical organization and safety.
- **Behavioral and Neurobehavioral Methods:** Traditional behavioral therapies are conformity-driven paradigms that rely on consequences and rewards to force conformity, a top-down approach that can cause intense somatic distress for a prenatally altered nervous system. In contrast, compassionate neurobehavioral approaches represent a massive, life-giving leap forward by shifting the focus from behavior to brain function, helping families depersonalize challenges and adjust cognitive expectations. Yet, even these supportive models can be beautifully expanded by integrating a bottom-up neurodevelopmental lens, which actively integrates primitive reflexes to calm the body's alarm center and build new neural

pathways. The beauty of the 4D Framework and the Vortex Model is that they dismantle these professional silos and put them all together. This framework integrates Dimension 1 (D1): Neuroprint / Physical, Dimension 2 (D2): Metabolism / Energy, Dimension 3 (D3): Environment, and Dimension 4 (D4): Time into a single, unified lens. Within this aligned framework, we can appreciate both the historical pioneers and the modern clinicians who bridge these fields:

- **Dr. Carol Brown (Cognitive Optimization through Play):** Carol's distinctive focus is proving that "no brain is so damaged it cannot be reached through games." Her Equipping Minds approach uses simple, familiar symbols (colors, shapes, card games) to perform rigorous cognitive workouts. Because the brain is training with "what it already knows", it doesn't trigger academic anxiety. She also created the "I See You" verbal feedback loop, a linguistic read-back tool that acts as a physical scaffold to prevent working memory links from dropping under stress. (In our recent conversation, Dr. Brown emphasized the critical, foundational role that OTs play in integrating these physical neural pathways so that cognitive training can succeed).
- **Dr. Claire Coles (Overturning the ADHD Assumption):** A pioneer in the FASD field from Emory University with over five decades of research, Dr. Coles' distinctive focus is proving that individuals with FASD have fundamentally different cognitive and learning pathways than those with ADHD. This research has been crucial in showing that standard ADHD behavioral and stimulant treatments are often a poor fit. She famously likened the learning styles of the two groups to different drivers

in traffic: while individuals with ADHD are like impatient commuters who impulsively change lanes, those with FASD are like drivers who patiently inch forward, content to stay in line. Dr. Coles also developed the evidence-based Math Interactive Learning Experience (MILE) program, proving that structured, multi-sensory support and parent training can systematically improve both academic skills and behavior.

- **Toni Hager (The Proprioceptive Squeeze):** Toni's distinctive focus is using intense deep pressure (such as systematic full-body joint squeezes) to stimulate the proprioceptive nerves deep in the joints. By bypassing damaged superficial tactile pathways, she physically teaches the brain where the body is in space, building neural highways "backwards" from sensation to coordinated movement.
- **Dr. Janet Oliver (Embryonic Protection & Gentle Encouragement):** Janet's distinctive focus goes deeper into the embryological timeline, identifying how pre-reflexive states, specifically the Fear Paralysis Response (FPR), shape our daily body culture. She shows that generalized anxiety is not a mental disorder but a physical sensation of being unsafe in gravity and space. Her clinical signature is "gentle encouragement," monitoring the physical threshold of the nervous system and pausing at the first sign of somatic stress to keep the delicate wildflower from folding its petals tight in a protective shutdown.
- **Dr. Lyelle Palmer (Reflex Integration Ramps):** Lyelle's distinctive focus is highly structural and biomechanical. He targets unintegrated primitive reflexes (like the STNR and Moro) through repetitive, physical movements. His practical

mastery is represented by brilliant, low-cost physical tricks, like placing stickers on a child's fingernails so their eyes have a moving visual anchor to track, or having an individual fall backward onto a mattress ten times before bed to exhaust and calm an overactive startle reflex.

- **Antonia Rathbun-Lindsey (Visual Language & Somatic Body Culture):** A registered art therapist and family clinician with over thirty years of experience, Antonia's distinctive focus is using non-verbal, visual art media to bridge cognitive and linguistic processing gaps. She developed the concept of "body culture" (the unique physiological norm of living in a prenatally altered body) and pioneered using the Expressive Media Continuum to map bodily sensations when the brainstem's alarms uncouple feelings from words. Her clinical signature is "dosing the environment" (adjusting lighting, space, and media textures) to signal physical safety to the brainstem before placing any cognitive demands, monitoring the physical threshold of the nervous system to keep the body's survival quills from rising. She famously reminds us that art in habilitation is not about analysis or a finished product, but about restoring connection: "We use art to restore... to connect, not correct, to connect. Because relationship is remedy."

Sensory Nerves First; Motor Skills Follow

One of the most profound mistakes of modern clinical intervention is attempting to train a motor skill without first stabilizing the sensory pathways. Most physical, occupational, and behavioral therapies focus almost exclusively on motor outputs. If an individual struggles with hand-eye coordination, they are drilled on writing; if they struggle to walk, they are handed a walker or placed in a wheelchair. Toni Hager points out the systemic flaw in this approach: "What PT and OT, any therapist you go to, they look at your outcome, your motor skills. They don't look at your sensory, how it got there, and what shape it got there... We have sensory and we have motor. And we actually have sensory nerves and motor nerves. So we worked a lot on the sensory channels."

Before a motor nerve can execute a coordinated action, the sensory nerves must receive, filter, and organize incoming environmental data. Just like a delicate arctic wildflower folding its petals tight against a rolling plume of toxic volcanic ash, our sensory pathways will shut down and refuse to process when the environmental load has become too hostile to bear. To prove this, Toni shares the incredible story of a family raising adopted children with FASD who did childcare for a little boy with severe Cerebral Palsy (CP). The little boy was non-ambulatory and spent his life in a wheelchair. Because the other children in the home were doing their daily neurodevelopmental exercises, which they simply called "program", the little boy naturally wanted to be included and participate too. Instead of focusing on walking as a motor outcome, they started at the very base of the brain's sensory-tactile system: deep pressure. Toni's method for building this neurological highway "backwards" is highly physical: you take the hands, feet, fingers, and toes, and you squeeze them as tight as you can, moving systematically up the limbs to the shoulders and stopping at the knees. This targeted, deep squeeze stimulates the proprioceptive nerves located deep in the joints, which tell the brain where the body is in space. By stimulating his tactile pathways every day, the little boy with CP began to develop actual calf muscles. Soon, he was able to stand up and sit down during church services. Eventually, this child who had been written off by traditional physical therapy began walking entirely on his own! This same physical mismatch explains why so many children are punished for "poor posture" or slouching at their school desks. Dr. Lyelle Palmer explains that when a child has an active Symmetrical Tonic Neck Reflex (STNR), bending their arms to write or read a book automatically forces their legs to stretch straight out under the desk. It is a physical reflex they cannot control. Trying to force a child to sit up straight and write when their arms and legs are locked in an involuntary reflex loop is biologically impossible and only drains their energy. As Jodee Kulp, Dr. Janet Oliver, and clinical art therapist Antonia Rathbun-Lindsey have proven, we cannot expect a child to "write with quiet hands" or "walk with quiet feet" if their tactile, proprioceptive, and vestibular baselines have not been integrated through safe, repetitive, bottom-up sensory stimulation.

Primitive Reflexes as Physical Survival Alarms

A massive chunk of what society pathologizes as "bad behavior", "aggression", or "oppositional defiance" is actually the direct, physical expression of unintegrated primitive reflexes. A newborn baby is born with over forty primitive reflexes designed to help them survive their first months of life. As the brain matures, these reflexes are meant to be integrated into the higher motor pathways. However, prenatal alcohol exposure, birth trauma, and chronic stress frequently prevent these reflexes from integrating. They remain active, trapped in the lower brainstem like smoldering embers in the body. Toni Hager's clinical experience with complex neurodevelopmental profiles led to a simple, liberating principle: "You fix the reflexes, the function improves."

Consider the Moro Reflex, the infant startle response. When those physical roots are left with active, unintegrated primitive reflexes, they act like the smoldering embers of a forest fire buried deep underground that people mistakenly think is completely out. It takes very little (a tiny sensory spark like a slamming door or a sudden touch) for those hidden coals to flare back up, heating the surrounding soil and forcing our California poppy into instant, reflexive closure to survive. By using Toni's and Lyelle's somatic exercises as targeted cooling protocols, we systematically calm those active reflexes and quiet the heat beneath the surface, stabilizing the soil so the poppy can safely open its petals and thrive in its own season.

The nervous system flares into instant defense simply to protect itself. It is a devastating form of clinical gaslighting to accuse an individual experiencing a reflexive survival response of "secondary gain" or "faking it for attention." They are not choosing to behave poorly, their physical survival alarms have been thrown. As Dr. Janet Oliver explains, when a Moro reflex remains uninhibited, the sensory-motor impact is exhausting. While a typical brain recovers from a surprise in seconds, a prenatally exposed nervous system can startle and feel the leftover tremor of that for 20 minutes. Like, that's too much startle. This persistent physical tremor is an automatic, involuntary motor response, not a behavioral choice. It keeps the body in a constant state of discomfort and somatic tension. As Liz Kulp so vividly described to Toni, a neurodevelopmental rage is an unstoppable somatic launch sequence: "It starts at your feet and goes to your knees. By the time it's reached your knees that rocket's taken off. We can't stop it. You just happen to be in front of us."

No behavioral sticker chart, standardized drill, or cognitive lecture can stop a rocket that has already cleared the launch pad. The only effective intervention is **preventative habilitation**, using targeted, somatic movements to integrate the reflexes and calm the survival alarms in the brainstem before they are ever triggered. To help reset these overactive alarms and promote restful sleep, Dr. Lyelle Palmer recommends a simple, literal exercise to exhaust the startle response before bedtime. Have the child or adult sit on the edge of the bed and fall over backward onto the mattress ten times in a row, sitting up completely after each fall. This repetitive movement triggers and exhausts the active Moro startle reflex, which relieves physical discomfort, relaxes the muscles, and allows the body to fall asleep naturally.

Beyond unintegrated primitive reflexes, our body culture is also shaped by the **Fear Paralysis Response**. Dr. Oliver clarifies that this is not a motor reflex, but an embryonic response that emerges at five weeks after conception, before reflexes are even established. When a vulnerable brain stem experiences chronic sensory or emotional overload, the fear paralysis response triggers an absolute somatic shutdown, everything physically contracts. Just like a delicate arctic wildflower folding its petals tight against a freezing wind, this embryonic contraction is an automatic, physical reflex to survive when the sensory load has become too hostile to bear. In real life, this biological protector often manifests as selective mutism; a child or adult may be incredibly articulate and expressive at home, but the moment they step into a noisy, sensory-rich classroom or grocery store, the fear paralysis is thrown, and they completely lose the ability to speak or respond. These unintegrated biological loops explain why traditional talk therapies cannot ease the chronic, systemic distress of FASD. As Dr. Oliver astutely notes, "generalized anxiety as a whole, starts at the body space level" and the reflexes that govern it. It is a physical sensation of being unsafe in gravity and space, and it can only be resolved by physically retraining the nervous system to feel secure.

Choosing Relationship Over Conformity; The Power of Play

If we are to step out of the top-down, conformity-driven box that has failed our community for decades, we must change how we define the therapeutic space. We must move away from the expectation of forcing a typical standard that never existed. Toni Hager's work was fundamentally successful because she and Jodee chose relationship over conformity, and connection over correction. They anchored their work in Jodee's beautiful concept of isness, a term she first used in Episode 53 of her podcast to describe a state of pure being, free from judgment. In practice, isness is the act of observing, accepting, and honoring a person exactly as they are in the present moment, without any ego-driven agenda to fix, change, or force them to fit a neurotypical standard. We do not force a differently wired wildflower to bend to a standardized ruler. We red-pen the "disses" out of the learning-disabled textbooks, evaluate their unique Scattered Profile, and build safe, permanent environmental ramps to support their biology. And we do this through play. Toni reminds us that for children under twelve, neurodevelopmental support must never feel like clinical labor: "You can incorporate a lot of the activities by making it fun... And what do fast kids like? They like activity and they like new activity."

Dr. Carol Brown shares this exact core rule of play. In her work at Equipping Minds, she insists: "You have to be having fun. And if you're not having fun and they're not having fun... the brain will shut down."

When we push a child to work at a level above their current developmental capacity, we trigger immense frustration and their survival defenses lock. Play is a somatic circuit-breaker. As Patti famously notes: "Play disarms the defenses in the brain. You cannot be angry and playful at the same time. You cannot be fearful and playful at the same time."

Laughing and playing actively engage the desire, care, and play centers of the brain, signaling directly to the brainstem that the body is completely safe. This is why Holocaust survivor and educator Tom Kramer told Dr. Brown words that she has never forgotten: "Carol, no child is so damaged they can't be reached through games."

No matter if the trauma is physiological, psychological, or developmental, play-based neurodevelopmental tools can bypass the defenses and systematically rewire the brain. To make this training accessible, Dr. Brown operates under a beautiful, simple theory: "We can only train the brain with what the brain knows."

This is the core of Dimension 3 (Environment). Instead of stressing an overloaded brain with complex, unfamiliar academic concepts, we use simple, known elements like colors, shapes, card games, and familiar animals to perform cognitive workouts. By training with what is already familiar, we take the anxiety out of the room, allowing the nervous system to focus its metabolic energy on myelinating and strengthening the underlying cognitive highways of working memory, processing speed, and visual tracking. Play-based neurodevelopmental tools are simple, inexpensive, and easy to use at home. For example, to build eye-hand coordination in a child whose eyes struggle to track smoothly across the midline, Dr. Lyelle Palmer suggests drawing small pictures or placing tiny, colorful stickers directly on their fingernails. Because the child can visually focus on their own hands, it acts as a visual anchor that teaches their eyes how to follow and track their fingers during daily activities. This play-based habilitation must always be guided by what Dr. Oliver calls "gentle encouragement." We can never force or push the nervous system beyond its limits; instead, we monitor for physical stress signs, like a flushing face or drifting eyes, and stop to let the system rest before a protective alarm is triggered. Habilitation is not about forcing conformity, but about slowly, gently helping the brain learn that it is safe.

The Interweaving of the Dimensions: An Illustrative Example

Because all four dimensions are fluid, interacting realities, they are constantly shifting and interweaving over Time (D4). Understanding this dynamic interaction is critical, if we look at any single dimension in isolation, we limit our ability to build a successful workaround. To illustrate how these factors dynamically interact in real life, we can look at the common clinical phenomenon of **sporadic mastery**. For many individuals, a skill that is executed with effortless perfection one day (or even one hour) can completely vanish the next. To traditional helper systems, this inconsistency looks like defiance, manipulation, or "secondary gain." But through the 4D lens, we see that mastery is not a static, permanently locked ability, but a temporary physical alignment of three shifting dimensions over Time (D4):

- **D1 (Neuroprint / Physical):** Is the somatic baseline currently free of unintegrated primitive reflex or sensory pathway interference?
- **D2 (Metabolism / Energy):** Is there enough physical charge in the battery at this exact minute to cover the metabolic cost of this task?

- **D3 (Environment):** Is the current sensory space matching the individual's sensory profile, or is it actively draining their energy? If a child can tie their shoes or process a complex direction at 10:00 AM, it may be that their D1 physical reflexes are calm, their D2 battery is at 80%, and their D3 sensory space is quiet. If they lose that exact same skill at 4:00 PM, it is not a failure of character or memory. It speaks to differing factors across all 4 dimensions. By using the 4D Framework to assess these shifting factors, we can stop blaming the individual and start building the supportive, permanent environmental scaffolding they deserve.

The "I See You" Visual Scaffold: Bridging Working Memory

To see how D3 scaffolding works in direct response to D2 metabolic depletions, we can look at some of the brilliant, non-pharmacological tools developed by these pioneers. For concrete thinkers, memory and follow-through represent some of our most exhausting biological hurdles. When our Dimension 2 (Metabolism / Energy) is depleted, our short-term working memory functions sporadically, dropping crucial steps of an instruction like lost cargo. To bridge this somatic gap, Dr. Carol Brown developed a powerful, immediate scaffold in response to Dimension 3 (Environment) called the "I See You" verbal feedback loop. Whenever giving a direction, instead of hoping the instruction "sticks", the partner describes the action in the present tense: "I see you putting your shoes in the closet. What do you see yourself doing?"

The individual repeats it back accurately in the first person: "I see myself putting my shoes in the closet."

This simple read-back loop completely changes the individual's self-perception. While it might initially sound simple, it is grounded in ancient philosophy and modern high-stakes science. In Chapter 10 of his Confessions, St. Augustine wrote extensively on memory, noting that our ability to retrieve and execute a plan relies on our mind's capacity to "see" ourselves performing the action in our internal space. This is the exact same "read-back accuracy" method mandated for soldiers, firefighters, surgeons, and air traffic controllers. Under extreme stress, the human brain naturally freezes and drops processing links. High-stakes professionals are never permitted to just nod and say "Okay" to an instruction; they must repeat the command back word-for-word before they are allowed to execute it. Applying the "I See You" loop in your home is not childish, it is a professional, neurological scaffold that prevents working memory freezes and ensures success. We also see this exact processing gap on the other end of the timeline. When Carol's son Clayton was 16, after tens of thousands of dollars of traditional therapies, he made a profound observation: "Mom, I just can't process it as fast as it's coming at me."

He added: "Mom, I feel like they throw a frisbee on one side of the room and I go to catch it and they throw it on the other."

This is what "processing delay" actually feels like to an individual under load. In our Dimension 2 (Metabolism / Energy), trying to digest rapid-fire, multi-step verbal commands is physically exhausting. By using a structured read-back scaffold like the "I See You" loop, we slow down the interaction, ensuring that the "frisbee" is caught safely before the next one is ever thrown.

When we nourish the biological roots with sensory safety, rhythmic movement, and play, we are not simply managing a condition. We are actively facilitating neuroplasticity, restoring self-compassion, and allowing our loved ones' Wildflower Intelligence to bloom beautifully, exactly as they are.

Chapter 20
Podcast Guests

- **Antonia Rathbun-Lindsey** – Episode 131 *(Unlocking Emotions Through Art: Therapists Perspective with Antonia Rathbun Lindsey)*
- **Dr. Carol Brown** – Episode 139 *(Neuroplasticity Through Play: Transforming Cognitive Development in FASD with Dr. Carol Brown)*
- **Jake Tjapkes** – Episode 119 *(Navigating Life with FASD: A Personal Journey with FASD podcaster & educator Jake Tjapkes)*
- **Dr. Janet Oliver** – Episode 93 *(Trigger Points: How Reflexes Shape FASD Journeys, with Dr. Janet Oliver)*
- **Jodee Kulp** – Episode 53 *(Kickstarting Season Two of Living with FASD, with author Jodee Kulp)*
- **Toni Hager** – Episode 137 *(Organizing the Neurodivergent Brain: The Hager Vortex & Sensory Integration with Toni Hager)*

"For those of us who choose to unmask
and embrace our wildflower intelligence,
the time is now:
to dance with the seasons rather than the clock,
to reach beyond boxes,
and to care for our minds and bodies
as we were uniquely knit together.

To everyone who experienced alcohol before birth
—this is your time."

Thank you Patti from Jodee

Acknowledgments

This project would not have been possible without the help of a great many people.

I have been blessed to talk with so many people who gave their time and shared their stories, their passion projects and their perspectives on the Living with FASD: Candid Conversations with Patti Kasper podcast these past 3 years. Thank you for your wisdom and for your passion. Thank you for allowing me to share your words not only with the listening and viewing audience, but also in "a future book project." That time has come, in the pages of this book as well as the sequel launching in 2027.

I have been blessed by my family, who have complained very little through the endless hours of my being locked away in my office, banging away on the keyboard. Your support of my passion projects means more to me than you realize. Thank you for sharing me with the world.

I have been blessed with the friendship and support of a group of women, all FASD authors and advocates. We affectionately call ourselves the FASD Meliorists, due to our belief that we have been called to this legacy work: to give of ourselves to make a difference in the world, or at least the world of FASD. To this end, we never know when something we utter will light a spark in another of us, only to be held to the light, and refracted back again, made brighter with new constructs. One shining example of this was Antonia's use of the word "wildflower" that morphed into an elaborate metaphor as I beheld it.

Jodee Kulp, thank you for publishing this work and for being my absolute champion, co-worker, and dearest friend. Thank you for constantly stretching me, for knowing exactly what to throw back to me to figure out on my own so I could grow, and for knowing exactly when I truly needed a safety net. I could not have completed this work without you. Your profound wisdom of "isness" (of choosing relationship over compliance and connection over correction) has transformed how I view myself and how I coach others. I also hold your daughter Liz's beautiful, enduring legacy in my heart on every single page. Her somatic, whole-body journey remains a powerful indictment of an unaccommodated medical system, but her tenacious spirit is a triumph that continues to light our way.

Antonia Rathbun-Lindsey, you are an inspiring teacher, a clinical pioneer, and a somatic guide. Your uncompromising attention to specificity has ensured biological accuracy throughout these pages. Your vast, thirty-year clinical experience in family therapy, art therapy, and qualitative research has helped polish this book until it shone. Long before our "4D" taxonomy was formally named, you were on the ground proving to managed care systems that clinical "body culture" requires somatic workarounds, not behavioral compliance. Thank you for being so incredibly generous with your precious time, your clinical wisdom, and your close friendship. My life is so much richer for the time we have spent together!

Deb Evensen, thank you for being a steadfast pillar of hope, an educator par excellence, and a sister in this storm. Your presence in my life as a fellow Meliorist has been a profound gift. Your pioneering work in school systems and across diverse, multi-cultural communities has shown me that my 4D Framework is a universal tool that works beautifully across cultures and in classroom settings. Your enduring belief that taking the time to truly learn about FASD is what makes an educator's job easier has deeply shaped my own approach to tailoring workarounds.

To the "Meliorists" (Jodee, Antonia, and Deb): the four of us each bring our own unique educational backgrounds, professional specialties, lived experiences, and personalities to this space, yet there is a beautiful, overlapping heartbeat in all that we do. Your steadfast belief in the potential of this book has helped bring my legacy work into the light of day. I love you all deeply and am honored to walk beside you as your partner, your co-worker, and your friend

To Carl Young: You really are a Meliorist at heart, my friend! Despite a punishing researching and writing career of your own, you not only took the time to read my preview, but you wrote a foreword that both made me cry and left me speechless, which never happens! Your belief in this work, in my 4D Framework - as shown by your immediate application of it into your consulting and training - is the ultimate validation! Your generosity in building the tools and templates found in this book and in the companion study guide, *Discover Your 4D Life: The FASD Living Experience*, out of such genuine collaboration has touched my heart. I cannot thank you enough for either, let alone both.

I am blessed to live a purpose driven life. This book has been a calling that has brought me back to its central purpose when I have been in danger of getting lost down numerous rabbit trails and squirrel chasing sessions. My gratitude goes also to my God, who keeps revealing assignments for me to work on.

Patricia Kasper, MA

Afterword

Although observation and logic show us that *not* all behavior is chosen, the byline of Behaviorism that it is all choice still permeates the Western Industrial and Technological mindset at every level. We are at a crossroads, facing a crisis of beliefs; if the facts of FASD and other neurophysiological conditions indicate Behaviorism is not a comprehensive solution for what we encounter, the problem has been, "What framework can replace this approach?"

That question is now being answered as data from 50 years of research converge with the wisdom of Living Experience of FASD & other neurodiversity. Patricia Kasper's 4 D framework provides a viable lens for organizing and enacting change.

In the 37 years I worked with all ages living with FASD, other neurotoxin exposures and neurodiversity, the reality of how one lives well over time with a chronic condition became clear: we and our families build our workarounds based on strengths—any given trait can work for or against us depending on the environment and expectations within it. As Patricia reminds us, "The only Normal is a town in Illinois." That said, research by Hogenkamp and others into regulatory bandwidth, mentioned in the 4D framework as D2 (reflecting configuration and one's energy capacity), gets managed over time with significant implications. Patricia's 4D framework makes building one's roadmap easier by helping persons living with FASD, families and professionals map out what needs to be different and which shifts maximize one's way forward. Spending energy where most needed, rather than wasting it on what doesn't work, is central to carving out our own living niche and maintaining headway.

I have had the honor of contributing to Patricia's message in this book because of great confidence in Wildflower Capacities. I have watched and lived how these resurge after the wildfire times we face in life. It is my fervent hope that this practical 4D Framework will inform global health policy, research and clinical practice, family support, future education and community understanding at this time in history when protection of diversity is essential to planetary sustainability. Finally, if what arrives is 'for' us, let nothing good be wasted as we support individualized ways to improve health and quality of life for everyone we love with FASD and reduce risk of harm for coming generations. Always, the trick in hard times is to keep ourselves focused on the next right step. The 4D framework can really help with that.

Antonia Rathbun Lindsey, MA, ATR, LMHC, BCPC, ret.

Author of "Parenting Your Porcupine: A Toolkit for Children with FASD, Other Drug Exposures & Neurodiversity"

APPENDIX

— APPENDIX A —

Facing Forward with the 4D Framework

Living the 4D framework we bump up against old ways and have to bring conversations to a new place, which is not always easy. Conversations shift from the debate about what's not working here to discussion about how to support neurobiology. Let's move together from a moral lens (choices/blame) to a biological frame (capacity/support).

1. The Visual Trap

The Myth: "They don't look disabled, so they shouldn't need accommodations."

Leading into a conversation: "Just because we can't see the disability doesn't mean it's not physical. On the outside a person has symmetrical parts, but the inside is where the disability lives. Prenatal exposure to alcohol alters the brain's physical wiring before birth. It usually does not change how a person looks, but it always changes how they function, turning mundane, everyday expectations into major neurological obstacles."

The Direct Response: "I understand the confusion; because there are no physical markers, the disability is invisible. However, the barriers are very real. What people with brain injury need are workarounds in the environment that fit their stamina and abilities."

2. The Defiance Delusion

The Myth: "They are choosing to be difficult/defiant."

Leading into a conversation: "Most people think that all behavior is chosen, but forget that defensive behaviors are often reflexive and involuntary. When someone looks resistant, confused or stuck, these are symptoms that they have reached their neurological capacity limit rather than a conscious choice to disobey. They are overwhelmed, not defiant."

The Direct Response: "When behavior seems defiant or rigid, we are seeing dysregulation, a neurological symptom. People don't 'choose' to be overwhelmed; it's very uncomfortable. Let's discuss how we can tweak the activity or environment so things work better."

3. The Masking Trap

The Myth: "They are fine at school/work/in public, so the parents are exaggerating at home."

Leading into a conversation: "Please be aware that when someone with a brain injury uses their limited metabolic energy to 'mask' in public, by the time they get home, they are neurologically exhausted. A 'good' day out often costs them a crash at home. It can take hours or days to recharge their battery."

The Direct Response: "What you are seeing in public is a 'mask of normalcy'; it takes immense energy to perform while hiding their neurological challenges. What we see at home is their collapse afterward. The family is their only safe place to implode or explode when they are running on empty. Families see what is hidden. People with other illnesses collapse at home too after trying to hold it together out in the world. Let's talk about a code to use so they can have breaks or support in both places, home and at school (or at work). It doesn't cure things, but it can make daily routine more manageable."

4. The Graduation Myth

The Myth: "They will grow out of this by adulthood."

Leading into a conversation: "When the assumption is that these struggles are choices which developmental 'maturity' will resolve, we are ignoring the fact that FASD is a lifelong neurological disability; it won't resolve by adulthood any more than blindness or cerebral palsy. FASD impacts the whole body, so we need to think beyond temporary fixes; this is about ongoing support that will grow with them as they mature, past age 18, 25, and beyond."

The Direct Response: "FASD is a permanent neurodevelopmental condition. We don't expect someone with a physical handicap to outgrow it by 18, and we shouldn't expect a person with brain injury from FASD to be cured by 18-21 either. After injury, the brain doesn't grow back in; instead it needs to use the circuits which work best to compensate. We focus on workarounds for living with a lifelong brain difference."

5. The "Smart Enough" Myth

The Myth: "They have a high IQ, so they should be able to manage their life."

Leading into a conversation: "We need to distinguish between book knowledge and applied living skills. Intelligence is not the same as adaptive function. We need to support them around the gap between what they know and what they can actually do with what they know."

The Direct Response: "They can state the rule but still not know how to carry it out. Ability to talk can hide what gets stuck in the walk, putting the words into action. It helps to keep the focus on the doing, not all the talking. Instead of long explanations, reminders and other workarounds can help intelligent people with brain injury succeed.

6. The "Close Enough" Myth

The Myth: "Let's just label it Autism/ADHD; it's easier for funding."

Leading into a conversation: "I understand you have services for other diagnoses. However, once a partial or convenience diagnosis is in their chart, it can alter the course of treatment later, causing medical maltreatment, or preventing eligibility for certain care. The problem here is that this is a whole body, lifespan medical condition which presents like a mental health problem. It's harder than that as a lifelong condition with a unique profile."

The Direct Response: "Using a standard Autism or ADHD playbook ignores certain distinct symptoms of FASD that are different. Support for the neurological differences with memory, language processing and waxing/waning functioning typical of persons with a brain injury are vital here. Neurocognitive fatigue is a big factor for our support planning. We propose strategies suited for brain injury instead."

7. The Stigma Cycle

The Myth: "The parent caused this/is a failure."

Leading into a conversation: "We are here to focus on the fit between this person's unique neuroprint and their daily environment. Family dynamics with a chronic condition do matter, however, our focus today is on how to move forward with clarity and care."

The Direct Response: "Many women continue to have menstrual cycles for two or three months into their pregnancies, which means we cannot assign blame to women for the condition of FASD. It is the alcohol that caused this, in every case. Having an attitude of judgement does nothing to help the current situation. We need to work together to support the individual to identify workarounds to create a better fit between individuals and their environments."

8. The Lying and Denial Myth

The Myth: "People with FASD are inherently liars, thieves, and criminals."

Leading into a conversation: "There is a common, terrifying myth that people with FASD cannot learn from mistakes and are destined for the streets or the justice system. In reality, their highly suggestible and compliant nature makes them exceptionally eager to please, making them targets for harm and exploitation. They don't mastermind criminal activity but are often targets for those who do. Since they want to fit in and belong, we need to focus on helping them protect themselves against bullying and scams."

The Direct Response: "Lying is about getting over on someone to take advantage. Instead, confabulation is about filling in memory gaps; often with several impossible or conflicting excuses that don't match each other inside of a single conversation. It is a big sign of impaired memory; it's common to FASD, other head injuries and dementia. Let's talk about how we handle this so they can protect themselves from being targets of criminals and scammers."

9. The Life Expectancy Myth

The Myth: "The average life expectancy for individuals with FASD is only 34 years."

Leading into a conversation: "When the prevalence data shows that there are 21 million adults in the US alone living with the effects of prenatal alcohol exposure, it is nonsensical to believe that people with FASD die by the age of 34 years."

The Direct Response: "That grim statistic stems from a single, out-of-context study of severe, unsupported cases. Individuals with FASD are living, aging, and thriving long past their thirties, forties, and fifties."

10. The "Just One Drink Won't Hurt" Myth

The Myth: "Light drinking or having a single glass of wine during pregnancy is completely harmless."

Leading into a conversation: "The science has confirmed there is no safe amount of alcohol when one is pregnant. Cultural history aside, alcohol is a neurotoxin, which, like lead or other poisons, crosses directly into the fetal bloodstream and causes damage which cannot be undone."

The Direct Response: "Even a single drink is still neurotoxic to the developing fetus which cannot filter out the poison. Minimizing this risk for social participation reflects outdated information. Fun can still be had without drinking when one is in the window of preconception or conception. Mocktails and other swaps are popular alternatives that pose no risk to fetal development."

11. The "100% Preventable" Myth

The Myth: "FASD is 100% preventable, implying that anyone affected is the result of a completely avoidable personal failure."

Leading into a conversation: "Prenatal alcohol exposure very often begins prior to suspicion of pregnancy. through the complex lenses of addiction, trauma, and the reality of early pregnancy timelines before awareness sets in."

The Direct Response: "Using the '100% preventable' slogan places a crushing burden of shame on individuals on the spectrum; it tells them they should not be alive. Peak years for drinking overlap the childbearing years which is how FASD happens; let's change social messaging during preconception and conception without shaming people who now live with FASD."

12. The "Violent or Criminal" Stereotype

The Myth: "Individuals with FASD are inherently dangerous, violent, or destined for criminal behavior."

Leading into a conversation: "People with FASD are teachers, therapists, firefighters, doctors, parents and have many other roles in society."

The Direct Response: "The vast majority of individuals with FASD are not violent or dangerous. The criminal stereotype arose from a few highly publicized, extreme cases. We can't compare untreated and complicated outcomes with everyone who lives with this condition. Every case is unique and so are individual supports that help success."

13. The "Incompetent Parent" Myth

The Myth: "People with FASD or mothers affected by the condition are incapable of successfully parenting or nurturing a child."

Leading into a conversation: "We celebrate the unique workarounds and capacities in people with FASD and other neurodiverse conditions that help them parent successfully and lovingly."

The Direct Response: "Having a different neurotype does not preclude someone from being a wonderful parent. They may parent slightly differently by utilizing specific workarounds, and often have extra capacity to love and nurture, help and support others."

14. The "Certain Kind of Woman" Myth

The Myth: "FASD only affects specific marginalized populations, lower socioeconomic groups, or those struggling with severe addiction."

Leading into a conversation: "We acknowledge that prenatal alcohol exposure crosses all racial, cultural, and socioeconomic boundaries, including middle- and upper-class households."

The Direct Response: "FASD does not discriminate based on wealth, race, or background. Assuming it only happens to 'other people' blinds society to its widespread prevalence across all communities."

15. The "Alcohol's Safe Because It's Legal" Myth

The Myth: "Because alcohol is legally sold and marketed as a lifestyle accessory, it must be safe and harmless."

Leading into a conversation: "Alcohol is a neurotoxin, poison, and solvent used in industry. Oversight of it as a product focuses only on the tax revenue it generates, leaving public health at risk."

The Direct Response: "Legality does not equal safety. Alcohol bypasses FDA medical scrutiny and is regulated by tax bureaus because of lobbying and revenue, hiding the severe biological risks behind a lifestyle marketing model."

Tips for "Pushback" Success:

1. **Don't Argue, Pivot:** When someone says, "They're just lazy," don't argue about whether they are lazy. Say: "Lazy is a character judgment; let's talk about the executive functioning deficit that makes multi-step tasks impossible for them."
2. **Use the "We" Language:** Use "we" to bring the other person into the "solution" side of the conversation. (e.g., "How can we structure this environment so the individual can succeed?")
3. **Hold the Frame:** If they keep trying to return to moral failure, calmly reset: "I understand why you think behavior is all about choice; but this isn't. It's about brain injury causing some brain tasks to be impossible to complete without workarounds, and

stress reflexes where we might not expect them. Let's think about the biology at play. Stress signs show us where their energy alarm goes off. Think of being rushed to get to the airport and traffic began piling up on the freeway. You see a sign there is construction or an accident, but there are "surface streets" you can take as a detour. As it turns out, traffic is worse on the surface streets, which are now carrying much more traffic than designed for. Traffic lights, and congestion from people needing to turn left. Your gas gauge is dropping low, and now you are anxious not only about getting there on time but also about running out of fuel as well. Horns start to blare, distracting you. What had you been thinking about? What was that route? You're getting warm and uncomfortable. Someone cuts you off and you suddenly understand road rage. The freeways in our brains are those heavily used neural pathways that get used often throughout the day; traffic runs relatively smoothly because there are no traffic signals and there are far fewer places to jump onto or off from the route. Just as detours add time and fuel consumption in our commutes, so too do detours in our brains. Prenatal alcohol exposure can affect the way our brains are wired similar to a bridge being out along the highway. We must allow the extra time and recharge opportunities (gas stations) in order to reach our destination (complete a given task). We must appreciate that stress levels are elevated and provide people with grace.

— Appendix B —

NDIT & 4D Framework Clinical

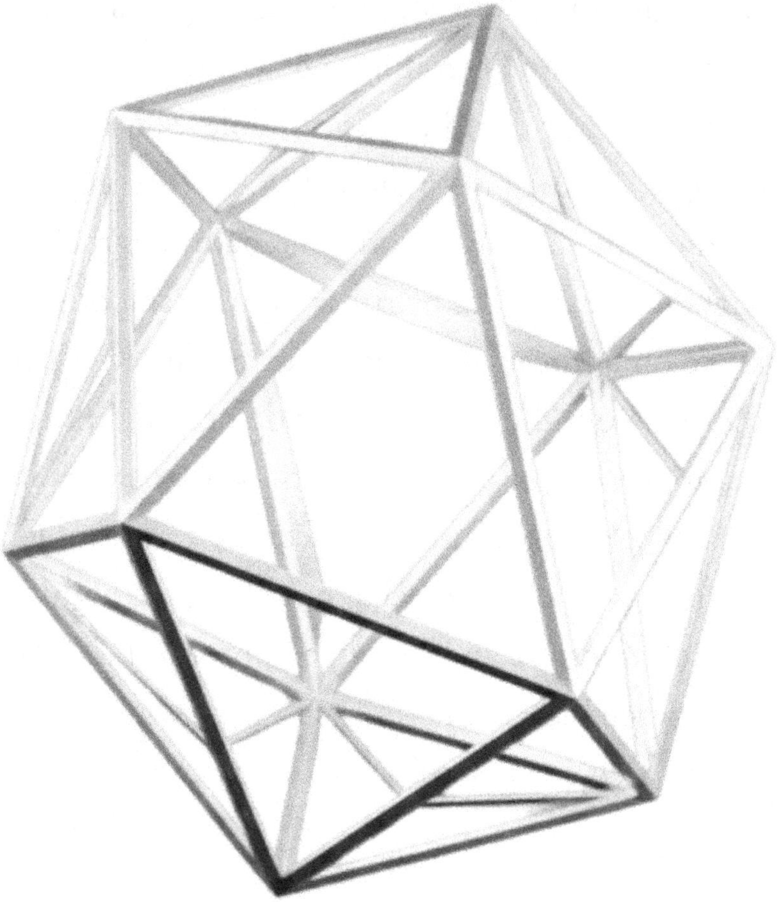

1. Clinical Foundation: CDC FASD Guidance & NDIT Modality

Fetal Alcohol Spectrum Disorder (FASD) is a lifelong, full-body medical condition caused by prenatal alcohol exposure, affecting an estimated 5% to 8% of the North American population. Traditional behavioral modification models (e.g., sticker charts, point systems, and conversational talk therapy) frequently fail because they attempt to enforce compliance ('software updates') on an organically altered brain injury ('hardware'). Effective clinical intervention requires shifting from behavioral management to neurodevelopmental habilitation.

The Centers for Disease Control and Prevention (CDC) emphasizes that FASD treatment is most effective when it adheres to five core principles. Neurodevelopmental Informed Treatment (NDIT) is the clinical modality that operationalizes this guidance, while Patricia Kasper's 4D Framework provides the step-by-step operational blueprint inside NDIT.

CDC FASD Treatment Mandate	NDIT Operational Focus	4D Framework Integration
1. Individualized Tailored to exact brain profile	Focuses on specific client routines & adaptive gaps	D1 (Bio-Structural): Maps the jagged Scattered Profile across 6 functional facets.
2. Strength-Based Focuses on assets, not deficits	Engages desire, curiosity, play & authentic 'isness'	Wildflower Intelligence: Leverages unique creative & relational strengths.
3. Concrete Visual, direct, non-abstract	Provides visual learning supports & clear scripts	Hardware Translation: Replaces 'Why' questions with What/Where/When/How.
4. Repetitive Consistent, predictable pacing	Structures predictable environmental routines	D4 (Lifespan Trajectory): Long-horizon pacing & supported interdependence.
5. Parent Training Caregiver coaching focus	Coaches caregivers to be 'Sanctuary Architects'	Environmental Scaffolding: Shifts onus from fixing person to changing room.

2. The 4D Operational Blueprint Inside NDIT

Dimension	Biological Reality	NDIT Clinical Target	Key 4D Workaround & Tool
D1: Bio-Structural			
(Hardware)	Systemic teratogenic exposure causes organic brain damage & 428 physical comorbidities.	Differentiate organic hardware gaps from bad choices or ODD.	Scattered Profile Facet Map: Plotting 6 functional domains to eliminate high-IQ masking traps.
D2: Metabolic Tax			
(Battery)	Manual override consumes massive energy; sleep apnea & sensory strain drain reserves.	Regulate nervous system & prevent After-School / Work Collapse.	3:30 PM After-School Reset Protocol: 45-min dim room, deep pressure, protein snack, zero demands.
D3: Environment			
(Scaffolding)	Mismatch between room demands & neurological capacity triggers fight/flight/freeze.	Build spatial architecture & sensory safety; change the room, not person.	Personal Regulatory Nest & Cry Recipe: Noise reduction, soft lighting, laughter and weighted pressure ramps.
D4: Lifespan			
(Trajectory)	Asynchronous development; cognitive bloom in midlife paired with somatic wear & tear.	Provide long-horizon pacing; transition from independence myth to interdependence.	Life-Role Transition Audit & Neuroprint Passport: Portable 2-page summary for medical/legal teams.

3. Setting-Agnostic NDIT & 4D Clinical Implementation

NDIT and the 4D Framework are not restricted to outpatient therapy offices. They apply universally across all practice domains, transforming how professionals interact with FASD neuroprints in any setting:

Practice Setting	Common Environmental Friction	4D Habilitative Micro-Shift
Outpatient & Clinic	Fluorescent lighting, waiting room noise, rapid verbal questioning, short session times.	• Implement 30-Minute Fatigue Threshold Rule. • Eliminate 'Why' questions; use concrete What/When/How. • Supply dim lighting options & visual step cards.
Home Visits & Family Support	Background TV/ noise, chaotic transitions, caregiver fatigue, expectation-capacity gaps.	• Audit home for sensory toxins. (toxins are unique to each person) • Establish non-negotiable diurnal reset protocols. • Shift parent from 'Disciplinarian' to 'Sanctuary Architect'.
Schools & Special Education	Over-stimulating classrooms, rigid compliance charts, public behavior displays, auditory overload.	• Replace compliance goals in IEPs with environmental modifications. • Provide sensory nests & scheduled movement breaks. • Honor 'can't without support' over 'won't'.
Acute Care & Medical Hospitals	Atypical interoception masking pain, medical gaslighting, fast-paced clinical directives.	• Utilize Neuroprint Passport during intake. • Recognize stoicism or calm demeanor may mask a burst appendix or acute somatic crisis.
Legal, Probation & Foster Care	Suggestibility, acquiescence ('yes' bias under stress), confabulation under interrogation.	• Never rely on raw yes/no questions. • Ask client to explain in their own words. • Provide concrete legal business card protocols (Boulding method).

4. NDIT & 4D Clinical Screening & Practice Audit Use this checklist to evaluate whether a treatment plan, therapy modality, or educational program aligns with NDIT and 4D principles, ensuring safety and efficacy for individuals with FASD:

Audit Category	Evaluation Criteria / Core Question	Alignment Status
1. Hardware Alignment (D1)	Does the provider acknowledge the organic brain injury and 428 physical co-morbidities, or are symptoms treated as willful defiance and character flaws?	☐ Aligned ☐ Needs Revision
2. Energy Protection (D2)	Does the session schedule respect time-of-day battery reserves (e.g., managing sleep apnea strain and avoiding post-school/work collapse)?	☐ Aligned ☐ Needs Revision
3. Environmental Scaffold (D3)	Is the physical environment audited for sensory toxins (lighting, noise, clutter), and does the provider build portable sensory ramps instead of forcing compliance?	☐ Aligned ☐ Needs Revision
4. Lifespan Perspective (D4)	Does the plan focus on long-horizon resilience, Wildflower Intelligence, and supported interdependence rather than forcing isolated independence?	☐ Aligned ☐ Needs Revision
5. Caregiver Partnership	Does the intervention coach caregivers as Sanctuary Architects and supply concrete scripts, visual tools, and non-judgmental support?	☐ Aligned ☐ Needs Revision

The Habilitative Mandate: We are not asking for a seat at the table of the traditional behavior paradigm. We are building a new table.

By combining Neurodevelopmental Informed Treatment (NDIT) with the 4D Framework, clinicians, caregivers, and self-advocates move from correcting behavioral output to nourishing biological roots, protecting metabolic reserves, and honoring Wildflower Intelligence across the lifespan.

— Appendix C —

Environmental IEP

Deb Evensen • Antonia Rathbun Lindsey

Name: Age: Date:

Strengths	
Where does your child do well?	
What activities or tasks are easy?	
When do they show positive actions?	

Whats Working	
When does your child do well?	
What are they doing at this time?	

Environmental IEP

DEB EVENSEN • ANTONIA RATHBUN LINDSEY

What's Working	
When are they doing?	
Is it structured or unstructured?	
Who else is there? (How many? Same age?)	
What's the environment like? (Noise smells)?	

What's Not Working	
When are they doing?	
Is it structured or unstructured?	
Who else is there? (How many? Same age?)	
What's the environment like? (Noise smells)?	

Environmental IEP

Deb Evensen • Antonia Rathbun Lindsey

What Would Help?	
What changes could make things better?	
How can the environment change?	
What tools or strategies can help?	
How can routines or schedules improve?	

Plan for Changes	
What steps will reduce challenges?	
How will the environment be modified?	
What actions will support strengths?	
What resources are needed?	

— Appendix E—

4D Neuroprint Passport

A Person-Centered Guide to Capacity, Regulation, and Environmental Fit

This passport is not a clinical diagnosis or a static list of deficits. It is a living operating guide—a practical tool designed to share who I am, how my nervous system stays regulated, what my energy reserves require, and how we can co-create an environment where I can thrive.

<table>
<tr><th colspan="2">PASSPORT HOLDER PROFILE</th></tr>
<tr><td>Full Name</td><td rowspan="3">Best Communication Channels:
☐ Written / Text
☐ One-on-One Verbal with Visuals
☐ "I See You" Loop</td></tr>
<tr><td>Preferred Name</td></tr>
<tr><td>Primary Support Allies</td></tr>
</table>

DIMENSION 1
MY PHYSICAL BASELINE & SOMATIC SIGNALS (D1)

Focus: Unique nervous system, sensory pathways, reflex roots, and alarm signals

Somatic Baseline **Processing Rhythms** ☐ Highly articulate verbally, but drops multi-step sequences when overloaded ☐ Non-verbal or selectively quiet in high-stimulation or unfamiliar spaces ☐ Relies on tactile anchors, physical movement, and hands-on engagement	**Notes on my physical baseline.**
What My Body Looks Like When Regulated Safe Breathing & Posture: ____________________ Facial Expressions & Eye Contact: ____________________ Physical Signs of Ease: ____________________	**Early Warning Indicators** (My Petals Beginning to Close) Visible Cues: e.g., flushing, slouching, pacing, glazed eyes, shallow breath

Reflex Roots & Physical Startle Sensitivity

Startle Response	**Physical Grounding**
☐ High / Prolonged Moro Tremor	☐ Deep Pressure / Joint Squeezes
☐ Sensitive to Unexpected Touch	☐ Clear Space (No Touch)

Physical Triggers to Avoid

DIMENSION 2
MY METABOLIC ENERGY LEDGER (D2)

Focus: Biological battery, energy expenditures, drains, and deposits

Daily Battery Baseline & Burn Rate	Heavy Metabolic Taxes (Top Drains)
☐ Rapid Burn (Needs pauses every 60–90 min) ☐ Moderate Pacing ☐ Highly Variable **Signs of a Depleted Battery** ☐ Cognitive processing delays ☐ Increased irritability / tearfulness ☐ Autonomic shutdown (laying flat / non-verbal) ☐ Other:	☐ Sustained eye contact ☐ Multi-step verbal commands ☐ Background noise / cross-talk ☐ Masking & forced compliance ☐ Unexpected changes ☐ Prolonged rigid sitting Other drains:

Restorative Energy Deposits (Recharging)	
Quiet / Solitary Reset:	**Sensory Sanctuaries:**
Rhythmic Somatic Activity:	

DIMENSION 3
MY SENSORY & RELATIONAL ENVIRONMENT (D3)

Focus: Physical, auditory, visual, and relational scaffolding

Sensory Profile	Environmental Accommodations & Shielding Tools
Lighting ☐ Soft / Natural / Dimmable ☐ Sensitive to Fluorescents **Sound** ☐ Requires Quiet / Ear Defenders ☐ Thrives with Rhythmic Audio **Space** ☐ Open Perimeter / Clear Exit ☐ Cozy / Bounded Nook	**Physical Tools Used:** headphones, fidgets, tinted lenses, weighted pads Other: **Ideal Workspace / Room Setup:**

Relational Environment (Coming Alongside Me)	
Relational Demeanor ☐ Calm, unhurried, low-arousal voice ☐ Warm & playful	**Instructional Style** ☐ Use "I See You" verbal loop ☐ 1 step at a time with generous wait pauses ☐ Backward chaining
What to Avoid Under Overload ☐ Raising volume ☐ Demanding eye contact ☐ Crowding space / blocking exits ☐ Debating or lecturing	**Notes:**
Please understand I need these to regulate in stress	

DIMENSION 4 MY TEMPORAL RHYTHMS & LIFESPAN HORIZONS (D4) Focus: Circadian windows, transition pacing, and developmental horizons	
Daily Circadian Rhythms Peak Clarity Windows: Vulnerable / Low-Reserve Windows:	**Transition Support & Processing Pacing** **Advance Notice:** ☐ 5-Minute Visual Cue ☐ 15-Minute Gentle Check-In **Wait Time:** Please offer me ______ seconds of uninterrupted quiet processing time.
Cumulative Fatigue & Lifespan Horizons	
Signs of Allostatic Load (Cumulative stress):	**Developmental Rhythm Note:** Honor where my scattered profile sits today without arbitrary deadlines.

Notes for providers:

— Appendix E—

Glossary
The 4D Framework

Working glossary for readers, caregivers, educators, and support teams. Definitions reflect how the terms are used within the 4D Framework and are not intended as diagnostic criteria or medical advice.

A–D

Accommodation — A change to a task, setting, communication method, schedule, or support level that reduces barriers and allows a person to participate more successfully.

Adaptive skills — Everyday functional abilities used to manage life, such as self-care, communication, safety, routines, money, transportation, relationships, and work or school demands.

Allostatic load — The cumulative wear on body and brain systems from repeated or ongoing stress and the effort required to adapt to it.

Anoxia – lack of oxygen to the brain. This can happen due to airway obstruction or constriction, such as when the umbilical cord is wrapped around the baby's neck during delivery.

Asynchronous development — A developmental pattern in which abilities grow at different rates across domains; chronological age, verbal skill, IQ, and practical functioning may not align.

Biological architecture issue — A framework term that shifts the focus from blaming a behavior to understanding the underlying neurophysiology, health, sensory, and functional conditions shaping it.

Biological energy economy (D2) — The framework's second dimension: the available energy a person must allocate across mental, physical, emotional, sensory, and daily-life demands.

Bristle attack — The framework's description of a sharp, defensive, or explosive response that may occur when energy reserves are low and the nervous system is overloaded.

Capacity — What a person can realistically access or do under present conditions, considering neurobiology, energy, environment, support, and time.

Confabulation — The involuntary creation of an explanation or memory when the brain cannot retrieve or organize the needed information; it is not deliberate deception.

Convergence and confirmation of evidence — A process of understanding a person by looking for patterns across multiple observations, settings, histories, and sources rather than relying on one isolated indicator.

D1 / Neuroprint–Physical — The first dimension of the framework, concerning the individual's neurocognitive and physical profile of capacities, vulnerabilities, strengths, and functional gaps.

D2 / Metabolism–Energy — The second dimension, concerning energy production, allocation, depletion, recovery, and the energy cost of daily demands.

D3 / Environment — The third dimension, concerning the sensory, relational, physical, social, and systemic conditions that either support safety and access or increase strain.

D4 / Time — The fourth dimension, concerning immediate fluctuations in function as well as developmental change, habituation, adaptation, and lifespan needs.

Deep Pressure -- Firm, physical touch—such as a tight squeeze, a full-body hug, or the weight of a weighted blanket or service animal—applied to the body to stimulate deep sensory nerves and joint receptors (proprioceptors). This simple technique tells the brain exactly where the body is in space, releasing calming hormones like oxytocin and signaling safety directly to an overloaded brainstem. For individuals with FASD, deep pressure acts as an immediate physical brake to help quiet overactive primitive reflexes, ease physical discomfort, and prevent or de-escalate a survival-state bristle attack.

How to apply it in real life:

- **The Limb Squeeze:** Taking a child's (or adult's) hands, feet, fingers, and toes and squeezing them firmly, moving systematically up the limbs to the shoulders and stopping at the knees.
- **The Shoulder Press:** Firmly pressing down on the flat muscle at the top of the shoulders (sometimes called the "salt cellars") to trigger the release of feel-good hormones.
- **Weighted Tools:** Placing a weighted blanket, weighted lap pad, or nesting pillows snugly around the body to provide a continuous sense of physical containment.

Animal-Assisted Grounding: Allowing a trained service dog or family pet to lie across the lap or shoulders, using their physical body weight to anchor a racing nervous system

Defiance delusion — The mistaken interpretation that a person's difficulty is primarily willful refusal, rather than a possible signal of overload, unmet need, skill gap, or limited capacity.

Developmental timeline — The person's actual pace and pattern of growth in skills and adaptive functioning, assessed by stage and capacity rather than age alone.

Dysregulation — A state in which the nervous system is under more demand than it can manage, reducing access to thinking, communication, flexibility, self-control, or coping skills.

E–N

Energy-aware pacing — Planning activities, expectations, transitions, and recovery around the person's available energy rather than assuming a stable, unlimited supply.

Environmental accommodation — A practical adjustment to sensory or situational demands, such as reducing noise or glare, changing timing, adding visual supports, or creating a predictable exit plan.

Expressive media — Nonverbal or less language-dependent ways to communicate and regulate, including movement, art, music, drama, gesture, nature, creativity, and animal interaction.

Flexed accommodations — Supports that are adjusted up or down in response to a person's changing capacity, setting, stress load, and current demands.

Fluctuating skill levels — Variation in the ability to use a learned skill from one time, setting, or energy state to another; learning a skill does not guarantee consistent access to it.

Functional gaps — Areas where a person experiences difficulty carrying out a task or life demand, even when other abilities or strengths are evident.

Functional parameters — The practical conditions under which a person can participate or perform: what supports access, what overloads the system, and what level of demand is manageable.

Gradual hand-off — A planned transfer of knowledge, self-advocacy, problem-solving, and care responsibilities from supporters to the individual, at a pace matched to capacity and support needs.

Habituation — Building familiarity, tolerance, and more reliable access to a task, routine, support, or environment through repeated, appropriately paced experience.

Habilitation — An approach that develops or strengthens functional skills, workarounds, routines, and supports while recognizing that ability may wax and wane.

High-support needs — A level of need in which a person requires substantial, ongoing assistance, supervision, adaptation, or coordinated support to participate safely and meaningfully in daily life.

Hostile Attribution Bias – A cognitive and perceptual tendency to interpret benign, accidental, or ambiguous social actions and environmental stimuli as deliberate, threatening, or hostile intent. Within neurodevelopmental conditions such as FASD, this reaction is often driven by sensory overload, trauma, or an activated survival reflex rather than calculated malice.

Interdependence — A support model that values reciprocal connection and shared help rather than defining success solely as complete independence.

Invisible tax — The often-unseen energy, time, planning, emotional labor, and financial cost of navigating environments or systems not designed for a person's needs.

Masking — The effort to hide, suppress, compensate for, or perform around neurodevelopmental differences to meet external expectations.

Masking tax — The accumulated energy and health cost of masking; apparent success in public may be followed by exhaustion, shutdown, dysregulation, or reduced functioning elsewhere.

Moro Reflex (The Startle Reflex): A primitive startle response that serves as the lowest, most foundational primitive reflex and the "gateway" to all other reflexes. It is biologically designed to trigger involuntary survival reactions across three distinct physical pathways:

- **Auditory:** Involuntary physical jerking or jumping in response to sudden loud noises.
- **Visual:** Startle responses triggered when something unexpected suddenly appears in the peripheral field of vision.
- **Balance:** An unconscious sense of instability triggered by changes in seating, posture, or physical orientation.

Why it matters for FASD: In typical development, this reflex integrates and goes dormant as the higher brain matures. However, because prenatal alcohol exposure alters the central nervous system's physical wiring, the Moro reflex frequently remains active into childhood and adulthood. An unintegrated Moro reflex keeps the sympathetic nervous system locked in a permanent fight-or-flight state. Because the body experiences a constant physical survival alarm, it remains in a state of ongoing discomfort and tension. This chronic alarm drains the body's daily metabolic battery (D2) causes severe sleeplessness, and triggers involuntary, defensive bristle attacks at the first hint of an unexpected sensory trigger

Neuroprint—The framework's term for a person's unique neurocognitive and physical pattern of strengths, vulnerabilities, processing differences, functional capacities, and support needs.

Neuroprint audit — A structured review of a person's Neuroprint: what supports functioning, what creates barriers, which strengths can be used, and where gaps require accommodation or skill-building.

Neuroprint Passport — A concise, person-centered guide that communicates key needs, strengths, stress signals, accommodations, regulation supports, and helpful ways others can respond.

P–Z

Parameters — Clear, realistic boundaries around what a person can currently manage, including the amount, pace, complexity, duration, or sensory load of an activity.

Preventative Habilitation -- using targeted, somatic movements to integrate the reflexes and cool the autonomic primitive reflexes before the alarm is ever triggered.

Pivot points — Reflection and application opportunities that help readers turn a framework concept into a practical adjustment, observation, or next step.

Primitive Reflexes – Refers to the 40+ reflexes that develop while in the womb, designed to help them survive their first months of life, and are integrated into higher motor pathways at various points during infancy.

Relational scaffolding — Support provided through trusted relationships, co-regulation, modeling, shared routines, prompts, and gradual skill-building.

Safety cues — Features of an environment or relationship that help the nervous system register predictability, connection, reduced threat, and the possibility of rest or engagement.

Sensory Pathways/Systems (The Senses): The physical network of nerves that act as highways, gathering information from both the outside world and the inside of your body, and carrying it directly to your brain. Before your brain can learn a new skill, regulate an emotion, or execute a motor action (like writing or walking), your sensory pathways must first receive, filter, and organize this incoming data.

While most people are only taught about five external senses, our bodies actually rely on eight distinct sensory systems to navigate life:

- **The External Senses: Sight (visual), hearing (auditory), touch (tactile), smell (olfactory), and taste (gustatory).**
- **The Vestibular Sense (Balance):** Your internal sense of balance and gravity, which tells your brain if you are moving, spinning, or standing upright.
- **The Proprioceptive Sense (Body Awareness):** Your joint and

muscle receptors, which tell your brain where your limbs are in space so you do not have to look at them to move.

- **The Interoceptive Sense (Internal Signals):** Your internal organ signals, which tell your brain if you are hungry, thirsty, tired, cold, or in pain.

Why this matters for FASD: Because prenatal alcohol exposure alters the physical structure of these nerve pathways, our senses do not always filter incoming signals smoothly. If too much information floods a pathway at once, such as loud background chatter, bright lights, or unintegrated movement signals, the brainstem misinterprets this sensory overload as an active physical threat. This triggers an automatic, involuntary survival response (such as a bristle attack or total regulatory shutdown) rather than a conscious choice to misbehave. Supporting an individual always requires stabilizing their sensory pathways first before expecting a voluntary motor or behavioral output.

Sensory minefield — An environment containing multiple sensory demands—such as noise, visual clutter, crowds, unpredictable movement, or touch—that may overwhelm a person's processing capacity.

Sensory Waterfall — Feeling bombarded by sensory input to the point of paralysis.

Somatic regulators — Body-based supports that can assist regulation, including movement, breathing, rhythm, sensory changes, grounding, rest, and other physical strategies.

Sporadic mastery — Inconsistent access to a skill: a person may demonstrate the skill at times but not reliably across demands, stress levels, environments, or days.

Strengths-based adaptation — Designing supports around what the person can do and what helps them engage, rather than centering only on deficits or compliance.

Support team — The network of family members, friends, educators, clinicians, service providers, and others who coordinate to understand and support the person.

Systems-based approach — An approach that considers the interaction of person, body, relationships, environment, services, culture, policy, and time instead of locating the problem only within the individual.

Timeline (short-term) — The immediate changes that affect functioning within hours, days, or situations, such as stress, sleep, sensory load, transitions, or energy depletion.

Timeline (long-term) — Lifespan changes in development, health, adaptive skills, accumulated stress, habituation, and the effectiveness of supports.

Unique neurotype — A respectful description of an individual pattern of neurological development and functioning that may differ from dominant expectations without reducing the person to a diagnosis.

Vortex Model – a neurodevelopmental model created by Toni Hager and Jodee Kulp, developed in the late 1990s. Sadly, this simple framework never caught on, but it was the basis for the popular Brain Domains.

Waxing and waning ability — The natural rise and fall of functional access over time; support should flex with the person's current condition rather than treating inconsistency as a moral failure.

— Appendix F—

The Wildflower Field Guide of Metaphors

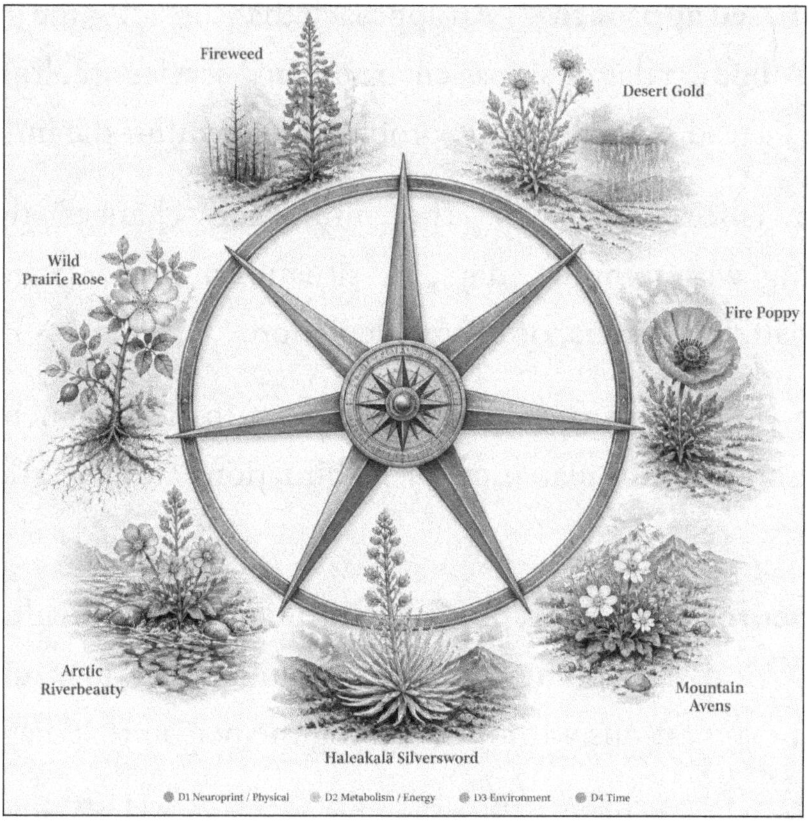

Traditional systems of care are designed for cultivated garden roses. They assume a predictable soil, an even climate, and uniform blooming schedules governed by rigid developmental charts. When a neurodivergent nervous system enters these environments, the mismatch is immediate: our jagged processing profiles, variable energy reserves, and unintegrated survival alarms are mistaken for brokenness or willful refusal.

A differently wired brain will not adhere to a neurotypical baseline. The goal of care is never to force a native plant to conform to the greenhouse ruler. Instead, we turn our gaze to the untamed landscape, where nature has perfected the art of thriving in complex, demanding terrain.

The Seven Botanical Mirrors The seven species in this guide are not delicate curiosities; they are tenacious survivors equipped with specialized biological adaptations. Each one mirrors an essential truth of our lived experience across the 4D Framework:

- **Fireweed** *(Chamaenerion angustifolium):* Anchoring underground rhizomes through scorched earth to reclaim the landscape following crisis (D1: Neuroprint/Physical & D3: Environment).
- **Desert Gold** *(Geraea canescens):* Preserving finite fuel through dormant dry seasons until saturating rains permit brilliant blooms (D2: Metabolism/Energy & D4: Time).
- **Fire Poppy** *(Papaver californicum):* Folding petals tightly to shield vulnerable centers when environmental heat flares buried alarms (D1: Neuroprint/Physical & D3: Environment).
- **Mountain Avens** *(Dryas octopetala):* Hugging the ground in dense mats and tracking the sun to gather radiant heat in alpine gales (D2: Metabolism/Energy & D3: Environment).
- **Haleakalā Silversword** *(Argyroxiphium sandwicense)*: Donning silver-haired sensory armor to reflect punishing radiation on barren volcanic cinder (D1: Neuroprint/Physical & D3: Environment).
- **Arctic Riverbeauty** *(Chamerion latifolium):* Rooting deep in shifting gravel bars and yielding pliant stems to survive flash floods without snapping (D1: Neuroprint/Physical & D3: Environment).
- **Wild Prairie Rose** (*Rosa arkansana)*: Weathering blizzards through twenty-foot woody taproots, guarding boundaries with sharp thorns, and offering late-season nourishment across decades (D4: Time & D1: Neuroprint/Physical).

Use this guide as an interpretive compass. When behavioral friction flares or a day grinds to an unexpected halt, step back from the urge to correct. Ask which wildflower is standing before you, what its biology is protecting, and what shelter the surrounding soil must provide.

Fireweed

(Chamaenerion angustifolium)

Primary Dimension: D1 (Neuroprint/Physical)

Ecosystem Anchor: D3 (Environment)

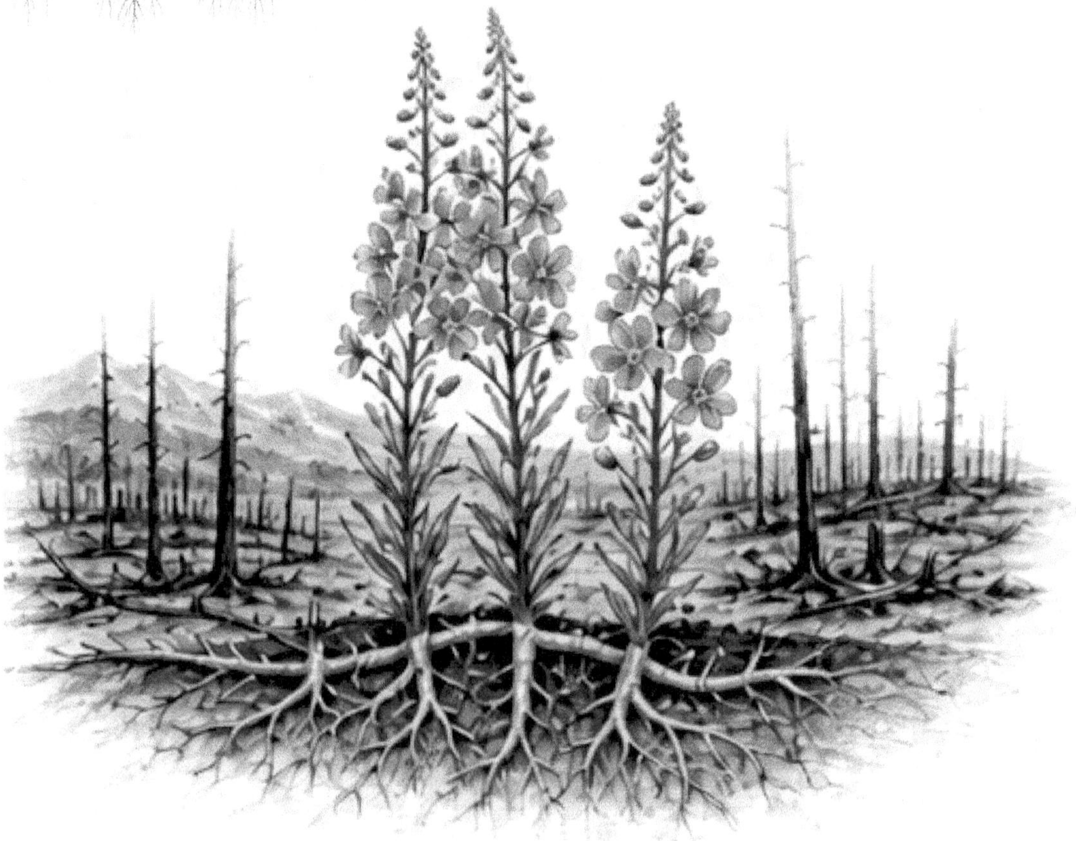

The Botanical Reality When wildfire roars through an ecosystem, it incinerates the canopy, bakes living soil to ash, and leaves a scarred expanse where survival seems impossible. Yet before the smoke clears, bright magenta spires rise from the soot. Fireweed does not wait for pristine conditions. Beneath the blackened crust, it weaves a tenacious web of underground rhizomes that knit fragile ground together, preventing catastrophic erosion and locking in moisture. It is nature's first responder, stabilizing scorched earth so life can return.

The Neurodivergent Mirror: D1 (Neuroprint/Physical) We know what scorched earth feels like. It is the devastating silence of an estranged relationship or broken marriage buckled under invisible friction. It is the sickening shock of a lost career, an eviction, or the hollow ash of autistic or FASD burnout where the body refuses to leave the floor. When systems and relationships scorch our lives, the world sees only ruin. But beneath the surface lies the subterranean root system of our neuroprint: an innate biological tenacity holding the self together when outward structures collapse. The persistence society labels "oppositional" or "rigid" is often our deep rhizome holding fast against total disintegration.

The Ecosystem We Require: D3 (Environment) Fireweed cannot bloom under a dense, suffocating forest canopy; it demands open light, room to breathe, and uncompacted soil. An adult emerging from catastrophic burnout cannot heal under the heavy canopy of unsolicited advice or demands to immediately "bounce back."

- **Allow the crash to settle:** Leave aside non-essential demands, social noise, and conversational pressure; when a nervous system is scorched down, let it rest.
- **Let the Ground Cool:** Stop expecting instant productivity; protect the metabolic battery and allow biological baselines time to settle without judgment.
- **Offer Unfiltered Light:** Provide steady, kind presence that signals safety but places no demands for decision-making during this time of depletion. Trust the rhizome to rise and reclaim the landscape from underground, upwards.

Desert Gold

(Geraea canescens)

Primary Dimension: D2 (Metabolism/Energy)

Temporal Anchor: D4 (Time)

The Botanical Reality Across the scorched, rocky washes of the desert floor, years can pass without a single green shoot breaking the gravel. To the casual eye, the landscape appears dead, barren, and utterly empty. Yet beneath that parched gravel lies a brilliant evolutionary strategy: the dormant seeds of Desert Gold. The seed wastes no drop of its internal reserves trying to grow in an unyielding drought. It waits. Only when a rare, soaking rainfall penetrates deep into the soil does it break dormancy, exploding overnight into a sea of brilliant yellow blossoms. It understands that survival is entirely an economy of energy.

The Neurodivergent Mirror: D2 (Metabolism/Energy) You know what drought feels like in a neurodivergent body. It is the exhaustion of operating on a five-percent battery, staring at a simple pile of unopened mail or a dirty kitchen sink, completely unable to generate the physical spark to move. The world looks at our quiet days and labels us unmotivated, depressed, or lazy. But dormancy is not death; it is metabolic preservation. Just as Desert Gold retreats into its shell to protect its life, our nervous system dials down non-essential functions when our biological fuel is depleted. Our sporadic mastery is not defiance; it is the natural rhythm of a living battery.

The Ecosystem We Require: D4 (Time) Desert Gold cannot be coerced into blooming by dragging a watering can across the sand on a schedule; it requires a deep, penetrating saturation that respects its seasonal clock. An individual running on empty cannot be revived through motivational lectures or high-stakes pressure.

- **Honor the Dormancy:** Recognize that fallow periods are valuable resting states, biologically necessary as protective phases, not character flaws.
- **Remove the Demands of Drought:** Cut the cognitive and sensory load when reserves are dry, stopping the energy hemorrhage before complete autonomic collapse.
- **Trust the Rainfall:** Provide respect and as a sign of relational safety over time. Trust that when the metabolic battery recharges, a bloom will follow.

Fire Poppy

(Papaver californicum)

Primary Dimension: D1 (Neuroprint/Physical)

Ecosystem Anchor: D3 (Environment)

The Botanical Reality Unlike plants that favor soft loam, the Fire Poppy lies dormant under dense chaparral duff for years, even decades, waiting for intense heat. Only the smoke, chemical cues, and thermal shock of a passing wildfire break its stubborn seed coat. Yet once it rises, its flaming orange petals are intensely delicate. At the first return of extreme heat, harsh drying winds, or hostile weather, the Fire Poppy does not fight back or harden its tissues—it folds its petals tightly inward to shield its reproductive core. It knows that survival lies in immediate closure, waiting for the surrounding ash to cool.

The Neurodivergent Mirror: D1 (Neuroprint/Physical) We recognize this lightning-fast defense. In a neurodivergent body, our unintegrated primitive reflexes and survival alarms smolder just beneath the surface of daily life. A big dose of mismatched sensory load—-an hour under fluorescent flicker, an abrasive tone of voice, a crowded hallway bump—-ignites the reflex of protection, fending off or shutting down. The sudden rage, explosive outburst or non-verbal freeze is not planned, malicious or a character flaw; it's the touchy alarm which went off to protect the vulnerable system.

The Ecosystem We Require: D3 (Environment) You cannot force a closed poppy open by prying at its clenched petals. Demanding logical explanations, imposing behavioral penalties, or shouting over an active survival response only fans the flames.

- **Cool the Smoldering Soil:** Stop all verbal exchange and demands for eye contact! Lower the ambient lighting, turn off TV or radio or devices, quiet the room. Let them withdraw and hide.
- **Provide Somatic Safety:** Provide a spot to hide or withdraw into. Allow nesting or swaddling while the stress hormone level subsides. Avoid shaming comments or restraint.
- **Wait for the Cooling Breeze:** Trust that when the environmental heat drops and physical safety is restored, the petals will gently unfold on their own.

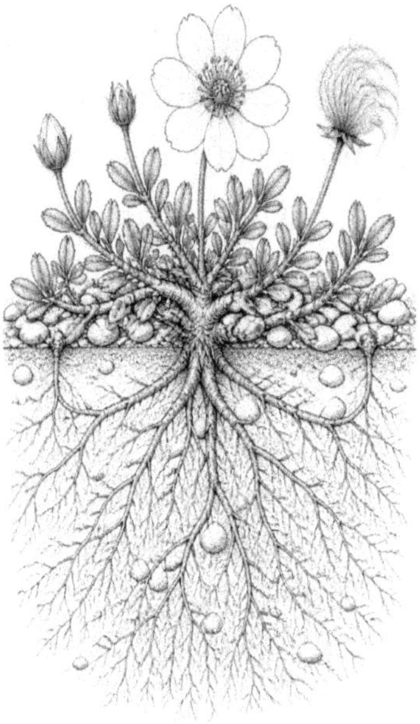

Mountain Avens

(Dryas octopetala)

Primary Dimension: D2 (Metabolism/Energy)

Ecosystem Anchor: D3 (Environment)

The Botanical Reality High above the tree line on exposed Arctic tundra and alpine ridges, biting gale-force winds strip moisture from every living cell. In this unforgiving climate, Mountain Avens does not try to stand tall against the storm. It hugs the ground in dense, low-growing mats, tucking itself into the micro-topography of the soil to escape the wind's razor edge. Most brilliantly, its creamy white petals are shaped like parabolic mirrors that are heliotropic—like sunflowers, they track the sun's low arc across the sky. The petals collect light, focusing radiant warmth into the center and raising the plant's internal temperature above the freezing air. It survives by mastering its energy economy.

The Neurodivergent Mirror: D2 (Metabolism/Energy) We know the exhausting alpine chill of a non-stop world that demands speed and efficiency—always "on," all day, every day, without downtime. Mechanization has accelerated the pace while sacrificing service; people must fit their assigned slot or be pushed aside as systems narrow. When sensory overload and demands for rapid-fire task or social responses sweep over us like an Arctic blast, we drain our metabolic reserves trying to mask or withstand frozen judgment and exclusion. The instinct to retreat, hide, nest, wrap in a weighted blanket, or wear noise-canceling headphones is not childish avoidance; it is biology hugging the ground. Like Mountain Avens, we seek low-friction pockets and safe warmth to keep our core-energy battery from draining to zero.

The Ecosystem We Require: D3 (Environment) Demanding that an individual brave the freezing wind without shelter guarantees hypothermic collapse. We support this energy-conserving wisdom by:

- **Building the Windbreak:** Reducing atmospheric chaos—dimming harsh lighting, lowering conversational volume, and clearing space for quiet retreat.
- **Encouraging the Nest:** Validating the physical tools (weighted items, tactile anchors, soft texture, hydration, headphones, etc.) that ground the body against turbulence.
- **Tracking the Sun:** Identify and pivot toward the natural interests, calming relationships, and joyful activities that pour warm energy back into the biological batter.

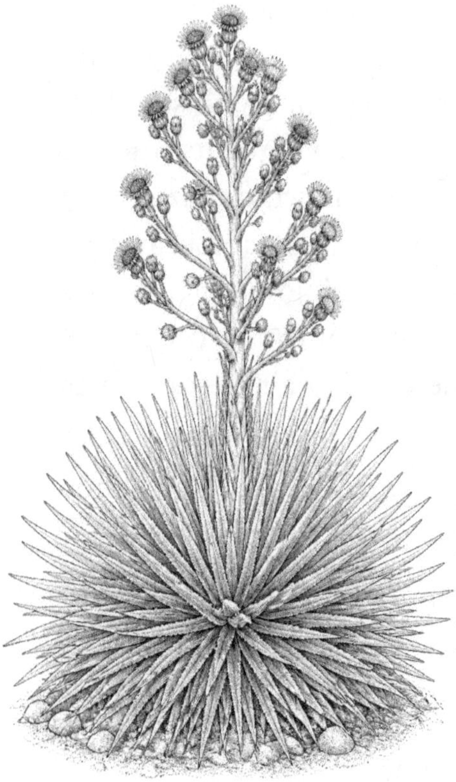

Haleakalā Silversword

(Argyroxiphium sandwicense)

Primary Dimension: D1 (Neuroprint/ Physical)

Ecosystem Anchor: D3 (Environment)

The Botanical Reality High on Hawaii's windswept volcanic summits, the Haleakalā Silversword grows in an environment that would incinerate ordinary vegetation. Anchored in porous, razor-sharp volcanic cinder, it endures blistering ultraviolet radiation by day and sub-freezing temperatures by night. To survive this extreme ecosystem, the Silversword creates its own protective armor. Its thick, succulent leaves form a dense rosette covered entirely in microscopic, silvery hairs. These hairs act like an array of mirrors, reflecting lethal UV rays away from the plant, insulating its tissues against freezing mountain air, and locking in precious moisture. It thrives in a barren moonscape by living with a built-in shield.

The Neurodivergent Mirror: D1 (Neuroprint/Physical) We know what it is to live with hypersensitivity in a caustic world. With a vulnerable nervous system, the modern indoor environment of homes, school or offices is full of harsh contours: screaming fluorescent tubes, buzzing appliances, device 'notifications', chemical smells, generators that emit electromagnetic fields, invasive social scrutiny. We are literally awash in mechanized inputs, compared to natural settings free of engineered structures. The tools we reach for — the noise cancelling headphones, tinted glasses, wide-brimmed hats, weighted clothing, intentional social boundaries — are not antisocial quirks or signs of weakness. These are our silver hairs, our essential physical armor to deflect the sensory pollution that constantly assaults our internal system.

The Ecosystem We Require: D3 (Environment) The Silversword is so delicate beneath its armor that even casual human trampling can crush its fragile root system and kill the plant. Navigating public systems safely requires:

- **Respecting the Shield:** Never demanding that someone remove their sensory accommodations (sunglasses, headphones, tents, hammocks, quiet nests) to prove respect or compliance.
- **Guarding the Perimeter:** Protecting physical space and personal boundaries against uninvited touch or rapid intrusion.
- **Preserving the Cinder:** Allow individuals the space to stand firmly in their unique armor without forcing them to fit environments that assault their biology.

Arctic Riverbeauty

(Chamerion latifolium)

Primary Dimension: D1 (Neuroprint/Physical)

Ecosystem Anchor: D3 (Environment)

The Botanical Reality Along the roaring glacial rivers of the far north, the riverbed is in constant, violent motion. Gravel shifts, icy meltwater surges without warning, and the terrain changes with every flood. A rigid plant with a brittle stem would snap and be swept away in seconds. Arctic Riverbeauty thrives here by embracing dynamic flexibility. It stays low to the stones, sending deep, tenacious taproots down between the rocks while growing limber, pliant stems that yield to the current. When the glacial waters flood, it does not fight the torrent; it lies flat against the gravel, bends with the rushing water, and rises unharmed once the surge recedes. It thrives because it anchors deep and bends without breaking.

The Neurodivergent Mirror: D1 (Neuroprint/Physical) We know what it is to live in a world where the emotional and sensory water levels are always shifting without warning. A sudden change in routine, an abrupt transition, or an unexpected conflict can feel like an icy flash flood engulfing us. Traditional systems demand that we stand rigid like concrete pillars, expecting us to "just push through" onslaught. But forced rigidity can collapse us into total shutdown. To adapt we have to hold on to a deep anchor, a core of safety, while yielding to overcome, and come back up for air after the flood. We have to breath at the top of the wave, then sink under and wait as it passes.

The Ecosystem We Require: D3 (Environment) Demanding instant conformity in the middle of a flood guarantees disaster. Supporting this resilient flexibility requires:

- **Providing Anchoring Rocks:** Establish predictable, concrete daily anchors—clear, simple routines, visual schedules, and dependable safe people.
- **Allowing the Bend:** Set aside non-essential expectations and yield during a surge, rather than forcing compliance.
- **Patient Waters:** Give the current time to settle, trusting that equilibrium will resurface once the torrent passes.

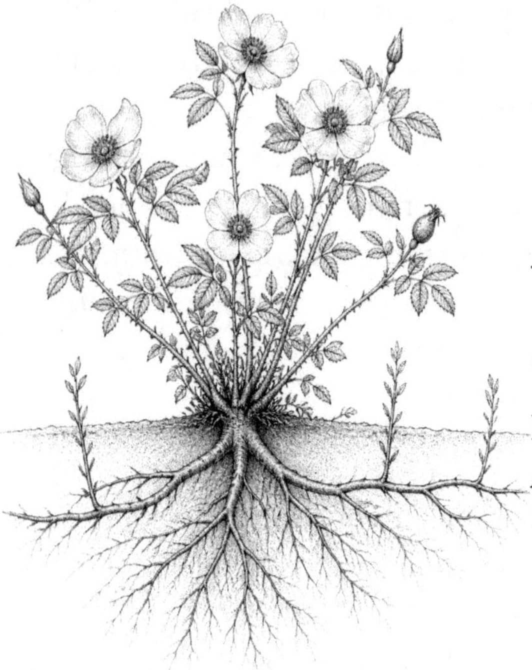

Wild Prairie Rose

(Rosa arkansana)

Primary Integration: The Complete 4D Archetype (D1, D2, D3, D4)

The Botanical Reality Across the sweeping northern plains, where sub-zero blizzards strip the land in winter, and scorching winds bake the summer earth, the Wild Prairie Rose refuses to yield. It survives neither by fragility nor delicate greenhouse pampering. Beneath the soil, it anchors a massive, woody taproot system plunging ten to twenty feet deep, outliving prairie fires, droughts, and decades of surface devastation. Above ground, its woody canes bristle with sharp thorns that guard tender growth against grazing predators. In high summer, its sweet pink petals open in calm defiance, but its true biological crown arrives in late autumn when it produces durable, scarlet rose hips. Packed with vital nutrients and vitamin C, these hips cling tenaciously to bare branches through howling blizzards, offering life-saving winter sustenance to the entire prairie ecosystem long after every other flower has withered.

The Neurodivergent Mirror: The Complete 4D Lifespan The Wild Prairie Rose is our capstone archetype because an enduring neurodivergent life cannot be understood through a single lens—it touches all four dimensions simultaneously:

- **D1 (Neuroprint/Physical): The Woody Taproot & Protective Thorns.** Our jagged physical neuroprint runs deep. The protective "thorns" we develop—our non-negotiable personal boundaries, sensory retreat tools, and somatic self-advocacy—are not hostility or antisocial defiance; they are physical hardware adaptations designed to shield our vulnerable autonomic core from predation and chronic trauma.
- **D2 (Metabolism/Energy): Metabolic Preservation.** This hardy perennial does not squander precious energy attempting continuous, forced blooms. It allocates its metabolic reserves with disciplined precision: resting deeply through the freezing winter, timing its bloom, and converting late-season energy into dense, concentrated fruit rather than showy, fleeting foliage.
- **D3 (Environment): Weathering the Prairie Winds.** The rose demands neither cultivated potting soil nor sheltered greenhouse glass. It flourishes in wide-open, uncompacted prairie soil with

room for deep roots to run. When an environment provides low-friction relational safety, steady scaffolding, and freedom from crushing behavioral containment, our roots anchor firm against institutional gales.

- **D4 (Time): Asynchronous Blooming & The Late-Season Harvest.** Above all, the rose honors lifespan development. Society demands that we bloom uniformly into maturation by the arbitrary timeline between eighteen and twenty-one. Yet our deepest brilliance—our lived wisdom, fierce advocacy, and generous late-life gifts—matures across decades. Like the winter rose hip, the richness of our neurodivergent trajectory often bears its most nourishing fruit in midlife and beyond, feeding our communities through interdependent connection.

The Ecosystem We Require: Whole-Person Habilitation

- **Respect the Thorns:** Validate firm boundaries, somatic pauses, and accommodations without demanding compliance or assimilation.
- **Protect the Energy Reservoir:** Structure daily life to safeguard finite biological fuel and prevent unnecessary energy hemorrhage.
- **Clear the Horizon:** Build spacious, low-friction spaces that allow deep roots to run without institutional barriers.
- **Honor Decades Over Deadlines:** Release the tyranny of chronological benchmarks, providing steady, lifelong scaffolding that celebrates our authentic, asynchronous bloom.

— Appendix G—

Living with FASD Podcast Guest Episode Directory

- Aeris Wren — 128
- AJ Locashio — 110, 120, and 134
- Alice Foote — 125
- Allison McCormick — 89
- Angela Geddes — 121
- Antonia Lindsey — 43, 51, 61, 68, 73, 77, 85, 86, 100, 131
- Barb Clark — 97, 118, 138
- Bruna Neptune — 84
- Carl Young — 91, 104, 129, 138
- Dr. Carol Brown — 139
- Carolyn Kiel — 108
- Chris Troutt — 60
- Dr. Claire Coles — 133
- Danielle Finnigan — 40
- David Boulding — 31
- Dr. David Gilbert — 56, 75
- Deb Evensen — 14, 59
- Donnie Winoker — 45
- Eileen Devine — 112
- Elena Schmitt — 49
- Elizabeth (Liz) Kriston — 17
- Dr. Elizabeth Cleveland — 80
- Dr. Emily Hargrove — 41, 76
- Fatima Iqbal — 7
- Gina Schumaker — 72
- Helen Simpson — 111
- Dr. Jack Rocco — 63
- Jake Tjapkes — 119
- Janet Oliver — 93
- Dr. Jeffrey Wozniak — 95
- Dr. Jennifer Fraser — 116, 122
- Jennifer Henszel — 117
- Dr. Jessica Rutherford — 52
- Jodee Kulp — 34, 45, 53, 81, 85, 86, 123, 135
- Jody Crowe — 64
- Joel Sheagren — 47, 62, 91

About the Author

Patricia Kasper is an educator, advocate, trainer, and speaker who combines professional experience with lived experience as a person with Fetal Alcohol Spectrum Disorder (FASD). She helps families, educators, service providers, employers, and communities understand FASD and the practical supports that help people thrive.

Through advocacy, education, consultation, public speaking, and her podcast, Patricia shares a hopeful, person-centered message: FASD is often invisible, behavior is communication, and people with brain-based differences deserve dignity, understanding, and opportunity—not judgment.

Patricia is also the creator of the 4D Framework, a practical training model that helps people respond more effectively to individuals with FASD and other neurodevelopmental differences. Her workshops shift the question from "What is wrong?" to "What is needed?"

Patricia is available for keynotes, workshops, staff training, caregiver education, podcast conversations, and consultation. For speaking, training, podcast information, and 4D Framework resources, contact Patricia through her professional channels.

www.ingramcontent.com/pod-product-compliance
Lightning Source LLC
LaVergne TN
LVHW060440061126
851857LV00016B/1681